VOLUNTARY MADNESS

ALSO BY NORAH VINCENT

Self-Made Man

VOLUNTARY MADNESS

My Year Lost and Found in the Loony Bin

NORAH VINCENT

VIKING

VIKING

Published by the Penguin Group

Penguin Group (USA) Inc., 375 Hudson Street, New York, New York 10014, U.S.A. · Penguin Group
(Canada), 90 Eglinton Avenue East, Suite 700, Toronto, Ontario, Canada M4P 2Y3 (a division of Pearson
Penguin Canada Inc.) · Penguin Books Ltd, 80 Strand, London WC2R 0RL, England · Penguin Ireland,
25 St. Stephen's Green, Dublin 2, Ireland (a division of Penguin Books Ltd) · Penguin Books Australia
Ltd, 250 Camberwell Road, Camberwell, Victoria 3124, Australia (a division of Pearson Australia Group
Pty Ltd) · Penguin Books India Pvt Ltd, 11 Community Centre, Panchsheel Park, New Delhi – 110 017,
India · Penguin Group (NZ), 67 Apollo Drive, Rosedale, North Shore 0632, New Zealand (a division of
Pearson New Zealand Ltd) · Penguin Books (South Africa) (Pty) Ltd, 24 Sturdee Avenue, Rosebank,
Johannesburg 2196, South Africa

Penguin Books Ltd, Registered Offices: 80 Strand, London WC2R 0RL, England

First published in 2008 by Viking Penguin, a member of Penguin Group (USA) Inc.

10 9 8 7 6 5 4 3 2 1

Names and certain characteristics of individuals, hospitals, and other facilities have been changed to pro-
tect people's privacy.

LIBRARY OF CONGRESS CATALOGING IN PUBLICATION DATA
Vincent, Norah.
    Voluntary madness : my year lost and found in the loony bin / by Norah Vincent.
        p. cm.
    ISBN 978-0-670-01971-7
    1. Vincent, Norah—Mental health.   2. Psychiatric hospital patients—United States—Biography.
3. Journalists—United States—Biography.   I. Title.
    RC464.V56A3 2008
    362.2'1092—dc22   2008029034

Printed in the United States of America
Designed by Carla Bolte · Set in Celeste

TO TEDDY

————————

CONTENTS

CURRICULUM

In November 2004, just as I was finishing the research for my book *Self-Made Man,* I checked myself into a locked psychiatric ward in the hospital.

I never finished that research. Instead it was cut short by a depressive breakdown that scared me enough to convince me that it would be better both for me and for those around me if I didn't go on walking the streets looking for someone to hurt me.

It may sound unduly dramatic to suggest that writing a book would drive a person into the bin (though I'm sure there are at least a few hundred thousand Ph.D. candidates and other wee-hour scribblers out there who would beg to differ on this score), but in my case, it was quite literally true. I lost it, in medias research, so to speak, and for good reason.

The research for *Self-Made Man* had been unorthodox, to say the least, since it had entailed disguising myself and then living, dating, working, and recreating as a man. I became a man, at least as far as the people around me knew, but I remained a woman, and that psycho-emotional contradiction in terms pulled me apart at the seams slowly and insidiously for eighteen months, leaving me limp and in tatters, sitting semicatatonic in my pajamas outside a nurse's station in the hospital, torporously signing away my freedom and giving my consent to be forcibly restrained if necessary.

Real lives and lived experience are the laboratory of the immersion journalist, and the journalist herself is the guinea pig. Consequently, a lot can change between the proposal and the finished book, and always does.

That is the whole purpose, after all. If you knew what was going to happen in the end, there would be no point in starting. Setting out to prove a point only colors the experience and then skews the results more than your inescapable subjectivity and prejudices already do. You have to leap. You have to be a bit reckless. Maybe more than a bit. Maybe a lot.

This is at once the adventure and the peril of what I do, and, for better or worse, it means I follow where the rabbit hole leads.

Last time around it landed me in the bin. But once I got there, I realized that bins are pretty fertile ground for writers of my stripe, and not altogether uninteresting places to be locked away for a few days with a notebook and a crayon (or whatever other nubby stylus they'll let you get your certifiable fist around).

As I sat there in the ward that November, wondering how the hell I was going to talk my way out of that zombie parlor, I said to myself, "Jesus, what a freak show. All I have to do is sit here and take notes, and I'm Balzac."

And that was it. Bam. That was how the idea for this book came to me, and I to it. Of course, "idea" is the operative word here, since the book I set out to write and the book you are holding in your hands are two quite different things. But then, as I've said, being an immersion journalist, I expected that.

I started in that ward with the theatricality of it all, distanced from my own condition, contemptuous, trapped, yet interested. But interested the way a field entomologist is interested, stooping to see, a deigning species apart, marveling at the hive or the colony and poking it with her pencil to get a better view.

Somerset Maugham once wrote that quotation is a passable substitute for wit, and so for me, prurience was a passable substitute for something better. Imagination? Diligence? Insight? I don't know. I thought I was in a foreign country, and so, like every frisky tourist, whose intrusiveness is pure entitlement, I was curious about the customs—and possessive, too. I wanted these people to myself, to make them mine in word and sentence.

These were living dolls, characters ready-made for me, shuffling by in all their goggle-eyed magnitude and efflorescent distress. I liked them that way, and I watched.

I did not accept, then, that I was one of them, and that the foreign country, the theater, the rabbit hole, was not out there but in my head.

I spent four lost, interminable days in lockup that first time in the bin, getting worse, weeping at the sealed windows, yelping for rescue through the pay phone in the soul-destroying dayroom, wrapping into my room-mate's seamless paranoia, and, finally, out of sheer rage, altogether losing what was left of my tenuous grip.

Then, scared Soviet of being stuck in there for months, I resolved to slip the trap and ingratiate myself to the pen pushers and paper pilers of the system. I put up a front of cool argument and reasoned my way out.

I got home a wreck, and swore that, no matter how bad I felt, I would never willingly go into such a place again. Never.

And yet, there was the lure, the powerful lure of the spectacle, and the human drama, and what I saw as the outright wrongs of the insanitar-ium, wrongs that I so longed to expose and ridicule, and hold up to pub-lic scrutiny. I felt centripetally attracted to the subject matter, to what I couldn't help seeing as the thematic cornucopia of the bin.

I wanted to immerse myself in that. Be the patient once more. It wasn't a stretch, obviously, but it was daunting nonetheless. I knew that in order to write a book about madhouses, I'd have to spend much more time locked away, and in several different types of institutions.

Wouldn't that drive me mad again, madder than being a man had ever done? Or would it only reveal a madness already there, entwined. Was I the reason to do it? Mad me turning to face me in the mirror of other warped faces?

After all, there was far more to my backstory, more to my personal investment in the topic, than that first trip to the bin.

It began more than ten years ago when I first went to a psychiatrist complaining of persistently gloomy and vaguely suicidal thoughts. I was in my late twenties, still working as a glorified secretary in a job that I was overqualified for and understimulated by. I had gotten to that age when all well-loved children of the upper middle class begin to discover that the world is not made for them, that all meaningful questions are rhetorical, and that the term "soul mate" is, at best, a figure of speech.

I had had too many ill-conceived relationships defiantly not rise phoenixlike from the flames. I couldn't see spending the rest of my working life wearing pantsuits, but I didn't know how to convert my expensive education into the bohemian Kulturkampf I was dreaming about. I did not relish what I saw as my prospects for love or money. I was sorely disappointed by my oyster, and so I despaired, flagrantly, aromatically, in purple poetry and reefer.

What can I tell you? It was the 1990s. The *épatant* was the bourgeois, and Kurt Cobain was dead. Despair was an icon, and I was in my Saturn return. I was stuck at an age when a lot of people are stuck. I was morose at an age when a lot of people are morose. I was spoiled. I thought life was supposed to make you happy, and I wasn't going to drudge for a living.

Did I need medication? Or did I need someone to talk to? Someone, that is, who would do more than charge the going rate for nodding and whip out a prescription pad before the first fifty minutes were up. Was I physiologically depressed? At an innate biochemical disadvantage? Or was reaching for the pad just the way things were done because the doc had been well patronized by the drug reps and had plenty of samples in her file cabinet?

I don't know, and I never will know. I took my first Prozac and took flight.

I went out like a turbocharged dorm geek after the last exam, a recluse set loose on the world with the sudden hubris of ten presidents and all the pent-up primal urges I'd been sublimating since the onset of puberty. I was a stalled career flounderer set going again by a little green-and-cream-colored Pulvule that made me feel so good I called it vitamin P.

In fact, my brain was never quite the same after I zapped it with that first course of SSRIs. Those initial months on Prozac when I was thin-

thin and wildly productive and fascinated by everything and feeling every minute like I'd just been fucked—they didn't last and they never came again.

Pretty soon my brain adjusted, and pretty soon I got puffy and lethargic, taking four-hour death naps in the afternoon, gaining weight, and guzzling coffee just to keep my head up, and maybe, if I drank enough, get some fleeting glimpse of the former glory.

My doc upped my dose to the max, and then we added other antidepressants to amplify the effect, until I was a bug-eyed, constipated, jangle-nerved sloth writing rants in the closet at 4:00 a.m. because I'd slept all afternoon and a soft cell was the only place I felt safe. I got kinda twitchy and geriatric when I ate, my fork shaking wildly all the way from the plate to my mouth.

My doc and I tried a lot of other medications along the way, and I had all the classic side effects. I went hypomanic on the Prozac, so we added mood stabilizers to even me out. I lost interest in sex, so we tried another antidepressant, Wellbutrin, to bring me back. We switched, jiggered, and recombined, looking for that perfect pickle. But if one thing didn't give me a rash or panic attacks, then it made me gobble salty junk food in the middle of the night. I tried most of the majors, and burned through their effects. I got scrawny, then fat, petrified, then out of control, sexless, then sex-obsessed.

Finally, beset by attacks of crippling anxiety, I got a scrip for Klonopin. The velvet hammer. A relative of Valium and Xanax, and the best drug I know for what ails you, if you've given up on all the rest. Just pop it and bonk—you're out. Sweet dreamless sleep.

But even this didn't last.

Eventually the dope just doesn't work the way it used to. Even Klonny needs a boost to keep hammering you. And that's when they start referring to you in whispered tones as "medication-resistant."

So I ended up in the bin that first time, to do some serious recalibration. I was all used up. In the space of a few years, I went from being just another twenty-something having a good old-fashioned life crisis to being a psychotropic junky.

And that, crowded and distraught, is the short version of my history with what we might broadly call mental illness. I qualify the term "mental illness" here not so much because I am in denial anymore about my challenges, but more because I don't accept the terms by which mental illness is currently defined.

That is part of the point. I am asking the question of myself, and perhaps of you, as well as the culture at large. Am I mentally ill? Or have I been diagnosed as such because it means that the insurance companies will pony up for my meds and my stays in the hospital only if I am placed in a category in the *Diagnostic and Statistical Manual of Mental Disorders* (*DSM*), whether I truly belong there or not?

And what is "mentally ill," anyway? What can it mean to say that someone is mentally ill when the DSM, the psycho-bible, is, in my and many other far more qualified people's estimation, not a scientific document, but rather an entirely subjective and seemingly infinitely amendable and expandable laundry list of catchall terms for collections of symptoms.

There is, at least in the quantifiable sense, no such thing as schizophrenia, bipolar disorder, major depressive disorder, social anxiety disorder, and a whole host of other accepted diseases listed in the *DSM*. There is no real test for any of them (only questionnaires and symptomatic observation). They are unduly subject to political and professional fashion, and even lobbying by special-interest groups. Hence the successive redefining of homosexuality in 1973 and 1980, and, finally, its excision from the *DSM* in 1987.

We are nowhere near understanding the causes and mechanisms of mental illness well enough to develop reliable diagnostic criteria for any of them. We infer backward from the symptoms to the disease, which is why, when it came to doing the research for this book, it was so easy for me to gain admission to various hospitals on the pretext of undergoing a major depressive episode, even though in at least one case I was feeling quite well.

People have often asked me how I was able to do this so easily, and I always shock them when I say, "Anyone could do it."

Getting yourself committed is very easy. Easier than it should be.

This has been true for a long time. In 1972, psychologist David Rosenhan and a group of his colleagues and graduate students conducted an experiment in which eight participants, or "pseudopatients," none of whom had histories of mental illness or institutionalization, set out to see how difficult it would be to get themselves committed.

They presented themselves at various hospitals across the United States, saying that they were hearing voices. They said that the voices were repeating the words "empty," "hollow," and "thud." They claimed to be suffering from no other symptoms and otherwise behaved normally. All eight were admitted, seven with diagnoses of schizophrenia, and one with a diagnosis of bipolar disorder. None of the staff was able to identify the pseudopatients as imposters during their stays, though a number of patients were reported to have done so.

The pseudopatients were all discharged after an average stay of nineteen days, at which time their schizophrenia was diagnosed as being "in remission."

The results of the experiment were published in the journal *Science*, and the authors concluded ominously, "It is clear that we cannot distinguish the sane from the insane in psychiatric hospitals."

I am sure that another Rosenhan experiment, if conducted today, would yield equally worrying results.

But this book is not another Rosenhan experiment. Though it does cast an unabashedly critical eye on the system, the practice of psychiatry, and the prevailing view of mental illness, it does so solely through the lens of my experience.

If you are looking for evidence, you will not find it here, except in the notoriously unreliable form of eyewitness testimony. My own.

The formal case against the leviathan has been made already, and is still being made in the courts and the newspapers. A number of people, several of them professionals in the field, have written extremely well-documented exposés of psychiatry, psychiatric medications, the pharmaceutical companies, and the *DSM*. These books are far too seldom read, in my opinion.

I admire and support what these writers, dissenting doctors, and journalists have accomplished. Initially, I sought to follow their lead. I saw probing the phenomenon of mental illness today as an effective and provocative way to take the measure of my culture. But as I plunged myself deeper in the project, I, and it, took a sharp turn inward, becoming somewhat less about what I saw around me and more about my private struggle to find a way out of chronic mental distress, a distress that the system not only seemed unable to heal but, more often than not, had only made worse.

As you read, you will see that what begins as the mostly detached report of the proverbial journalist at large, first in a big-city public hospital, then in a private rural hospital, and finally, in an alternative treatment program, soon dovetails and then merges indistinguishably with the very personal account of a bona fide patient's search for rescue and, if possible, a touch of lasting self-awareness along the way. The journalist and the patient are both me: one doing a job, or trying to; the other slouching, in her own time, toward bedlam; and each, by turns, pushing the other up and along or dragging her down.

What follows is the record of that dual journey, shot through with observational inexactitude. This is what I saw and what I thought. It is what happened to me, inside and out. That's all. It is not, nor was it intended to be, an argument, a polemic, or an investigative report, though it is, at times argumentative, conjectural, and raw. It draws no hard-and-fast conclusions. It asks. It surmises. It prods. It also wanders, meanders, spirals, and circles back. But in the end, it does no more and no less than take you with me. And that, after all, is really what you're here for, isn't it? To come along for the ride.

That much I know I can promise you. A bumpy, loopy, sideways, up-and-down ride.

A journalist I once knew had a saying about our profession: The most you can hope to do is inform and entertain.

As an invitation to these pages, that sounds about right.

BEDLAM

Meriwether

Pseudonyms. It began with pseudonyms. Hastily scrawled on the dog-eared pages of a paperback book. Words circled, underlined, then crossed out by the exuberant young man who sat next to me that first long night in the ward.

His given name was Kristos, or so he said, but his pseudonym was Nil. Nil, as in nothing, nullity, none. It signified the end point of his quest, the resignation of his ego, and, as he said, "A far, far better name for a Buddhist, wouldn't you agree?"

We could not hit on a name for me. Or he could not sit still long enough to do so, and I didn't feel quite comfortable with the exercise. I was undercover, after all, but using my own name.

I still have the sheet of paper. "Possible pseudonyms," it says, written large and slantingly in Nil's hand, leaning sideways across the orderly printed text beneath. I am looking at it now, and in the light of day, or perhaps, healthful dissociation, the two *p*'s seem too large, the sibilant *s*'s too small, yet so inspirationally precise, and, of course, so blatantly— well—insane.

Written so imposingly, as they are, in that distinctive fecal brown Crayola marker—the only pen psych patients at Meriwether hospital are allowed—these are unforgettable words to me, words as indicative, damning, and, admittedly, histrionic as "Abandon all hope." They are the words above the doorway, the words of my descent and of Nil's. They say everything and mean nothing.

You could make a diagnosis on that basis alone, I suppose, if you were so inclined. As an artifact, Exhibit A, this page would not work much in Nil's favor in court, or in a doctor's hands. Nor does it pasted in my notebook.

It is the thing I turn to when I want to go back to my first night in Meriwether. Immediately back, as if transported to the all-night fluorescent lights of the hospital ward shining down on the off-white page, Nil scribbling and cocking his head interestedly at his own wild script, all the while explaining dharma, string theory, and the four noble truths.

Nil couldn't sleep and neither could I. He, because he was manic. I, because I was terrified, though trying hard not to show it. And because I was bedding down for the night in a foldout chair. All the gurneys in the hallway were taken, and the hallways were all that we had: U-shaped and lined with gurneys, with small alcoves on each end. One side for the women, one side for the men, the nurse's station in the middle, and alcoves at either end. The alcoves were filled with the chair beds, and each had a small picnic table with a TV mounted above it.

My chair was commodious as chairs go, like the contraptions you see in business class on a plane. It probably wouldn't have precluded sleep had it not been for the loud talk and laughter going on just feet away at the picnic table, which the night staff had colonized. They were flipping through tabloid newspapers, trading jokes and insults.

Their noise resounded in my head, the noise of a public place.

And that is very much how a big-city public hospital feels. Like an ugly big-city public place, a bus station, say, or a restroom in a vagabond park where everything is a bilious green or degraded shade of gray and nothing quite works the way it's supposed to, or is ever really clean, except in the strictly antimicrobial sense, as when you scorch cement and porcelain with bleach.

The noise wasn't the only barrier to sleep. It was freezing in there, too, and all we had to cover us were sheets and paper-thin sky blue pajamas. Hospital issue, all of it, including the Acti-Tred socks with stickum on the soles. I was wearing two pairs of those, and I had layered on a few extra johnnies for warmth.

Seven hours before, all of my possessions had been taken at the door, put in a gray metal locker, and tagged. I had been sitting in my chair ever since, pretending that I was on a flight to Australia instead of locked by my own doing in the holding pen of emergency psych.

I had been working my way up to this for weeks. I hadn't wanted to go. Who wants to go to a psych ward, much less one of the grungiest, scariest ones you can think of?

Dumb-ass journalists doing experiments, that's who.

Despite having been to the bin before, I hadn't been at all sure how to commit myself to Meriwether. That first time around, at the end of *Self-Made Man*, I had arranged it through my doctor, and I had only agreed to go because she knew the place—had trained there, actually—and because, according to *U.S. News and World Report*, it had been rated one of the best facilities in the country. I had been given the admitting nurse's number, had called, and had been told where and when to present myself for treatment. And, of course, I had needed/wanted their treatment. This, on the other hand, was self-inflicted and clinically unnecessary.

It was altogether different. I knew no one. I had no connection with the place, and, understandably, I was intimidated by its size and what I expected would be its desperate, unclean, cavernous recesses where the unwanted were lost and forgotten. Though I had put myself there purposely, and purposefully, the urge to flee set in immediately, nonetheless. I didn't want to get lost there, or even unduly detained for however long it might take, once I'd gotten my story, to convince the doctors that I didn't really need to be there.

That was the trick. Convince them that I did need to be there. Stay for at least ten days. Then convince them that I didn't need to be there anymore. And do all of that without seeming crazier than anyone.

I had a history of depression with occasional mild hypomanic episodes, or so the diagnosis of my former private psychiatrist had indicated, but when I checked myself into Meriwether I was feeling good. Quite good, especially when you consider how scary it is to throw yourself anonymously into what you can't help thinking of—per the liberties of one too many Hollywood movies—as the darkest heart of darkness in the concrete jungle.

I was not actually depressed, but I had to pretend that I was. A strange exercise for anyone, but especially for a depressive who has spent the bulk of her adult life trying to escape bleak moods, not court them. I wondered: Could I talk myself into a trough, when I had never been able to talk myself out of one? Would faking the mood bring it on for real? Was my "disorder" that suggestible? And, more to the point, were the doctors?

Certainly, I knew what to say, and how slowly and disconsolately to say it. Whether I was really well or ill, no one but I could really know. How would the docs tell the difference? As in all psych wards, when you check yourself in with only a backpack to your name, saying you are suicidally depressed, they take you at your word. There is nothing else to go on. Diagnoses are made on hearsay. What you say is what you are, even if you are not a reliable narrator. There is no test, nothing independently verifiable. Just the swordplay of soft interrogation.

I might have told them I was hearing voices, but then they might have given me Seroquel—which is what Nil was taking—or Haldol, or Thorazine, or some other heavyweight antipsychotic that makes you drool and twitch and doze off at the dinner table. But I didn't want to put myself in for that.

I could have told them that I had slept with five people in the past day, heard the birds speaking Greek, sold my mother into white slavery and spent the money on dinner. Then they might have opted for Depakote, the big gun of mood stabilizers. But again, I wasn't ripe for that. I'd been on Depakote before. I had gained way too much weight, for one, and didn't trust what it would do to me. That wasn't the way.

But the things you say in psych wards can become a menu for drugs. You have to be careful. I wanted to keep drugs to a minimum, so I reported the virtual truth of my history. Depression, possibly bipolar. I was on

20 milligrams of Prozac, and hoping to get away with nothing more than a dose boost on that—the devil I knew—and maybe a sedative for the p.m.

As it turned out, the medication question was going to have to wait for "upstairs," the ward itself, spookily referred to, where a team of pros could look me over and make the chin-stroking, wisely nodding call.

Down there in emergency that first night, I had managed to get some Klonopin by request, but I still hadn't managed to fall asleep.

Nil had migrated to the picnic table, and so was contributing to the noise. He was playing a highly unorthodox game of chess with one of the orderlies, who was complaining loudly and incessantly about Nil's strategy, which apparently entailed moving more than one piece per turn. His amped-up brain was skipping ahead three moves and making them all at once.

"You can't do that," the orderly kept saying, his voice rising in irritation.

The bright lights were kept on all night, so it was like trying to sleep in an interrogation room. The staff, too, went on all night, gabbing and laughing as if there weren't stranded sick people lying all around them trying to rest. We were invisible, discounted, like baggage or the dead, stowed and impervious. We could tell no stories, the assumption being, I expect, that we were all too drugged or nuts to notice or lodge a complaint.

There were four rooms in there, actually, with beds even, two of which were empty. Who qualified for them or why I wasn't sure. Perhaps the violent. After I'd been there for a few hours, I would have killed for a bed, or even just a closable door. I asked, at one point, if I could crawl away to one of the vacants for some privacy and quiet, but was told in typical bureaucratic futility-speak that it was impossible. I was, they said, not being formally admitted there, but only being held until a bed opened upstairs.

Somewhere around 3:00 a.m., however, one of the loud gaggle on duty announced that he could use a nap, and crawled off into one of these rooms for a snooze, pulling the curtains and all. Three hours later, just in time for shift change, he emerged, sighing and stretching satisfiedly.

I had managed to drop off somewhere around one o'clock, but had been woken at two for a chest x-ray.

"Why do I need a chest x-ray?" I asked the man who wheeled me in a seat-belted, wooden-backed wheelchair through a maze of green hallways and mauve doors.

"To check for TB," he said.

Oh, right. As you do.

In the middle of the night?

Passing back through the locked door that said Patient Elopement Risk and Triage in big white letters, I knew that I would not do well if I had to stay in the psych ER for another night. But I had no choice. It would all depend on when a bed became available on one of the main wards upstairs. This special, sequestered, locked ER was where they held you until then, where they processed your insurance or lack thereof, where they kenneled you, like it or not, because you were a risk either to yourself or others. It would take as long as it took.

We were in the bowels of the hospital. There were no windows. No air but the recycled variety, wheezing through vents. No light but bright fluorescents, unforgiving and somehow worse than shadows. Had they not secured my valuables, I might well have made a run for it from radiology. But then, of course, they knew where I lived, and I felt sure they would have followed up if I had made for home in my mad rags.

"Eloped" was priceless, though I suppose only we loons were inclined to do it alone and from a wheelchair, streaking through the streets in our blue issue, like B movie extras run amok.

But, God, it was a strong urge—run!

I thought—and I had this thought many times in the coming days—who wouldn't look crazy doing that? Yet who, under the circumstances, wouldn't do it, or at least want to?

I had given them urine at ten, films at two, and blood at six. I was, it seemed, contagion-free, excretion-wise anyway. And the lungs, I was told after breakfast, were clear.

Some time in the night, the cops had brought in a shirtless man in handcuffs. He had, apparently, threatened his family. I saw him come in, but since we were separated by sex, I did not see him again.

Somehow, though, perhaps because of his long hair and Zen demeanor, Nil had managed to stay on the women's side with me for much of the night. He told me he had been to the bin many times before. Since adolescence, he said, he had been in and out of places like Meriwether. He knew the routine well, which was a great help to me, who didn't.

I had managed to smuggle in a pen but had forgotten that I should not be seen with it, and so it was promptly taken by a nurse, officious and smug.

"You can't have that," she sighed, flicking her fingers to her palm impatiently. "Give it here."

I was a kid to her, cheating at school. And that is how it felt. I was not yet practiced at subterfuge, and surrendered the pen with a shrug. This was a false position, though, since I was not indifferent. Losing the thing made me panic. It was not a small loss to me, though, a petty one on her part, and she knew it, took pleasure in it.

Or was that the beginning of paranoia?

I didn't know what I was going to do if I couldn't write. Nil knew this feeling, and reached into the paper bag he had found to house his few pilferings from around the ward. They included, aside from the brown marker, the dog-eared paperback book that he was using as a notebook, some rolls and milk kept from dinner, and a small square blanket someone had snatched from the maternity ward, which he was using as a meditation mat. This was when I saw and used my first Crayola, the blunt tip acceptable in a place where a ballpoint was a weapon, or could be.

"You can do a lot of damage with one of these," a nurse had said to me, holding up her pen. As soon as she said it I had visions of stabbing a person in the neck, maybe myself. The jugular is pokeable and fatal, and what's more, neatly self-inflicting if you're so inclined. Just then, I was not. But too long in that place and you might be—probably would be. That was clear.

They had a metal detector at the door, though they did not put me through it. Maybe this was a perk of being white, or of being thought too thin to hide weapons in my flesh. Or maybe the guards were too busy with the fat Muslim woman in *hijab* to bother with me. They put her through twice. They didn't even pat me down. But as I told the admitting nurse, I've never been violent, so who's counting?

"Have you ever lost your temper?" she asked.

Was that a test? A bout of cognitive lock-picking? A measure of my faculties? Later, in this vein, they would ask me: Who is the president? What day is it?

Don't get smart, I decided. Be as honest as you can.

"Um . . . yes."

From where I was sitting, I could see another sign I enjoyed. "Please do not walk through triage area while triage in progress."

Was this triage in progress, or was that when you lost your temper?

"Do you have a psychiatric history? Do you know your clinical diagnosis?"

"Yes and yes," I said, looking away.

A man in the hallway had crapped himself, a brown seep the shape of Lake Michigan hanging low in his bottoms. He was shouting into the nurse's station, which was a fort of Plexiglas from which the RNs rarely emerged unbidden. Patients tended to loiter there and stare, ignored. If you needed something, you had to knock. Or shout. Or crap your pants, I guess.

I had gawped there, too, earlier, just for something to do, mesmerized by a computer whose crawling screen saver said—ungrammatically— "Always borrow money from a pessimist. They never expect it back." I spliced it like a chant in my head, coding it for meaning. "Always borrow . . . never expect . . . money, money . . . a pessimist's back."

This was one of those nutty hallmarks that began to make sense to me in there. Babbling. Boredom was a scourge and the enemy. You fended it off with anything, the brain leaping on word games for food: scrambles, iterations, puns. It was, oddly enough, a defense. Not so much the evidence of a mind gone awry, as the ditch of a mind trying not to, like a verbal rocking that puts confusion to sleep, the language center calming itself, whistling a tune in the dark.

No one moved to help the befouled man, so Nil, ever eager to be of service, offered shampoo.

"I need a towel," the man grumbled ungratefully.

"Sorry. Just shampoo."

"Can't you get me a towel?"

"I'm a patient, too."

The nurse put a statement in front of me. It said that I would not harm myself or others while being evaluated. I signed it—smiling—with her ballpoint pen.

Time had passed slowly after that. Sitting. Staring. And then more questions. The questions were much the same. Condition. History. Temper. First the nurse, then the doctor. The doctor explained what voluntary meant: (a) you can be discharged if and when the doctors agree; (b) if the doctors disagree, you can be discharged against medical advice—though how or if this ever happens is unclear, given that (c) if you insist on being discharged and the doctors still disagree, you must write a three-day letter expressing your wishes, in which case, you will be brought before a judge within seventy-two hours. In theory, at least, this is the law, but I made no use of it.

In short, voluntary did not mean free. It meant I had not come there in cuffs, but I could not leave when I chose.

"Do you understand?"

"Yes."

"Sign here."

Voluntary means will. An act of will. Free will. I will this and it is so. Or so it is in the free world. But there, in Meriwether, it meant a resignation of will, the last free act until they discharged you. And this, to my mind, was the worst part about being there, the worst part about being mad, or deemed mad.

Madness is a disease of the will, of judgment. That is what is impaired. And so, in there, along with so much else, your will was taken away, like a pen, because you could not be trusted with it. Yet your will is the thing that makes you feel human. Without it you cannot be well, which is why no one in there really got well, or, arguably, much better.

This is the paradox of asylums, and their fatal flaw. Put a person in a cage and you cannot help him. But leave him to his devices and he cannot help himself, or will not. Freedom is a prerequisite for healing a broken mind. It cannot be fixed against its will. Yet a broken mind is a broken will, a freedom that does harm, even potentially serious physical harm to itself and possibly others, a freedom that can attack or maim. So, how else to heal but by force?

I looked at my wristband. White, with my name, date of birth, my age, too (for the lazy), and a code I couldn't decipher. MXE. Again, it seemed like the most natural thing in the world to play at breaking this code: methotrexate enema; maximal xenon eczema (a rash of computers; could be bad). But that's what crazy people supposedly do, right? See cryptograms everywhere. And when you are looking, you will find them.

It's like learning a new word. Someone uses it—"Esperanto," for example—and you say, "What the hell does that mean?"

They tell you, and you are amazed. "It was a language made up by linguists in 1884. It was supposed to be something that the whole world could learn, so that we could all speak to each other."

"Really? I've never heard that before."

"Haven't you?" they say. "How odd."

Then, as if by public consensus, it's everywhere. Someone brings it up in conversation. A newspaper article tells you it's in *Finnegans Wake*. And then, there in Meriwether of all places, where the TV was blaring above my head all day and evening, it was the daily double on *Jeopardy!* No joke.

"What is Esperanto?"

Fuck me. Don't tell that to the nurses.

I have my pet theories like everyone else. Madness as the extension of sanity, the same propensities, only more so. A mental game gone too serious and scary, a dream we cannot wake from, or better, a somnambulist's midnight lack of sense running prime time and permanent in the day.

Maybe you, the normal man, walk into the kitchen in the wee hours and eat jelly by the tablespoon right out of the jar, and have no memory of it in the morning, only the weird evidence in the sink. Or maybe when you wake, you turn to your wife and say, "I had the strangest dream last night. I was flying in a tiger suit over Wall Street and your mother was there wearing a turban."

And she will nod at you understandingly, knowing the oddity and cogency of dreams. You get up and go to work, sit in board meetings. You are sane.

But a mad person will say the same thing in the middle of the day, all day long, and he will find it more convincing because unshakable after a shower and a cup of coffee. Is he wearing his subconscious on his sleeve, as he tells you (or usually himself, aloud) of tigers and turbans? Has his mind turned itself inside out, switched night and day, abstract expression and photo real?

Maybe our art is his life. Maybe he lives every day in the stream of consciousness we so admire in Joyce, with little breaks of coherence in between, the precise opposite of our daily grind, the stone-dry workaday that we relinquish so happily for a bit of science fiction fantasy on TV. Maybe the madman is a model of rationality in his dreams, while you are all over the map.

Breakfast came at eight. A small pack of raisin bran, a roll (processed "wheat" flour bleached to a fare-thee-well, with riboflavin, niacin, and God knows what else, preservative or homogenizing, chemically added back in), margarine, grape juice, and a four-ounce carton of milk. I was determined not to gain weight while I was in there, eating all that sugar and starch, and sitting all day. But I was equally determined to shit, daily if possible, so I downed the sugared cereal for fiber and passed on the rolls and juice. For good measure, I managed to get another milk and cereal off an unclaimed tray and made quick work of that as well.

After breakfast I sat some more, and thought, and watched, and listened. I was already in despair of that place, which was itself collectively despairing. Even the people who worked there had given up. Perhaps they most of all. It was written all over them. The way they fell asleep in front of the TV during their shifts, the way they moved and operated, slowly and sighing, as if only with great effort. The way they talked to us, with the tone people reserve for the retarded and the elderly of whom no improvement is ever expected.

We were held together there, the attended and the attending, the lazy and the infirm, and choice did not really come into it anymore. The staff were there of their own accord, just as I was, though what does that really mean? That they had many other, more desirable employment prospects? I doubt it. That they went home at the end of the day? But to what? A furlough at best, and an all too brief one. To doughnuts and coffee and movies of the week, to the sustenance of empty lolling. What lives was that place really sustaining? What was done on the outside? More of the sleeping and eating and lassitude that we were all practicing in there?

We were a reflection of them and they of us. Hardly different in kind, though surely in quality? You go crazy the way your culture goes sane. We were getting fat, eating junk food and rotting our brains in front of the TV, popping pills to make us palatable, and our lives palatable to us, inanity everywhere and we a party to it, dumbly coasting.

Contempt. They felt contempt. That was it.

"You want what? A cup? A toothbrush?"

Sigh. Lumber, lumber.

"Just a minute."

I had gotten through my first night, and the morning and partial day thereafter. I had succeeded all too well in penning myself in. It was done.

I was committed. Not just to Meriwether, but to the first leg of my long year's journey to three psych wards.

I was scared and—oh, how the magic had worked in one night—I was depressed. More than depressed. Caged. A trapped, too cognizant animal, tiptoeing my way to the clogged toilet, over the foul floor of the women's bathroom on flagstones of piled paper towel. It was just about as bad as I had imagined, maybe worse because I was there, not imagining, but stuck firm in the hours that dragged on so harsh and idle.

I looked for comfort in the gurney that I got, finally, only an hour or two before they came to take me upstairs. I lay on it, and then couldn't, because I didn't want to be another one of those lumps lining the hallways.

It wasn't just that I didn't want to resemble the rest of them, lying, as they were, face to the wall. It was that I didn't want to become them, because I feared that lying with your face to the wall in that place could *make you into* a person who lies with his face to the wall in that place.

Or was it the other way around?

Did the people make the place, or did the place make the people? Did the fact that these people were mostly poor, or at least of modest means, and sometimes even homeless, turn the place into a zoo, or did the zoo turn the people into animals? I knew, even in just one night, that the latter was true. You become your environment, and you become what you are expected to be. The lower the standard, the lower the result. The ruder the treatment, the cruder, the more animal, the man.

But did causality move in the other direction, too? This seemed true as well, even in the outside world. Public places become disgusting because no one cares about them. They belong to no one, even though ostensibly they belong to all. And so they decline. People litter. People piss. They deface whatever they can reach, leaving all those grimy little marks of insignificance that add up to a slum. What is not yours is not your problem, and then it is everyone's problem, or eyesore.

Or bedsore.

Yes, I thought. It goes both ways. Viciously. We shit where we eat, and then we become shit where we are eaten. We write on the walls, and then the writing is on the wall.

I wore the flimsy johnnies and the Acti-Tred socks, and they wore me. Down and out.

I lost my pen to the nurse and learned to write legibly with a marker, in fat, loopy, childlike cursive just like Nil's.

I went in well and turned ill overnight.

I was, and I was becoming, a patient at Meriwether Hospital.

I made it up to the ward that afternoon. Day two.

They took me up in the wheelchair, the same wooden one with the seat belt that I'd ridden to radiology the night before. No walking yourself between wards, apparently.

You're sick. You sit.

I have no idea what happened to Nil. I never saw him again. I didn't even say good-bye. He was and remains a ghost of that night. I'd almost believe I thought him up, except that I have that torn page from his "notebook," which, looking at it again now, I see was taken from a 2001 edition of a literary review called *Glimmer Train,* a publication that you'd be far, far more likely to find in a university library than just lying around in the asshole of Meriwether Hospital.

What poor tasteful soul had taken refuge in that artifact, I thought? Or had come in clutching it to his breast years ago? And had he left it behind purposely, a grim reminder of a time he was determined to forget? Or had it fallen from his grasp inadvertently while he gave himself up to a gurney and turned his face to the wall?

I took that page with me up to the ward, taking my own brand of refuge in it, as had Nil. I took it, and my notebook, and Nil's Crayola, which he had kindly given to me for keeps.

I went into a consult room and met my treatment team first thing.

The word "team" sounds good here—thorough—but wasn't really. They were more of the "How many mental health professionals does it take to screw in a lightbulb?" variety. Their effect was not increased by their number.

There was the unit chief, who made brief appearances twice during my stay (at the first interview and the last). There was Sarah, a medical student; Kim, a chirpy social worker, whom I never met again after the first interview; and Dr. Balkan, the staff psychiatrist, who would be attending to me most directly.

We gathered at a long conference table in what I remember as a poorly lit room, but this may just be my memory shading the scene to fit how I felt. I felt exposed yet shadowed, intruded on but not seen. There was too much attention and not enough.

This gloominess was, I think, the effect of the way these people did their jobs, like civil servants, dryly, colorlessly, in unison. They had procedures and they followed them. They asked me more of the usual questions about my history, my family, and what had brought me there. They wrote it all down on their notepads, and then they looked at me to see what they could see.

I don't know what they saw. A classic depressive? A charlatan? I worried that they might see through me. But a night in emergency had lowered me to the right level, or thereabouts. So what were they really going to see? Fear? Desperation? Distrust? Those were real enough.

I know that I did not see them any more clearly than I thought they were seeing me. I was jaundiced as hell. I went in there predisposed not to like them.

My first time in the bin in 2004 had soured me pretty soundly on ward shrinks. I'd been at the mercy of a prick on a power trip, the kind of buttoned-up banty rooster who gets off on control and then, when you resist him, tells you that *you've* got issues with control. It had taken me two days of forced calm and tactical parlay to convince him to let me out of that place, when all I wanted to do was leap across the table and bash his bald pate in. Again, who wouldn't look crazy doing that? And yet, who wouldn't want to do it when squaring off against a pug jailer with an advanced degree.

Aside from Baldy, I'd met my fair share of shrinks over the course of the previous fifteen years. One of the last ones in the string had been the genius who'd convinced me to go into the bin that first time, even though it was the worst possible advice she could have given me. She'd also been the one, back in my twenties when I'd first consulted her, to prescribe way too many medications way too soon, without telling me about their side effects or the dependency and withdrawal they could induce.

Coming into Meriwether, I had, let's say, a sore spot for doctors.

That's undoubtedly why, among the team, I liked Sarah, the medical student, best. She wasn't a doctor yet, and so she still had sense enough to doubt herself. She hadn't yet cultivated the persona that she would get with her degree, the nonstick coating that so many psychiatrists spray on an inch thick somewhere between memorizing the material at school and coming into contact with actual human beings. All too often, by the time you found yourself sitting across from them in the hospital giving them your sorry spiel, it was like talking to a diving bell.

But Sarah still had cracks. Now and again actual thoughts were getting through, thoughts that had not been placed there by others or rooted out by the training. Her face was frequently strained by the effort of appearing remote, professionally cool.

She wasn't.

Early on, when we were alone for a moment, I asked her something about her manner, about what she was learning to do, and how you could really hope to relate to another person as a person if you were practicing the art of galvanizing your own soul.

A blush spread over her cheeks. Would she learn to repress that later, I wondered, if it came so readily now? What a loss if she did. Sad, because it was such a pleasure to watch her thoughts bloom on her cheeks like hot little pools of appetite. Intellectual appetite. A noticeable idea coming through her ears in waves of sound, landing on her brain as chemical information, a wave becoming a particle, then the information some-how—God, how?—pouring itself into an emotion, giving rise to a physi-ological response, and then a color in her face. For me, it was the best part, the miracle of the brain that it could take my question not just as language but as implication and turn it to a rush of blood.

But if Sarah was going to make it in this line, she'd have to learn to check that evidence. Dry up. Cover. Get stupid.

The unit chief was stupid in that way, I thought. Not genuinely stupid. She seemed bright enough. Doctorly stupid, I mean. Stupid because cut off and rendered arrogant by her profession and her position. She was in charge, and she sat in her sovereignty with unnerving entitlement. But to me, she knew and controlled a lot less than she thought she did. She was catered to, but mistaken, like a fat newborn, thinking her little sphere was all the world and her will the axis it was spinning on.

She wasn't like other doctors I'd known in this respect. It wasn't Baldy's kind of entitlement, overweening and repugnant. And yet it was of the same strain, because doctors are trained by doctors to be doctors, and part of being a doctor is acting like one. She came off as if her sphincter had been tied shut like a reticule. Baldy was more the type you suspected might have buried people under his house, people like his high school valedictorian, or maybe, from his übermensch period, a landlady or two.

Who knows. Maybe she was a really nice cuddly lady at home, as tame as they come. But I didn't see her at home. I saw her on the job, and that is how I judged her, by how I saw her doing her job. It wasn't really what she said so much as how little she said. It was clear that she knew exactly just how little she needed to say to exert her influence. She sat heavily, like lead in a boat, pulling all the ballast toward her. The others deferred palpably, unthinkingly, as if by force of gravity or instinct.

Dr. Balkan was a type, too, and does not yield an inspired description, I'm afraid. She wasn't particularly bad or good. Not singular. Just a yeo-man, you might say, doing service day in, day out. Showing up. Trying, but knowing the limitations of talk in a place where most people were too delusional to have what the rest of us would think of as a conversation. She was doing her job conscientiously. She was efficient but not officious. Removed but not too proud. She listened, though maybe a tad hurriedly, during our ten-minute consults each day. She cared, you could see that, and she really did want to accommodate my desire for more therapy and fewer drugs, but there was only so much time in the day. And even if there had been a spare hour, she wasn't practiced at the long, slow muse, or probably much inclined toward it.

Anyhow, Sarah was different. She interested me. I almost wanted to save her, cut her free and say, "Go and be a person. Get out before it's too late." But then I was hardly a recommendation for that approach, at least in my present condition, or what she perceived to be my present condition.

But what did she or any of them perceive? This was part of the problem. My private conversation with Sarah had begun with me asking her about herself, about the way she handled situations where a patient asked you something about yourself or tried to establish an exchange. She had said that she hadn't quite worked out yet what to do on those occasions. She wasn't sure when and or if she should ever let the patient see her. I admired her for admitting even that much.

The dance with patients could be tricky, I knew. I mean, you wouldn't want someone like me blundering around inside your head. And I suppose there were always people like me who were wanting to do that, either for entertainment or because it was just too hard to have any kind of therapeutic relationship with a cipher.

I had both motivations, as it happened. I wanted to see what she'd do, what any of them would do if you challenged their remove, if you said in effect, "Be a person with me, will you? I'm not a petri dish." I wanted to relate to them, to connect as a human being. But I also wanted to get a reaction that wasn't preprogrammed. I wanted to poke an actual working apparatus. Stimulus, response. Action, reaction. Slap and gasp. Spit and grimace. Whatever worked.

This was the cross-purpose of it all, in my view. They saw me as a set of chemicals. They were dealing with my brain as an organ, palpating it with categories, forgetting of course that, unlike its illustrious sister discipline, neurology, psychiatry is not just the science of the brain as brain, but brain as organ of thought, seat of incandescent function, impalpable, the only organ in my body that can answer back.

So, talk to me.

But even their names and titles were too heavy for such intimacies. Doctor. Dr. It gets bigger with abbreviation. Degrees are magical that way. They make gods. The doctor who tells you what she knows, as if she knew it for certain. Yet, she is a deeply fallible, mostly chimerical being created by us to talk down to us when things are at their worst, because somehow that makes us feel better. In the absence of someone who actually knows what she's talking about, we are just as comforted by someone who sounds like she knows what she's talking about. That is enough. Just say it with conviction and it will make the boogie man go away.

Dr. Balkan suggested Lamictal, a mood stabilizer that I'd tried years before, but had quickly abandoned because of a swelling in my groin. A very small percentage of patients who try Lamictal develop a dangerous rash. According to the docs, it is the only side effect of the drug, but a very serious one. At the time, my groin swelling had made my doc nervous, so she'd advised me to stop the course. As it turned out, the groin swelling had been a side effect of another, nonpsychiatric medication that I had been taking.

"It's worth trying Lamictal again, then?" Dr. Balkan said.

Having done my homework on meds, I was skeptical. I'd read a lot about the undisclosed or unknown dangers and unpleasant side effects of so many of the pills my docs had been prescribing for me over the years, and I'd been appalled to read, first in books, then in newspapers, of how thoroughly corrupt the drug development and approval processes are in this country.

Pharmaceutical companies have their fingers in the pie every step of the way. They fund clinical trials of the drugs for which they hope to obtain FDA approval. They ghostwrite the papers that report the results of those trials. They provide most of the advertising revenue for, and therefore exercise undue editorial influence over, the journals that publish those ghostwritten papers. They pay large sums of money to many of the doctors and "experts" who advise the FDA, and often vote directly on which drugs to approve.

Their sales representatives call directly on primary-care physicians and psychiatrists, providing free samples of their drugs, as well as reams of so-called informational literature, which is actually carefully crafted promotional literature about those drugs. Often this promotional literature is the only source of information that most docs consult about the drugs they are prescribing and, more alarmingly, the conditions for which they are prescribing them.

The drug companies often go so far as to hire individual doctors as "consultants," paying them thousands of dollars and sending them on all-expenses-paid trips to exotic locations where they can attend conferences about the company's star drugs. Finally, the drug companies go directly to the consumer, flooding the airwaves with advertisements not only for their products but for the diseases those products are purported to treat. This is one of the major reasons why most people think they know—not just believe, but know—that serotonin deficiencies cause depression, even though there is no real scientific evidence to support this claim. But we know. We know because the drug companies told us so.

So you can see why I wasn't eager to take any more drugs, and why I was, in fact, attempting to wean myself safely off of the 20 milligrams of Prozac that I was already on when I came into Meriwether. (I had been on it for at least a year, sometimes at slightly higher doses, but usually right at 20 mg, where the side effects seemed least intrusive, but the benefits sufficient to keep me afloat.) You can also see why I didn't exactly trust that Dr. Balkan knew—or if she knew, would tell me—what I needed to know about Lamictal.

"What neurotransmitter does that work on?" I asked.

"I'll have to get back to you on that," she said.

A few hours later she produced something she'd printed off the Web, a typically useless document that betrayed how little anybody knew about what the hell this drug was doing or how.

Apparently, Lamictal acts on the neurotransmitter glutamate, blocking its release in the brain. Glutamate is the same neurotransmitter that appears to be activiated by the street drugs ketamine and PCP, or so the paper said. Lamictal was first approved for use as an antiseizure medication for people with epilepsy, and it is still used in this way.

That's all I could glean from the paper, and it wasn't really of any use, except to confirm my worst fears that when it came to understanding these meds and their real effect on our brains, we were all shooting a blunderbuss at a field of daisies in the dark.

I told Dr. Balkan that I wasn't comfortable with the drug routine and thought it might be best to go the therapy route for now.

She was insistent.

"Bipolar disorder is a chemical imbalance that is something like eighty percent inherited."

The idea was that I was unlikely to get better without meds.

Of course, the theory that there is any such verifiable chemical thing as bipolar disorder is far from proven. Besides, the idea that I had bipolar disorder at all was built on a pretty flimsy foundation, having come about because I had become hypomanic while on antidepressants. Enough people have done this that antidepressant-associated hypomania, or bipolar III, though it is not, as yet, listed in the *DSM,* is now an unofficially recognized mental disorder.

The side effect of a medication had become an organic disorder, poof, just like that.

I spent almost the entirety of my first two ten-minute daily therapy sessions going back and forth with Dr. Balkan about the meds. Finally, I succumbed to the fear that they might keep me longer than I'd planned if I refused to take anything, and said I'd take the dose.

As they are no doubt required to do, the nurses at Meriwether watched you take your meds. They wheeled around a cart full of pills and liquids, stopping in front of every room to dispense them. By the time they started giving me the Lamictal, on my third day up there, I'd figured out that they weren't terribly vigilant about making sure you weren't hiding anything under your tongue, or holding it in your mouth or palm. Besides, I'd requested a multivitamin, which they gave me at the same time as they gave me the Lamictal, so I was able to make it look like I was popping both pills into my mouth, when in fact, I was holding the Lamictal back, lodged between two fingers.

When the nurses left I went into the bathroom and flushed it.

After the triage hole, the ward seemed like a penthouse. It had big wide windows, albeit elaborately gated and locked. But you could still see through them enough to get a sweeping view of the city below. We were on the twentieth floor, and the width of the sky at that level was intoxicating to my trapped mind. Diffuse light pervaded the large rooms for most of the day, though no fresh air made it in, or very little. My bed, one of four in my room, was pushed up lengthwise against one of these windows, and I spent a lot of time, especially late at night when I couldn't sleep, sitting up in bed watching the lights glowing in the windows of skyscrapers. The seal on my window had a sliver gap in it somewhere near the bottom, and as I sat there, desperate for a lungful of unprocessed oxygen, I'd lean my face against the grating and listen to the slow whistle of the winter wind, feeling the momentary caress of the cold on my cheek.

In that place, where there was so much that you weren't allowed to do, leaning that way felt like stealing, like I'd get busted for breathing wrong when the head nurse, Mrs. Weston, strode into my room, as she periodically did, and searched the slim freestanding closet by my bed. It was more a power play than anything. She usually missed half of the contraband that was in there, that being a few pens I'd asked visitors to bring me, a couple of oranges taken from a box in the dayroom, a plastic bag for dirty clothes (possible suffocation risk), and a pair of pajama bottoms with a string tie (strangulation risk; the Ping-Pong table in the dayroom had no net for the same reason).

We got oranges around eight o'clock, as a snack after dinner, usually along with peanut butter and jelly sandwiches on Wonder bread. You had to eat all this in the dayroom, though, because we weren't supposed to bring food back to our rooms, lest it attract bugs and mice, or worse—that was the official rationale anyway—though that seems appalling in a hospital.

But, like everybody else, I used food as a form of succor, hoarding it for late-night snacks. It was about the only thing you could do in there that felt good, aside from masturbate, that is, and I don't know what they did with you if they caught you doing that.

The oranges served double duty, as they were especially useful for making what I dubbed prison potpourri. This was the kind of thing you learned to do when you had extremely limited resources and you were faced with the foul odor of the unlockable en suite bathroom that you shared with your three roomies, all of whom were less hygienic than one might have hoped. The odor was mostly of piss, strong concentrated piss of the kind you get on the floor and walls when you're overmedicated and underhydrated, have bad aim, and are not particularly concerned about flushing the toilet after use.

A janitor gave the bathroom a cursory going-over most days, often very cursory. That didn't always include mopping the floor, or if it did, it didn't help for long. The stench was overpowering, yeasty, and thick as no piss I've ever smelled, such that you had to keep the bathroom door closed at all times. Otherwise the whole room would smell like hell's own pissoir.

To make prison potpourri I'd take my oranges into the bathroom to peel them, standing over the toilet as I did so, thus allowing the pungent oil in the peels to spray the room with what amounted to a home remedy cleanser. For extra effect I'd stand in front of the steel plate mirror (no glass), hold each piece of peel up to the fluorescent light, and squeeze it as many different ways as I could make it bend, watching the fine spray spurt into the air. Finally, I'd throw the peels in the garbage and let them suffuse the room for as long as they could.

Standing there squirting my orange peels under the light, sometimes holding them right up to my face to get a really good look at the spray, and doing so with the kind of keen attention that other people devote to their taxes, I realized I was doing something that, if you came upon me doing it, big as you please, in my blue issues with their dodgy snap fly open, and my Acti-Tred socks half pulled off like clown shoes, you'd be inclined to think that I was mistaken in believing I needed to be anywhere but exactly where I was.

But all these elaborate bathroom cleansing plans were foiled for the day if Mrs. Weston stalked in. Usually, I was sitting on my bed, leaning into my grated window sipping the air, or writing in my notebook with a pen, propping it against my upbent knees to keep the writing instrument mostly out of sight. When I wasn't using one of my pens, I kept my stash of them safe in the front pouch of my hooded sweatshirt. But even in my bed, taking precautions, it was hard not to get caught using one, so my marsupial supply dwindled quickly.

Mrs. Weston had a keen eye for ballpoint pens. She could see them from the hallway, and before she got halfway across the room, she'd put out her hand imperiously to demand the precious item. She'd take it, then proceed with a vigorous search, flipping open my closet, pulling out the oranges she could see, and saying in her loud ward voice, "No food in the rooms, people. No food in the rooms."

The plastic bag was a much bigger deal, but she never found that, buried as it was under my underwear and books and papers (these latter items were not considered to be a risk). As I said, she was more interested in the symbolism of the act. She was a tall, imposing black woman in low-heeled boots and a semicasual pantsuit. Her voice was powerful, and she enjoyed using it as if she were herding third graders at recess.

I suppose it made her feel efficient to conduct her searches. It was probably in her job description to at least walk into every room in the mornings, just to be sure no one had died or stuffed someone else into a closet during the night. Still, the searches were intrusive, and always conducted with the same entitled attitude and condescending air that made me want to rig my closet with a dummy, or a leaning cup of piss, just to make Madam Suzerain think twice about where she stuck her nose.

But then I suppose that was part of why she treated us like kids, because given the circumstances—the rules, the restrictions, the unreasonable deprivations—you resorted to childish deceits just to meet your needs or show a bit of spunk. Pranks are the refuge of the powerless and the puerile, I guess. The elements of surprise and ridicule sticking out their tongues.

I found it unreasonable, for example, that they didn't let the patients smoke. It was illegal to do so in the hospital, and I was all for that, especially on our hermetic ward. But once patients had been in for a few days and earned the privilege, we would be taken in small groups to the roof once—or if the staff was especially organized, maybe twice—a day to get some fresh air. It would have been quite easy to allow smoking on those breaks. And you can be sure they didn't forbid it for health reasons, because when you saw the food they were serving to mostly overweight diabetics, you knew that, despite it being a hospital, this was no refuge for the metabolically convalescent.

Smoking was something almost everyone on the ward was dying to do. It was one of those few pleasures in a destitute's life that made the days pass. Forbidding it was a form of torture to most of these people, who were homeless psychotics and had been picked up by the cops for disturbing the peace. This meant that they were quitting of necessity cold turkey. Nicotine patches were available to them. But the addiction was clearly far more psychological than anything else, and being trapped in that place, miserishly squirreling away my oranges, it made perfect sense to me why that was so. And I was there of my own doing. They were not—which, of course, made the deprivations that much worse. The one thing they had, their freedom, had been taken away and supplanted by the worst possible substitute, the shuffling shoelessness of the institution.

There are few things more humiliating, more soul-destroying and depressing, than the process of being institutionalized. And the worst part is your own collusion in the process. It doesn't just happen to you. You allow it to happen to you. You partake. You adopt the mind-set of the place. You become docile, subservient, frightened, dull, unthinking, susceptible to the mysterious self-fulfilling power of the rule. You loathe the tone of your own voice as you mewl and cower to the dingbat shoving you your meds or taking away your pen. You are demeaned by the routine as you regulate your life by mealtimes, loitering in the hall at eight, twelve, and six. You change as you acquiesce to rudeness, becoming less, becoming small, a picker, a stealer, a scratching stray licking the hand that defeats it.

You do strange things. I tried, for example, to make shoelaces out of toilet paper, so that I could walk like a normal person instead of limping like a gangster because the tongues of my tennis shoes were curling absurdly to my toes. The laces tore, of course, but it was a way to pass the time, rolling the long strands of tissue between my fingers as tight and stringlike as they would go, and feeling, even though I failed to make the lashings tie or hold, the momentary elation of knowing that I could still exercise some form of creativity.

I learned to flick on the light over my bed with the teeth of a comb or the tip of the forbidden ballpoint pen so that I could read late at night when I couldn't sleep and the dayroom was closed. The light switches were in the hall and recessed so that only the staff could access them with a key or some other lean instrument, and thus enforce lights out at eleven and lights on at eight. Controlling light is no small matter, as they well knew. Just one of many daily benefits you take for granted in the outside world and never notice, but which take on an almost religious significance in the bin.

There are many other such things, things like, as I have mentioned, fresh air. Most of us never think about how little time we spend outdoors. We work in offices all day and colonize the couch at night. We rarely exercise the privilege of stepping out, and that is of course precisely because we know we can do it whenever we like. But when the door is locked and you have to rely on a lazy nurse to take you to the roof, only in groups of four (first come, first served), and only at specific times, for specific periods of time, you begin to get obsessive. You begin to think about the word "inspire" and its literal meaning, "breathe into," and then you think of God breathing life into clay to make man. And you begin to feel that God is on the roof, or some angel who saves you with cool respiration, so that you can face the long night of disinfected air and urine coming through the dusty vent in the bathroom. And that, my friend, is a crazy thought. It's exactly the kind of thing that any one of my ward mates would have told you on any given day, leaning close to you as if someone might be listening, whispering this heady, sacred secret of the universe: that God was on the roof of Meriwether Hospital just waiting to give you the breath of life.

Pacing was the same; a ritual made sacred by the trap. There was a long wide hallway in the ward. It ran the length, from the men's end to the women's, past the dayroom and the nurse's station, the dining area and the activity room. It dead-ended at the locked door that led to the doctor's offices and another locked double door that led to the adjacent ward. Usually the small windows in the tops of those double doors were covered with construction paper, but now and again it was ripped, and you could see into the north side of the wing, where other people like us were wandering around in their pajamas.

Most of us paced up and down that hall at various times of day. It was the only exercise you got, unless you did push-ups and yoga in your room, as I did, or a few jumping jacks and miniscule laps on the roof for the fifteen minutes you were up there. Roof laps were always punishing, though, because you had to do them in your stocking feet. You couldn't run in shoes without laces. The next day, my knees and the bottoms of my feet always felt like they'd been filled with broken glass.

Pacing calmed the mind, too, and assuaged some of the restlessness we all felt at being cooped up under the ever-watchful gaze of Mrs. Weston and her staff. And they *were* watching you. Believe me. You might think me paranoid for saying this, except that I got busted for enough petty misbehavior to know I was being observed. Sometimes the nurses would even object to your pacing itself, maybe because it made them nervous, especially because we often did it in pairs. But mostly they objected because they thought we were planning something. Which was, in fact, sometimes the case.

All the patients on the ward figured out pretty quickly that I was both compos mentis and a sap, meaning that I could be manipulated into getting my visitors to bring them just about anything they wanted, from candy, to phone cards, to cigarettes.

Mr. Clean was the worst in this regard. He was a six-foot, three-inch black psychotic diabetic, who was, to say the least, not exactly looking after his blood sugar. Not that the staff was helping much, but what could you do? The guy wanted candy and his cheap cigars, which they'd confiscated on admission. He loved McDonald's and pretty much anything else salty or sweet that he could shovel into his sparsely toothed mouth. He was obsessed with his few pleasures, as we all were.

"It ain't right to starve a person," he often said.

The whites of his eyes were yellowed and bulged out of his head like gone boiled eggs. His hair was long and nappy, and it always had lint in it. His belly was so incongruously round and protuberant that it looked as if he'd strapped it on for a part in a film. The front of his T-shirt was always dribbled with jelly or gravy or God knew what else—handprints, smears, and stains of all descriptions, crusty, oily, or wet.

I was his connection. He wanted cigarettes. Badly. So he spent a lot of time and energy coaching me on how to make this happen for him, stage-whispering as we walked down the hall.

"See, I'll save it till night. Then I'll take it in the bathroom and blow it into the vent. Nobody'll know. Just get me one, and some matches. Okay?"

His breath smelled like decaying meat.

Breathing through my mouth, I'd say, "I'll try, Clean. I'll try."

And then he'd lean in and go through the scenario again, adding detailed instructions about how to get something past the nurses.

"Just put it in the wrapper of the hamburger or in with the fries, then put it in the garbage in the visiting room, and I'll go and get it later. Then I'll just take it in the bathroom late and stand on the toilet under the vent and blow it up in. Nobody'll smell it. Just get me one, okay? Don't get a pack. And some matches. Can't do nothin' without matches."

If the nurses didn't explicitly hear what he was saying, they surely inferred it. It wasn't hard.

"Okay, you two," one of them would say. "In the dayroom or in your rooms."

Throughout the day he'd stop outside my room and moan.

"Norma?"

No answer.

Louder.

"Norma?"

I'd pretend I couldn't hear him or was too absorbed in my notebook to respond. But he was insistent enough to call attention to himself every time.

"You got any candy, Norma?"

Invariably the staff would see him standing there and tell him to leave me alone. Then, of course, after visiting hours he'd step it up, he and several of the others who'd sniffed me out as the soft touch. They'd prowl around so obviously in anticipation of a fix that it wasn't hard to figure out who was the source. Very quickly I got caught and taken to task. I had my roof privileges suspended for two days, but they let me off without suspending my visiting privileges as well.

One of my three roomies was a ciggie hound too, though more tactful than the others. I called her Tracy Chapman because of her comely face and short signature dreads. She was the only one of the three of them who didn't talk to herself most of the day and night, and with whom you could carry on a fairly normal conversation. She'd told me she'd been committed or "called in" to the authorities by her foster children, whom she claimed had done it to punish her for denying them extra funds to buy clothes and high-tech toys.

It sounded plausible enough. Calling in fake abuse wasn't unheard of, and at first blush she didn't seem nuts enough to need to be in the hospital.

Ellen was my second roommate. She was a short, sixty-five-year-old black woman who had been in the hospital for five months. She said she'd gained sixty-five pounds in that time, which seemed very likely, since she never left our room except for meals, which she ate with gusto. She hadn't even realized that it had gotten cold outside, having come in July and having sat in this regulated air for so long.

She could barely walk, her ankles were so swollen with edema. She wore a white rag tied around her head, a sweatshirt, sweatpants, and a pair of Acti-Treds on her feet. She sat all day and night in a plastic chair by the bathroom door. She never used her bed because she had some problem with mucous, or reflux—I wasn't sure which. She just said that the devil was in her stomach, and when she lay down he came up and she couldn't breathe.

When she wasn't sleeping she was staring at the walls, or at me doing my yoga or writing in my notebook. She saw everything I did unless I did it in the bathroom. After a while she started to feel like my conscience. Every time I looked up I'd see her staring at me in that blank unflinching way that went right into me, and then through me and past me.

When I still thought pleasantries applied, I'd smile nervously and say, "Hey."

She didn't respond, which was awkward at first, but came to feel natural and easy, even pleasant over time. It was actually a relief to stop making small talk. That was one of the things I liked best about hanging around my ward mates. Social conventions didn't apply. It was one of the

privileges of being "disturbed." It was probably one of the diagnostic criteria. But God, it was nice. I really liked being able to just end a conversation and walk away, or say nothing to fill the silence.

At night, Ellen wrapped herself in a sheet and put it over her head, so
that sitting there in the dark with the lights of the city coming through
the window and picking out the whiteness of her form, she looked like
a dead body, as if propped up by the staff for some sick joke. At first, I
didn't understand why she did it. My third roommate, Sweet Girl, did it
too, though she did it for much of the day as well. As time went on, and
I came to understand that privacy was one of the other major deprivations of that place, and one of those other things that most of us take for
granted in the outside world, I realized that they did it because it was the
closest they would ever come to having a room of their own, to reclaim-
ing the structural integrity of their minds as separate places that belonged
only to them.

Of course, in public hospitals, private rooms are an uncommon luxury.
And, of course, people who are a danger to themselves or others can't be
left unwatched. All of this I understand. I am not comparing Meriwether
to the gulag. And yet, as any Solzhenitsyn will tell you, watching is a
form of torture. Being watched is a soft violation that grows into a harder
one with every passing day. Like dripping water on a stone, the eyes of
other people wear you down, slowly, invasively. They leave a hole.

Lying there at night, unable to sleep, I'd look at Ellen and Sweet Girl
wrapped in their shrouds and think that I was in the morgue. In part it
spooked me, but most of the time it just made me terribly sad, because
the shrouds were not only for privacy. They were, I think, also a way of
saying no to what was happening. This was the pose of the abandoned,
the dress work of a despairing mind that was tired of being poked at and
observed, degraded by the treatment, and talked down to.

Yes, the "treatment." That deserves to be in quotes, and probably ital-
ics, too, because I mean it in both senses. I mean it disrespectfully, as

in pseudo, as in your treatment is a joke and an insult and an arrogant, dehumanizing, lazy nonsolution. And I mean it, too, euphemistically, in the same way that cartoon hit men mean it when they say, "Give him the treatment." As in work him over, make him easy, like pulp. Treatment as in, dealt with, put in place, made malleable, and put down.

Sweet Girl was in her early twenties as far as I could tell. I never found out for sure, but she talked often of having been a student at a local college, and she had the face and bearing of someone very young. She was beautiful—high-cheekboned, mahogany-skinned. She hardly ever spoke to anyone but herself, spending most of her time deep in scanning speech colloquy with an imaginary friend she called Patsy. Usually she was curled up in the fetal position on her bed under the sheet, though sometimes she'd sit bolt upright as if surprised by or aghast at something Patsy had said. Then she'd stare into the middle distance and argue the point until she was satisfied, or maybe make a trip to the day-room, where she'd continue the argument in front of the TV.

When I first heard her talking to herself, I thought it was a foreign or made-up language. But then, as I got used to it, I realized that it was English, just very fast English full of all kinds of shorthand and slang that presumably only she and Patsy understood. Sometimes she would coo and giggle and say discernable things like "I love you, too." Other times she'd blurt something about "your smelly cunt" or reprimand Patsy for saying something worse.

"You're disgusting. Shut up."

I tried to listen in, but with little success. Besides, it seemed to me that eavesdropping was just another breach of privacy that I had no right to inflict.

Still, from the parts that I couldn't help overhearing or taking note of, because they were shouted, or repeated, or chanted almost like a prayer, it seemed to me that somewhere along the line Sweet Girl, or perhaps her renegade brain, had done what any of the rest of us might have done in her position. I had no way of knowing what her reality was like in the outside world: where she lived, with whom, under what circumstances. The information was not forthcoming from her.

But she had clearly created a world of her own inside her head, an alternative to what I can imagine must have been a brutal, or at the very least unpleasant and alienating, world on the outside. Maybe she hadn't been abused. Maybe she had only been strange, unpopular among her peers, alone for too long with an unshared and unshareable view of the world, socially inept, and cripplingly shy. (This seemed undeniable from what I saw in our encounters.)

Or maybe the docs were right, that it all stemmed from an innate chemical imbalance, as faultless as autism or retardation. Whatever the reason, whatever the cause, she had produced for herself what seemed to me to be an eminently adaptive response to unbearable isolation. Unlike me—who spends way too much time thinking about all the things I wish I had done or had yet to do—Sweet Girl was not a prisoner of too much consciousness.

She was in her own world, peopling it with friends.

And sometimes, fairly often, I envied her for it. She was socially hermetic.

My envy, of course, led me to wonder whether the lucidity and the sanity we were so eager to impose on her were really so preferable to her world. Would they make her feel better? Or was consciousness—brutal, imposing consciousness—precisely the thing from which her mind was fleeing with all its creative energies awhirl?

Is this a romantic view of madness? Probably. Or maybe just a realistic view of reality.

Can we really say that our lives are in every way preferable to the madman's? We spend our lives running from consciousness, too. Every chance we get. Our lives are full of guzzled substances and vapid entertainments, the generically familiar, homogenized, franchised world, all a distraction from the emptiness at the heart of ourselves and our heavy, heavy awareness of same.

Yes, awareness.

We as a society wanted to make Sweet Girl aware. We wanted her to know that she was a lost soul, or an outcast, or unloved. We wanted her to dwell on all the unbearable truths that her florid mindscape had kept her from really knowing. We wanted her to face the weather like the rest of us, even if it meant waking up to a nightmare. Or at the very least, the lackluster present tense.

But maybe, just maybe, awareness is overrated, and Sweet Girl knew that as well as we did.

Now it's arguable, on the other hand, that she was, as the medical model would have it, a prisoner of too much unconsciousness. Her strange mentality may well have been exactly what kept her isolated from the world, and therefore intolerably lonely and dysfunctional. God knew, in her present state, she was not functional in the world's terms. She could not hold a job, or most jobs. She could not sustain relationships or pay rent. And, as the smell of her would often attest, she couldn't even manage to bathe or change her clothes.

Sanity, of whatever sort she could achieve on medication, would presumably allow her to do those things. But if that was true, it was also true that the "sanity cure" was a cure only in the sense that it would damn her to living with and like the rest of us. That is, holding a less than blissful job at best, and paying bills, and perhaps marrying with a 50 percent chance of getting divorced. It would allow her to fit, or pass as fit, as so many of us do, and maybe that was better than falling out the bottom of society because no one knew what to do with you.

Certainly, I had seen in other fellow patients the stress and pain that mental illness had caused in their lives, the loneliness and isolation that only made them take sterner refuge in delusions.

Mother Teresa was a classic example of this process at work. She was a forty-two-year-old Puerto Rican woman who, a year or so prior to land-ing in Meriwether, had left her three teenage children with relatives back home on the island and come to the mainland United States.

At the time of her admission, she had been living in a homeless shel-ter and working on and off at a fast-food restaurant. One of the other patients, a recovering alcoholic and depressive named José, had given her the nickname Mother Teresa because she was, to say the least, extremely religious, a pathological proselytizer and self-styled saintly minister to the godless and suffering.

A few weeks before I met her, she'd been arrested for disturbing the peace in the lobby of an office building in one of the outer regions of the city. By her own admission, she'd gotten a little excited and started run-ning up and down the main floor of the building, laughing and singing and declaring herself the bride of Christ. She'd gone out to this part of the city, she told me, because she had seen Jesus flying that way, calling her to follow.

When I met her, Mother T's delusions were many and various, though all biblical in origin and extremely pressing. She couldn't stop herself from describing her visions of Jesus and the second coming and trying to convert or preach to pretty much everyone she saw.

This, more than anything, was responsible for the crippling loneliness she felt, and spoke of tearfully, on the few occasions when she wasn't talk-ing about Christ. She wanted very much to find a husband. She had been married very young and had had her three children, but her husband had left her not long after the children were born, and he was no longer in her life. She missed her extended family terribly. Before she left Puerto Rico, she had been living with her mother, father, and siblings. She spoke often of wanting more than anything to be reunited with them. But it seemed they were unable to deal with the wild vicissitudes of her illness and had sent her packing.

There was a pay phone on the ward accessible to any patient, but long-distance calls required a calling card, and most of the patients, including

Mother T, didn't have the money for one. I did have one, though, so one afternoon I suggested that perhaps she might feel better if she gave her family a call. Maybe they could patch things up. She was very excited by the prospect, dialing the number eagerly as I walked away.

But only a few minutes later she appeared in the doorway of my room, crying.

"They told me to shut up. That I'm crazy and I can't come home. They don't see Jesus as I do. They don't understand."

After an episode like this, Mother T would spiral vigorously back into her delusions. As I watched her deal with the pain of her family's rejection, and later with other rejections and crushing disappointments, I saw her grab hold of her visions and her perceived special connection to Christ like a buoy in a raging sea. They kept her afloat. They were a refuge from the cruel knowledge that no one wanted her.

"It's okay," she would say, her sobs abating, "I have the Lord and he knows me, and his plan for me is the most important thing. I must be here to do his work."

"Yes," I would say, stroking her back. "Yes. That's right."

"Ah, and you know, Norita, he is so beautiful. His eyes are like fire. Clear fire. And when his spirit descended, and my crown came down on my head, oh, it was . . ."

"Heavy?" I said.

"Very."

"I bet."

I put my arms around her.

"It will all be okay," I said.

And then came a reprimanding voice shouting from the nurse's station:

"NO TOUCHING. Down the hall, there. You two. No touching."

"What?" I said, looking at Mother T as she pulled away. "Is that a rule?"

"Oh yes," she said. "It is a rule."

A necessary rule in some ways, as I came to learn, in a world where people had few or often no natural boundaries, and where tempers were likely to flare into violent altercations over almost anything. Keeping the patients from getting sexually or amorously involved with one another was a wise policy, and giving vitriolic patients as few pretexts as possible for overreaction was a prerequisite for keeping order.

But depriving lost and desperate human beings of the healing comfort of something as innocuous as a hand on the shoulder or, in extremis, a kindly hug was, at moments like that one with Mother T, just another form of gratuitous deprivation, just another reason why this place made you feel less than human.

I realize that this may sound hopelessly naïve, and I also realize that there was a lot about my fellow patients' histories and conditions that I didn't and couldn't know, but it seemed to me that a lot of the therapy they needed was of this simple tactile and sympathetic kind. Not because they were crazy, mind you, or because such therapy could cure them, but because they were human and everybody benefits from sympathy. Yet, as far as I could see, it wasn't even being tried. Basic human contact, most of which need not always come in the form of touch but rather in the form of engaged (not clinical) listening and the occasional sympathetic response, was not much in the repertoire.

I spent a good deal of my time in Meriwether trying to offer this to my ward mates, not spontaneously, but in response to the artless promptings of people like Mother T and Mr. Clean and even Sweet Girl (when she emerged), all of whom sought me out, not just for cigarettes and candy, but because, as Mother T said once, "Your eyes are so calm."

I am not calm by nature, but, as you might expect, psychosis and its attendant restlessness are as distinct from run-of-the-mill high-strung as depression is from the blues. In a place like Meriwether, Zelda Fitzgerald would seem serene, and so did I. My ward mates seemed to have a nose for the less afflicted. They picked me out right away as being *not* one of them, and they took what they could get from me.

One of the women in the room next door to me, Cherise, a Meriwether veteran, and the person who taught me how to flip on my light with a comb or a pen, nailed it the first time she spoke to me: "You keep nodding, and your head's going to fall off."

She was dead-on. I did a lot of nodding. Maybe out of politeness. Or maybe because it seemed useless and hurtful to disdain someone's delusions, as I remember seeing one of the surliest nurses do.

"I am not your Jesus, okay?" he shouted to Mother T one night as she interrupted his bleary TV watching on shift. "So leave it."

I thought it was cruel and unnecessary, like correcting a grown person's grammar. What for? To humiliate her? Establish your own superiority? Your power? Your remove? Were these even in question?

What possible good could it do to trample on someone's defenses? It wouldn't work anyway, either because, as the docs maintained, the visions and beliefs were spontaneous and chemical, or, as seemed at least partly true in Mother T's case, precisely because they were defenses. They were elaborately crafted and strongly fortified walls against the world. Attempts to dismantle them were perceived and responded to as threats, assaults as grievous and harrowing to the psychotic as a mugging would be to us.

Making them see it your way would fail. It wasn't the way in. On the contrary, I often found that validating the delusions, learning and mapping their contours, nodding, not in toleration, knowing better but in earnest, won you a person's trust, and once you had that, increasing lucidity often followed.

That, I suppose, was part of what led me to believe that the delusions were a defense in the first place. All the people on the ward whom I got to know and befriend spoke to me exclusively in riffs and riddles when I first met them. They didn't know me. They didn't trust me. But without exception, they spoke to me coherently, and often without digression, by the time I left.

Undoubtedly, you can attribute some of this to the medication. I was in

Meriwether for ten days, and many of them had already been in the hospital for some time before I got there. Ideally, the plethora of drugs they were all on might have had a chance to kick in by then. But I noticed they kicked in temperamentally; as Sarah, the med student, acknowledged to me in one frank conversation, they worked only up to a point. They tended to tone down the voices and visions but not to banish them.

Depending on the day's stresses and the encounter at hand, whether it was a quiet exchange between two friends or a confrontation with a nurse or another patient, the lucidity factor would go up or down. If Mother T was feeling relatively secure and supported, she could deviate from the God talk. But if her parents had just hung up on her or someone had roughly rebuffed her preacherly advances, she would pace the halls agitatedly and insist that I read aloud portions of the epistle of Jude.

Another patient, Deborah, was the same way. When I walked into the ward for the first time, this very short, unabashedly potbellied, pewter-maned, and mustachioed woman stood directly in front of me there in the bright pacing hall. She looked me lewdly up and down, wolf whistled, and walked away. It scared the living shit out of me, and it was meant to.

During my first few days there she cursed under her breath whenever she was near me and rambled on about how the staff was trying to infect her with HIV. She thought she had sailed the Nile as a queen and was convinced that there was a bomb in the pay phone at the end of the hall. She was like a lot of the other patients in that way. She had her pet obsessions and irritations, and she'd stop you in the hall or the dayroom and rant about them in bursts. Usually the rants weren't long, and I'd just say "Okay," or "Makes sense," or "I hear ya," and then she or whoever it was would seem satisfied and walk away.

That was the getting-to-know-you phase. The test.

Deborah's first test was the whistle. Then there were her frequent iterations of the word "shitpot," a term of execration that she applied mostly to blacks and Hispanics whom she deemed, in her temper tantrums, to be inferior.

"Your people were servants on the Nile," she'd say, forgetting, of course, that Cleopatra herself was not exactly white—or from suburban Connecticut, as Deborah apparently was.

Deborah would get into "shitpot" tiffs with her Hispanic roommate, Carla, a tattooed toughie who had a habit of getting uncouthly down and dirty with her boyfriend in the visitor's room, and who looked to be the type for whom the ballpoint pen rules were made. Deborah didn't like Carla, not because she was Hispanic but because she was rude, and prone to her own fits of temper. When the two of them butted heads over nothing, Deborah walked away muttering, or sometimes shouting, "Puerto Rican shitpot."

For a while afterward, that's all you could get her to say.

"Calm down, Deborah," the nurses would say. "Calm down."

Carla, too, would storm around agitatedly, usually crying and whining.

If this went on for too long or was too disruptive, the person in question was "medicated." Usually, there was a warning period. The nurses would say, "Do you need to be medicated?" or "You're going to get medicated if you keep that up."

Then, a group of five or six large men would appear on the ward wearing dark purple rubber gloves. They would usher the party or parties in question, one at a time, into the seclusion room, or sometimes into their own rooms, hold them down if necessary, and give them the hypodermic. A few minutes later the team would disappear as quickly as they had materialized, and the patient would either remain supine where they had left her, falling quickly into a torpor, or emerge peevishly, rubbing her ass.

I have no idea what they gave them, but it worked so well that the person would usually pass out facedown on her bed, with one foot still on the floor, shoes half kicked off, pants fumblingly unbuttoned and abandoned about the hips.

Deborah always wore her one pair of jeans or her Meriwether issue pajama bottoms unfastened at the waist, because her belly was too big to fit into them. She often wore a large polo or T-shirt draped over the top, and on her feet she wore Meriwether issue shoes, black Chuck Taylor-style low-top sneakers with Velcro straps. Whether she was really from Connecticut, there was no way of knowing, but she spoke like someone who had been raised in a fairly wealthy family in the northeast.

She often whistled songs from *West Side Story* and *Top Hat* as she walked back and forth down the hallway, smiling at me mischievously as she passed, and winking.

Her hair was shoulder length and pin straight, and she was only a little over five feet tall. Like Clean, she was diabetic and her belly was similarly localized and protruding, perfectly round and proud like a baby just about due. Also like Clean, she enjoyed her sweets, especially fruity beverages like the blueberry juice shakes that my visitors sometimes brought me and packets of peanut M&M's, which I learned to request on her behalf.

Looking back, it's hard to believe that I was ever afraid of Deborah. She was like some errant WASP homunculus who had tripped sideways out of her good breeding via Great Aunt Eugenia's bad genes and landed on the street. As it turned out, she had a big soft spot for me, and when the antics fell away, she was perfectly harmless.

"I just want to follow you around and look at you," she'd say. "You're the freshest face I've seen."

She said she had a room somewhere in the city, but she spent most of her time on the street, in the parks, or sitting on benches feeding the pigeons. Like Mother T, she'd been hauled in by the cops, probably for loitering or disturbing the peace. Like many of the other people on the ward, she'd been to Meriwether several times before, her last visit having been only two months prior to this one. Probably like most of the rest of them, she was on a cycle. She came in here, got meds, meals, and shelter, broke the choke hold of the delusions, left with some prescriptions, hit the street, stopped the meds, lost control, got arrested, landed back here, and did it all over again.

She usually stopped taking the meds when she was out, for the same reason that everyone else did. The side effects were too bad. The fog, the sluggishness, the tardive dyskinesia—abnormal involuntary, spasmodic movements, especially of the face, lips, and tongue—and the overall shaking parkinsonism that so many of the dopamine-blocking antipsychotic medications induce. Deborah, like Clean and many of the others, was on Haldol, among other drugs, a moldy old neuroleptic first used in the 1950s and developed on the basis of an entirely unproven theory that psychosis is the result of abnormally high levels of dopamine in the brain. There is great debate within the scientific community about the safety and effectiveness of these drugs in reducing hallucinations and controlling delusions. If they work at all, they work because heavily sedating and inducing Parkinson's in a person is a little like hitting them over the head with a frying pan, medicine practiced Three Stooges' style. The blow will probably stop the agitation and devivify the psychotic experience, but, as with the antidepressants, not because it's redressing a chemical imbalance, but because it's creating one, one that some have argued amounts to brain damage, and is in no way precise, but tends instead to shut down the system wholesale. It's the theory of person as pinball machine: unplug them and they'll stop binging.

It works. But then, lobotomy worked, too.

And most of the people I met, Deborah included, did stop binging, or at least they stopped binging as loudly and insistently as they had when I first met them, but at the cost of one hell of a hangover. And that's from only one drug.

They were all on cocktails of antipsychotics and mood stabilizers: Haldol, Zyprexa, Depakote, lithium, Klonopin, Seroquel, Thorazine, and Risperdal, to name only a few. Depending on the time of day—we were given medication three times a day, at eight, five, and nine—and whether a person had been forcibly medicated or not, the patients were more or less sluggish, retarded, zombified, mush-mouthed, or dead to the world, drooling big lakes of syrup onto their bedsheets, as Sweet Girl did every single night I was there. She used to wake up in the morning—it was more like noon, really, when she could finally pry herself out of her cocoon—and when she lifted her head, there was a long, viscous rope hanging from her mouth to the mattress like a snot umbilical.

I suppose if you looked at and dealt with people doing this kind of repulsive crap all day, you'd be hard-pressed to see them as fully human, too. That's how it must have seemed to the staff, and that on top of the exasperation of having to shove someone like Sweet Girl into the shower because she smelled bad enough to make your eyes water. It wasn't likely to engender respect. And even though I felt defensive of my fellow patients, sometimes I could really see the other point of view.

I'd look at Clean, for example, in all his foul, pestering regression, and catch myself thinking, "You should be put through a meat grinder and fed to cats and dogs." I'm not proud of that, but I thought it. I thought it vehemently and with relish and with the most visceral disgust and hatred I have ever felt for another human being. Because as much as Clean could inspire the profoundest pity in me, his childish, relentless, mindless life force made me loathe him. Watching him eat, listening to the slurping, slapping noises he made as he sucked the anemic meat and drippy fat of a deep-fried chicken wing off the bone, I wanted to make elaborate and creative use of my ballpoint pen in all the forbidden, murderous ways that the staff had ever seen or imagined.

I wasn't on Haldol or any of the other doozies my ward mates were ingesting three times a day, so I enjoyed a comparatively stunning range of motion and mental agility. I had not been reduced to repellency. Yet. Or was I deluded? When you spend your days with society's rejects, the indigent insane, who are by turns caught in the chloroform embrace of modern medicine, chemically infantilized, swathed in institutionalized helplessness, then coughed out the bottom of the system stoned and spiritless to languish on the street until the next arrest, you begin to wonder about your perspective on what's acceptable. These people are not acceptable as is. They are made mildly more acceptable when tranquilized or debilitated, or they are made less of a nuisance anyway, which is most of the point. Like kids on Ritalin, we medicate them mostly to make life easier for us, not them, to make them easier to handle, and the sight of them less guilt- or revulsion-inducing.

Casey came on to the ward on my third day, reeling in disbelief. She might as well have been wearing a sign that said, "I don't belong here." She was in shock, trying to figure out how she had gone from breaking down in tears in her therapist's office to being committed to a public ward with a bunch of homeless psychotics. I remembered the feeling well. I'd felt the same way that first time I'd found myself in the bin.

Her story was very similar to mine. She'd gotten depressed, said something vague about suicide, and had unwittingly set the whole confinement system in motion. Only instead of committing herself under advisement, as I had done, her doctor frog-marched her down to Meriwether personally and checked in via emergency.

She'd spent her first night in the same hole as I'd spent mine. Same in-flight foldout chair. Same loud staff at the picnic table all night. She even confirmed that one of the night orderlies had once again taken a three-hour nap in one of the empty beds.

The next day she'd been shuffled up to the twentieth floor with the rest of us and gotten dumped in a room with Deborah, who made her usual memorable first impression.

"How'd you like me to break your neck for you?" she said, and Casey put her face under her pillow and cried.

I couldn't help smiling at this. Not outwardly, of course, when Casey told me—as she told me all the rest of it, while standing in my room with her arms crossed—but inwardly, to myself, knowing that Deborah was just giving Casey a little comedown from her superiority complex.

Casey had this air about her, not just of someone who didn't belong in Meriwether because she wasn't sufficiently crazy, but of someone who believed she didn't belong here because she had too much class.

She didn't mean to insult anyone. She was a nice girl. But underneath, she thought she was better than the rest of us, and her bearing betrayed her. Or, I should say, them, not us, because she had sought me out as a refuge. She appeared in the doorway of my room and said, "Can I talk to you for a second?" She had quickly concluded not only that I wasn't loopy beyond recall, but that I was another college-educated, middle-class person whom she thought was on her level. And that was the vaguely prissy vibe she gave off. Of course, I'm sure I gave off more than a whiff of that myself. I know I had done so under the jaundiced watch of Baldy my first time around the maypole.

You can't hide what you are, or what you think you are, and crazy people don't have a filter, so despite the fact that you're standing there semi-petrified, with your hands in your sweatshirt pocket, the sweatshirt that, to add insult to injury, has the name of your college emblazoned on it in purple, you'll come across as the snooty brat that you are, and are secretly proud of being, and the likes of Deborah will sense that a mile away and a mile deep, and will say outright the things that normal people are just thinking. Let me break that long, white cultivated neck for you, princess, and then we'll see whether you don't feel that you belong here in the pig pile with us grunts, after all.

So Casey showed up in my doorway, having ferreted out a fellow princess, and asked if we could talk. I invited her in, against the rules. I invited her in, as I had done with no one else, because I was secretly, snobbishly as sure of her as she was of me. I knew she was safe, and unlikely to spit up, or freak out, or ask me for more than I was willing to give. And we conversed without fear, with the comfy *cordon sanitaire* of our shared superiority drawn perfectly around us, while Ellen in her chair and Sweet Girl in her shroud talked and burped to themselves on either side of us, lost in their own shifting worlds.

Casey told me how she'd gotten there, and asked me how the hell to get out.

"Here's the thing," I said. "You gotta stay calm or you'll only make it worse. Be polite. Be cooperative. Palm your medication. Keep to yourself. And call legal services. Call your parents, and tell them to call your therapist and put the fear of God into her. Whatever you do, don't lose your temper and don't be disrespectful. You're dealing with egos here, and you don't want your doctor knowing you think she's a quack or she'll pull the power trip on you and draw out this whole horror show a lot longer. Believe me, I know what you're going through. I've been there."

Ellen, as if on cue, and for contrast, stood up on the other side of the room. She was having a bit of trouble. The devil in her stomach was on the rise. She was standing in front of her chair and stroking her throat, saying:

"I need to vomit, but it won't come up."

"Should I get the nurse?" I asked.

Ellen nodded.

One of them was passing in the hall, so I called to her. "Listen, Ellen is having trouble, can you help?"

She poked her head in.

"I need to vomit," Ellen said again.

"Okay," said the nurse. "So go into the bathroom."

"It won't come up," said Ellen.

The nurse looked at her quizzically, said something unmemorable and noncommittal, something like, "Just give it a minute," and then walked away.

Ellen stood in the doorway helplessly, still stroking her throat, looking down the hall after the nurse. After a moment, she walked into the bathroom and closed the door.

Casey and I turned back to our conversation.

"God. This place," she said.

"So what do you do for a living?" I said.

She was a grade school teacher in the city in her second year at a tough school. Lots of behavioral problems. Lots of parental neglect. The usual.

"Well, there's your problem right there," I said. "That's depressing. You don't need medication. You need to change your job."

"I know. I know."

Deborah's head appeared in the background over Casey's shoulder. She'd stopped in the doorway to get my attention. She pointed at Casey's back and put her hands to her throat, miming strangulation. I shook my head, smirking, as if to say, "Yeah, yeah," and waved her on. Casey turned around. Deborah smiled innocently and moved off.

Ellen emerged from the bathroom.

"Anything?" I said.

"A little."

"Good."

Casey went on. She had an MA in education and was only in her second year of teaching. She was in her late twenties, that same time of life that had delivered me up to my first depression. No mystery there.

"What drugs have they got you on?" I said.

"Last night they gave me something called Seroquel."

"What? Are you kidding me?"

"It made me feel really weird."

"Did you discuss this with the doctor?"

"No. It just showed up on my chart. I didn't know what it was, so I asked. They said it was to help me sleep."

"Unfuckingbelievable. They're giving you Seroquel to sleep? Jesus, that's an antipsychotic. Don't take that shit. Really. That's hard-core. Just hold it in your cheek and spit it in the toilet."

"I'm afraid to," she said. "What if they catch me and they use it as an excuse to keep me longer?"

"Look," I said, "sit down right now and write your three-day letter."

I had to explain what a three-day letter was and try not to make it sound like a bad thing that she'd have to write it in Crayola. I gave her some of my paper, though it occurred to me that the missive might have more of the desired prisoner-of-conscience effect if she wrote it on toilet paper or a scroll of rough brown paper towel from the bathroom.

We were just finishing up the details when a loud splatting sound brought the conversation to a close. Ellen had managed to bring the devil up in earnest on the floor of our room.

After that, Casey sat with me at meals, trying to avoid the Chinese man who ate like a starving animal, and Clean, who had found in Casey another hapless soul to pester for extra pudding. Naturally, she wanted a buffer against Deborah, too, whom she found more unnerving at table, chewing suggestively.

Still, there was no getting around some unfortunate companionship in the dining room. There was the Hispanic man with the chesty cough who hadn't quite mastered the art of breathing and swallowing by turns, such that milk and masticated bread often flew from his mouth in long arcs of chunky beige spray that landed on the tables, floor, and chairs and any diners at close range. There was the other Asian man of indeterminate national origin, who had the long, sharp, yellowed fingernails of a Satanist, which he enjoyed sucking clean of the meal's accumulated mash.

There was Street Kid, a lanky, ninety-pound twenty-year-old who wore his baseball cap several sizes too big and sideways, like the rapper Flavor Flav. He "got medicated" often and heavily, prone as he was to tantrums. This put quite a damper on his hand-eye coordination; scooping the food from the tray to his mouth via fork, or any other means, was an elaborate procedure that often failed. He looked like he was moving underwater, and sounded that way, too. He spoke as if he had a mouthful of marbles, and he usually ended meals by wearing on his front, or depositing on the floor, a good portion of what he'd been served. This made him cranky, messy, and volatile. Not an ideal tablemate.

And then there were the talkers, who, though less offensive than the suckers and slurpers, could try you as much. Cherise was a big talker. So, I discovered, was Tracy Chapman, when the mood struck her.

Per her story, and seeming coherence, I'd been laboring under the misapprehension that she'd been unfairly committed by vindictive foster kids. That is, until one day at dinner, when, deeming her the least of the evils on offer at mealtime, Casey and I had chosen to sit next to her, only to learn that she was, in fact, way, way out there on Pluto after all.

She began innocuously enough, telling us that she'd been a model when she was a teen. It was possible. Then she said, "Let me show you a picture."

She pulled out a fashion magazine that she'd taken from the dayroom, where there was a pile of newspapers and other recent periodicals set out for patient perusal. This one was only a month old. She opened it to a splashy ad featuring a young dreadlocked girl.

"That's me," she said.

She pointed to a group photo on the next page, a gathering of celebrity women that included Madonna.

"And that's my posse. I was in with Madonna and all them."

Casey and I nodded.

"Oh. Uh-huh."

"That was before I got shot, though," she added. "The bullet went through the back of my head and came out my mouth. Ended my career."

So much for safe harbor.

Ellen and Sweet Girl were best at meals. They kept to themselves, ate passably, and if they spoke, it was usually, as in Sweet's case, to themselves. You weren't required to listen. Sweet didn't eat much, which was why they gave her a cup of Ensure with her meds every day at five. She wasn't much interested in solids. This made her a good source of extras for people like me who weren't eating the gristle burgers or the starch substitute. I could usually get her milk and her veggies if I moved fast.

You had to move fast. Meals were like a bazaar. The minute we sat down, you'd hear someone say, "Anyone got bread for a milk?" or "Dessert. Anybody not want their dessert?" Much of this was orchestrated by José, whom I had come to call the Spanish Yenta, because he was in everybody's business and fancied himself the mayor of the ward. He took to answering the pay phone regularly and coming to get you for your calls. He knew most people by name within the first day, and he started the bidding at meals, often walking between tables to make the trades.

I always promised my dessert to Clean, and usually my bread, unless I was hungry or feeling self-destructive enough to go against my principles.

By far the safest bet in dining, both for quietude and for extras, was the Yemeni woman, who didn't speak English, didn't talk to herself, and hardly ever ate any of her specially ordered halal meals. They were sealed in plastic, so I knew nobody had had his germy fingers in them, and they were usually tastier, if not always healthier than what I got. She usually just handed them over wholesale the minute we sat down.

I have no idea why she was in there. She cried a lot and mostly kept to herself, making copious use of the phone, presumably to beg her relatives for help. I don't know what or when she ate. Probably oranges and peanut butter sandwiches in her room late at night.

When she gave me her meals, I always said the only Arabic words I knew, "Allahu Akbar," and she always smiled.

Street Kid was another regular. Though barely an adult, he'd been to Meriwether three times already, in fairly quick succession.

Somebody told me, "Yeah. His family just gets sick of his bullshit and sends him on a little vacation with us."

Deborah and Mother T were repeats, I knew, but, it turned out, so was Sweet Girl. They were like family, actually. They knew each other's habits and quirks.

I found this out one night sitting with Kid and Sweet Girl in the day-room. Sweet was wearing a long khaki trench coat over her hospital issue, sitting in front of the TV having a heated conversation with Patsy. Something about God's knees and Bloody Mary.

Kid said, "Damn. Is she still doing that shit? She was doing that the last time I was here."

The Bloody Mary part was especially interesting to me, because it started with an exchange Sweet and I had had in our room one afternoon, and was one of the clues to her mental leaps.

There was a bit of graffito on the wall above my bed. It said "Darkside."

Sweet asked, "Norah. What does it say on the wall behind you?"

When I told her, she said, "Bloody Mary. Bloody Mary."

To me the leap seemed clear. Sweet was a college kid. She was remembering her reading. Mary Tudor was famous for her reign of terror, hence the moniker. The graffiti in the Tower of London is equally famous, prisoners scrawling their names and paltry testimonies into the stone.

Meriwether was a prison to Sweet. She was not there voluntarily. She was giving her own testimony. Oral history to a deaf world.

I liked the puzzle quality of these exchanges. I spent a good deal of time in Meriwether doing crossword puzzles from the newspapers, and I started thinking in clues and clever answers, because it seemed that that's how the people around me were thinking, too.

I remember looking at my dinner tray one night examining the hard plastic cover that always fit over the hot portion of the meal. It was manufactured by a company called A La Carte. And as I sat there next to the Yemeni woman, eating her halal chicken and peas, I thought, A la carte. Allah Cart. Clue: What is a God wagon? Answer: An Allah Cart.

It was a code. For Sweet, usually a safer way to speak to someone like me whom she didn't know but wanted to, a way around her crippling shyness and the shame she felt about her illness. Her internal monologue was punctuated by insults of the kind she'd clearly been hearing all her life:

Patsy: "You're crazy."
Sweet: "I'm not stupid."
Patsy: "Crazy pinto bean."
Sweet: "Go away. What did I ever do to you?"

She was afraid I'd say the same thing, which was why she backed away when I'd try a direct approach and say something stupid like, "When you talk, does someone answer?"

She'd get understandably defensive and say, "I'm okay. It's just thoughts. I'm fine."

Then I'd say something even dumber like, "I'm worried about you."

And she would say, "Thanks."

I could tell I was making a somewhat favorable impression, though, because every now and again she'd say something stunningly lucid that was meant for my ears. She could never say it directly to me, because that was too scary. She'd say it to herself, but slowly and deliberately so that it was clearly distinguishable from the scanning speech, and so that I could follow. Once, after one of our brief exchanges, I'd gotten up to go into the dayroom for something, and just as I was crossing the threshold into the hall I heard her say, "Talk to Norah."

But mostly she couldn't. It was too risky. Instead she went the long way around, inching her bed closer to mine whenever I wasn't in the room so that at one point her head was only about a foot from my own. At other times, her appeals for my attention were truly desperate.

One night I was standing in the doorway of our room talking to Casey about a recent meeting she'd had with her docs, when I heard Sweet call me in an uncharacteristically roguish manner.

"Hey, roomie. Will you get me an orange?"

She was under her covers, fully swathed.

"Sure," I said.

When I came back from the dayroom with two oranges, she was sitting on the edge of her bed naked. I handed her the oranges as if nothing was strange, and went back to talking with Casey. A minute later she was back under the covers, the oranges lying by her head, uneaten.

After that she often asked me for things, a sweatshirt or snacks, but she never used or ate them. If I'd been there longer, and if she'd been less sacked out on meds, sleeping most of the day, we could have made more progress, I'm sure. As it was, we did the best we could, talking in code or short bursts, with me usually taking refuge in the customarily blunt forms of exchange that sent her back to Patsy embarrassed.

Kid was far more functional than Sweet. When he wasn't overmedicated, he could hold a conversation, albeit one usually punctuated by goofy dance breaks and aptly chosen lyrics of popular songs.

"Get crazy. Get crazy. Everybody get crazy," he'd sing, spinning on his heels, and chicken-winging his arms, or moonwalking with little hops of pleasure in between.

He was another toughie like Carla, clearly bred half on the street, and probably involved in all kinds of nastiness that you didn't want to know about. When he wasn't collapsed on the rubbery furniture in the day-room, he was pacing the halls agitatedly, as any cooped up young kid would do, grumbling about wanting his possessions back or picking little tiffs with Deborah and others. Like so many other high school discipline cases, he'd probably been given some hybrid cockamamie ADHD-bipolar diagnosis at a very young age and been medicated into submission for the benefit of his homeroom teacher. We've all read about them in the paper, the problem kids who get slapped with five disorders by the time they're twelve, and horse-pilled by a culture that has pathologized everything from PMS to teen angst.

Clearly the kid had problems. But what might be causing those problems? Brain malfunction, acquired or inherited, recreational drug abuse, unstable or violent home and neighborhood life, or just plain time-of-life maladjustment and bad manners? It was anybody's guess. And that, of course, is exactly what his diagnosis was, a guess. A whole tangle of dysfunction and undesirable behavior blamed on his brain, on the behavior of neurotransmitters whose functions we cannot in any meaningful sense of the term measure, do not understand, and cannot regulate with any reliability or accuracy.

So we take a kid whose signs of "mental illness" were classic youthful irritability, impatience, restlessness, rebelliousness, selfishness, rudeness, agitation, and ebullience, and we turn him into a chemical waste dump before he's old enough to vote? Were his moods and outbursts more extreme than those of other young people his age? Sure. Was he unreachable? By no means. Not in my experience. Was he pissed off about the same things that the rest of us were pissed off about? Things like having your few prized possessions and pleasures confiscated and forbidden by lazy, mindless bureaucrats who treat you like a deficient dog; or being doped senseless every time you let out the understandable and mounting frustration you feel at being cooped up and forcibly medicated by a bunch of arrogant nincompoops whose diagnoses and treatments are conjectural. You bet he was. Was that reason enough to throw him into limbo and pump him full of meds that made him incapable of buttering a piece of bread or completing a sentence?

Was anyone even trying? Were the professionals at a loss? Or, as was the case with me, were they not in the business of making conversation?

With Kid it didn't take much. He wasn't delusional or paranoid. Or if he was, not so's you would notice. Not like the others. The medication was the biggest thing standing between him and making sense. He just wanted out, or he wanted a burger, or he wanted someone to pay uncritical attention to him for five minutes while he danced.

But time. That was the thing that no one at Meriwether knew what to do with. Yet it was the thing that dragged on and out like a life sentence. It was the thing that weighed so heavily in everyone's attitude, whether it was the docs who didn't have any of it, or the nurses who did, but had mostly perfected the art of doing as little as possible, or the social workers who were lost in shuffled papers.

Nobody had time for you. Nobody stopped and paid attention. And yet, caught as you were in the system of enforced desuetude, you were definitively stopped. A stopped clock. A broken thing. A forgotten case. And all you wanted or needed in the world was a moment, the briefest of actual acknowledgments to set you going again.

The Spanish Yenta said it best. He was due for discharge one afternoon toward the end of my stay. He was sitting, as I would later do, on one of the chairs in the dayroom, the ones by the door where you always sat anxiously craning and fidgeting when you were expecting a visitor. You did this because those chairs afforded a view of the ward doors, and a view through the small rectangular windows in the tops of those doors, of the hallway beyond, where your visitor would first appear like a blessed apparition of the outside world. The Yenta was sitting there, fidgeting, too, waiting for his discharge papers, fantasizing about the very first thing he was going to do the minute he got outside.

"I'm going to step out onto the street and stop the first person I see. I'm going to pull all the change out of my pockets and say, 'Can I buy a cigarette off you?' And they're going to say, 'Here. Take two. And put your money away.' "

That was it. Something gratuitous. A favor without the asking. A super-fluous act, however small, was recognition, was contact.

It was those attentive moments lost that hurt the most in Meriwether and made you crave them all the more. The times in the hallway with Mother T, when I could not comfort her with even a hand on the shoulder, or the times when someone as skittish as Kid would, in unbelieving thanks for a candy bar—as if this were the world—whip his arms out wide to hug me, big smile, then stop himself and pull back, remembering that touch was against the rules.

But, despite the sound of this, I don't romanticize any of it overmuch. You couldn't. The reminders were always there to bring you down. Kid was a royal pain in the ass. I wouldn't have wanted to be his parent. I doubt I would even have had the stamina or patience to be his peer counselor, let alone his therapist. That is, if you were really going to be a therapist, and sit down with him every day plugging away at his problems.

And yet, we had all given up on him too soon, or so it seemed to me. Without a fight? I don't know. There might have been one somewhere along the line, a long-drawn-out home-front attempt abandoned in favor of triage. But nobody in Meriwether was fighting anymore, if anyone ever had. It was the kind of place that atrophied optimists, turned them gray as dishwater and as unimaginative. These old pros were the epitome of hands washed, outlook poor, going through the motions on the punch clock. And that was an approach, a prognosis very sad to see in a kid as young and alive as Kid was.

To earn points with the nurses for cooperating, Kid went to community meetings and nodded off in his chair, too stoned to participate. When we went around the room introducing ourselves, he had to be elbowed awake. He'd marble-mouth his name or maybe make a brief complaint that was too garbled to understand, then tip back into oblivion.

He waited out his time. And we waited out ours. Mumbling, bumbling through.

In one of her best puns, Deborah cut right to the heart of this pre-
dicament, one in which, let's be clear, mostly resourceless, essentially
harmless people who had often committed crimes no more serious than
disturbing the peace were confined against their will, forcibly medicated
with drugs of dubious or at best limited efficacy and usually unfathomed
toxicity, and left to rot until the hospital needed the bed space, in which
case they were turned back out into the world twenty to eighty pounds
fatter (depending on length of stay), more polluted, emotionally disen-
franchised, and in despair. Practically deployed for a relapse.

One afternoon, during a patient karaoke session hosted by Sarah and
another med student, Deborah and I sat at a long table together hoping for
some Gershwin. Sarah turned to us and laughed.

"You two look like a panel of judges on *American Idol.*"

"Yeah," Deborah said to me, pointing to the med students. "They're
American, and we're idle."

Everyone had a version of this complaint. A woman whom I met on
my second day, but whom I saw thereafter only at meals, or ensconced
on the rubberized couch in the dayroom watching TV, said once in an
aside to me, "Welcome to Hotel Meriwether, where they give lessons in
authoritarianism."

Mother T's version was more empathic. She watched over the rest of
us, concerned, thinking that someday she would go before the Supreme
Court and argue our case or, barring that, lobby God, whose ear she had
her lips to.

She didn't like the way things were done at Meriwether either, and she
objected on other people's behalf.

When Len, the Chinese guy who refused his meds, made a show of
tossing his pills over his shoulder rather than into his mouth, the nurse
said threateningly, "I'll be back with an injection."

Mother T leapt to his defense. "The law says you can refuse treatment."

And in reply, the nurse actually said the wormish words, "I'm just following orders."

Mother T made a similar objection to me on my first night in the ward. The purple-glove brigade had taken Carla into the seclusion room, pricked her, and left her there to come down, or pass out, or pound the pads until she shut up. She'd been pacing the halls, crying, and cursing the Savior as a faggot.

"Gay motherfucker," she said looking up at God on the ceiling. "I hate your son."

Then, postinjection, she began keening in scales like a wounded bloodhound.

Mother T and I had been walking the length of the hall talking about her merciful God. As we passed the seclusion room she pointed at the door.

"This woman in here," she said. "It's not right to be in such a small room when you're losing your mind."

Ellen protested mostly to herself, spitting soliloquies under her breath or, occasionally, when I asked her about herself, spitting them only slightly more audibly at me.

"I'm sixty-five years old," she'd say, with trenchant economy. "And I've been here for five months. I sit in this chair and I pray."

She, like Tracy Chapman, thought she'd been shot in the head. I wondered if this was a common explanation among psychotics for the confusion and broken thoughts. She told me about what I can only presume was an imaginary, truant, or deceased son who, she said, brought her breakfast every morning, but was stopped at the hospital doors and turned back.

"They won't let him visit me," she said. "So he has to dump that breakfast in the garbage every day and go home."

When I heard things like this I marveled at what great mercies the mind seemed capable of. If you were spending your golden years languishing in a public hospital while your son, probably alive and well

and not giving a shit, had left you there for months on end, the breakfast pilgrimage was a beautiful lie to tell yourself, a sustaining image
of thwarted devotion, and a glimpse in one lonely, clinging mind of the
origin of human myth.

Myth was her form of revolt. That, and once, late at night, from beneath
her swaddling shroud, there came the soft, proud sobs that I could hear
her choking out and swallowing.

And Deborah, of course. She had lots to say on the matter, not just of confinement or things taken away, but of technique. Survival in the mind.

I asked her about Sweet, trying for a way in.

"What's she doing? What is all that talk?"

"She's doing the same thing you do. Just more extreme."

"Why?"

"Because when they take away everything that you care about, that's
what you have."

"Is it how she copes?"

"She's hiding," she said finally. "We all are."

She rolled up her sleeves and showed me the scars from where she'd
tried to open her wrists.

"I did this when I knew the police were coming for me."

That shut me up. I didn't have anything else inquisitive to say to that.
She looked at me for a minute, full in the eyes.

"You have your pen. You have your notebook. You have soft skin and
you have your mind. That's all you need. Keep it. Don't let anyone take it
away from you, because they will. Shit, I want your mind, too."

Like Deborah and Ellen, Clean also had his take on the matter. He
thought a lot about power. Like so many of them—Deborah, with her
ethnic shitpots, or Mother T with her not so extreme or uncommon
apocalyptica—he reflected the prejudices and obsessions of his culture.
He thought that all white people were German. Germany meant power.

Again, the authoritarian tinge to the "crazy" person's view, history cherry-picked for meaning, out of date, but symbolically in the ballpark.

"Norma," he asked me, "was Rome civilized?"

"Yes," I said, betraying my own distortions. "Once."

"And who's Rome now?"

"We are," I said.

Still, let's not get too high-handed about all this. The insane are not sages of ill repute, or martyrs of an empire in decline, standing nobly outside or above its vices, crying into the wind. They are deeply and indicatively of their culture, our culture. They are not ennobled by their suffering. They are like the rest of us. And so was I. I responded to them just as the system and everyone else did, even if for a moment I convinced myself otherwise.

They were not, for example, immune to coveting possessions simply because they had none. If I gave, they wanted more. Always more. (How American.) And very quickly they ceased even to be grateful, becoming as entitled as the rest of us to our accustomed bounty. And when I gave, I became The Giver, the smarmy Samaritan who gets off on giving, the goody-good whom everyone admires, the blessed, kind answer to their prayers. And I began to loathe myself in this position, smiling beneficently, handing out my balms and prizes, graciously accepting thanks, and thinking all the while that God was working up one hell of a performance report for me that quarter. Cha-ching.

But for a while, before the saintly stand-up gal routine started to make me sick of myself, and before it made me want to bury my greedy, grasping fellow patients alive under a pile of McDonald's french fries— There! Choke on it!—I played the role. I made myself the wish granter of Ward 20.

As I lay there, listening to Ellen cry that night under her shroud, I felt so goddamned overwhelmed by guilty thankfulness for the unjust accidents of birth that I resolved the next morning to make her happy, or at least backhandedly, gustatorily happy, the way a jailer grants the death row inmate a last meal and manages to feel magnanimous about it.

"If you could have anything to eat tonight for dinner," I said, "what would it be?"

"Fried chicken," she said. "And a Pepsi."

Ah, she was going to make this easy. How nice for me. I called my visitor for the evening and put in the order. I put in an order for Clean, too, who wanted cigarettes and McDonald's, and Mother T, who needed a Bible, though she was too resigned to ask for anything, and Deborah who wanted McDonald's too (they all did), as well as a *National Geographic*. By the end of my stay I was the delivery whore, passing out dollar burgers that I got by the half dozen, and fries, and sodas, and Hershey bars, and sticky buns and any other cheap sop I could think of or got a request for.

But before long, the predictable happened. It was like filling a bottomless cup. I gave Ellen her chicken and her Pepsi, and though she thanked me profusely, fifteen minutes later she flagged me down and said:

"You got anything else?"

This happened with everyone, to the point where I couldn't even eat my own snacks without rousing the scavengers. I'd have given away twenty candy bars minutes before, but the smallest rustle of a wrapper and they'd be on me.

"Have some?"

I hated myself for begrudging them, and felt like some kind of despicable closet pigger when I took to going into the bathroom to eat, coughing loudly to cover any suspicious sounds.

Finally, when I was taking my orders one day, and Kid asked for an iPod, I got the reality check I deserved. I decided this whole fellow man thing wasn't for me. There was just too much childish need for gratification and endless expectation of same. This was no solution. I was giving junk food to diabetics, recovering addicts, and sedentary near-vagrants whose meds were already well on the way to making them obese.

And all purely for the hit of pleasure it would give them and, more important, me.

The worst of it is that they came for me in other ways too. As soon as I extended my rubber-gloved helping hand to them, they grabbed hold. They latched on. They wanted to keep in touch on the outside. They wanted to be my friend. But I just wanted to help them from a safe distance and be rid of them. I didn't want their company. I was posing, or passing, but I didn't really want to know them. They were my subjects, and if I cared about them at all it was out of authorial self-interest and pity and moral vanity. Moral vanity being that great middle-class indulgence that makes us write checks to charities and do the right thing for the less fortunate, because doing so reinforces our fiercely guarded belief that we are good people. But when the less fortunate come banging on your door and your heart in real time, up close, blowing their not so fresh breath in your face, wanting to be a person instead of a project or a write-off, then your cherished little antibacterial ideals turn all squeamish and stuttery, saying "Well, but, . . ." "Yeah, but, . . ." and finally show themselves outright to be as vaporous and self-serving as they always were.

Where are the boundaries? What can help really mean? And isn't that why we leave it to the professionals, who, in turn, leave it to a lost cause, or to the pharmaceutical path of least resistance? Nobody wants to do the personal work. It's disgusting. What's more, it challenges—no, rakes up and scarecrows—every humanitarian illusion you have about yourself. It makes you know that at heart you are a little bit of a fascist like everybody else, thinking in the way, way back of your mind that wouldn't it really just be cheaper and better and utilitarian—now there's a word we can work with—to be rid of these people?

Yes, this is all very ugly—but so true. I don't want to know what's in your soul. Not really. And you don't want to know what's in mine. Keep back, we tell each other. Those are your problems, which is really just a polite way of saying, "Go starve somewhere else. You're ruining the view."

I couldn't do well by these people. Not that it was my job to do so, but it felt like my obligation somehow. And maybe, for some of the same reasons, nobody else could do very well by them either. It was just too much. Too hard. Too late. The question is there all the time. What to do? I can denigrate the system, impugn it with all the progressive zeal that makes my brain twitter with self-satisfaction, and I might actually be right. The psychiatric emperor has no clothes. But I would be lying, or pruning the full picture, if I said I didn't see why that system fails the chronics and admit that I abandoned them myself.

You got tired of their ceaseless intrusions after a while, and in order to draw boundaries that they would respect, you had to be a little mean.

I was on the pay phone with my shrink one day, the one I had on the outside, when Clean started orbiting me like some kind of demented circus balloon. Per Dr. Balkan's instructions, I was trying to make an appointment to see someone when I got out. I was trying to explain how I'd landed in Meriwether without even so much as a by-your-leave, or a drowning wave, or some indication that I was in distress. I didn't want to put him in a sticky position by telling him that I was A-OK fine and doing research, so the conversation was odd and halting, with me trying to avoid direct answers until I got out and could explain the whole thing. I didn't need Clean leaning in every two minutes to bug me about when my visitor was coming and whether or not he'd have cigarettes.

"Norma?"

I put my finger to my lips and pointed to the phone.

"Oh, okay. I'm sorry, Norma."

He walked away.

Two minutes tops and he was back.

"Norma?"

Again the finger routine, more emphatic this time. Another apology, another departure, then another approach.

And finally from me,

"Fuck, Clean. I'm busy here. Can't you see?"

It made you feel bad, like you'd slapped a puppy. But it had to be done.

Callousness was one of the things that happened to you along with the other effects of being institutionalized. Callousness and, what? Xenophobia, I guess.

To wit: it is significant that while I was making that phone call to my doc, I was holding the receiver with a paper towel.

I know. You'd be justified in thinking that maybe I was getting classically obsessive-compulsive along with the rest of them, always thinking about germs. You would think so, that is, until you remember that each year alarming numbers of people contract fatal staph infections while in the hospital.

But that is not the whole truth, or maybe not even the half of it. Not the real point.

The point is, I held the receiver with a paper towel because I did not want to touch the things that my fellow patients had touched. That is the beginning of spiritual disgust. It starts in the body, in the nose, and moves to the skin, proverbially crawling, sliding first paper, then walls between itself and the unclean, then verminous other.

And once that had happened, and you could admit it to yourself, that's when you started to understand why the nurses were as grouchy as they were, and as distant and demeaning. They'd learned, as I had, first, that setting limits was paramount, but second and more shamefully, that good intentions were the casualties of contact—the same theoretically exalted human contact that I had started out so in favor of, and had seen soiled somewhere along the way.

Life at Meriwether was lived in patterns. Patterns of marked time and lost time, and doobie-do this, and doobie-do that.

The Yenta turned to me in the dayroom one afternoon and said:

"What month is it?"

"December."

He looked surprised.

"God, time is passing me by. The drugs make me so out of it I can't think straight. It's like waking up from a dream."

"So you don't know how long you've been here?"

"December what?"

"Fifth."

He counted on his fingers.

"Then, nineteen days."

"How did you get here?"

"From rehab."

"How does that work?"

"I was in rehab in this really dark and dingy place, and I just felt like hell. Really depressed. I was talking with my counselor in this glass-enclosed room and I made the mistake of telling her that I wanted to bash my head right through the glass. So they sent me over here to emergency with a bottle of antidepressants. While I was waiting to be checked in, I went into the bathroom and took the whole bottle at once. They kept me in the ICU for a couple of days, having convulsions and spasms and weird shit."

"What are you on now?"

"Another antidepressant."

"Which one?"

"Effexor."

"Oh jeez," I said, and gave him a speech about the horrendous withdrawal that people who stop taking that drug can undergo. I told him what the docs probably weren't telling him. After I told him, he confirmed that, yes, I was right. The docs hadn't warned him.

I'd been on Effexor at one point, and had gone off it abruptly under a doctor's care. The doctor—actually, more than one doctor—hadn't warned me that withdrawal from Effexor can, and in my case did, cause, among other joys, vivid, prolonged nightmares, fever, sweats, chills, dizziness, crying jags, and what I can only describe as brain zaps, a kind of electric shock sensation inside your skull. When I started experiencing these symptoms, I went on the Web and found out that a lot of other people had endured the same torture.

"Just so you know," I told the Yenta.

He got his discharge a few days later, and that, presumably, was that. He would go on taking the same pills to live as he'd taken to try to die. Poison in therapeutic doses, didn't someone say? Medicating, no longer self-medicating, or something like that. Getting drugs to get you over the hump, or through the objectionable days, or to help you cope, or coast, or, as in Casey's case, to do double duty, to keep you going and to help you sleep.

Casey, like me, had been prescribed the antipsychotic Zyprexa on the outside, and for the same ass-backward reason. Antidepressants had made her hypomanic, so her doc had decided on a mood stabilizer.

But not just any old mood stabilizer—the pet mood stabilizer of the day. An antipsychotic that had been approved by the FDA to treat bipolar disorder. Zyprexa: the same trendy pill that, interestingly enough, was well advertised in the Meriwether ward. "Informational" (read: promotional) displays were posted, complete with detailed, four-color leaflets, on the bulletin board outside the dayroom. Some of the nurses even carried their papers around on Zyprexa clipboards stenciled with the same promotional information that was in the leaflets. Others carried clipboards or wrote with pens that advertised competing drugs like Abilify.

Like Mother T and others, Casey had gained a lot of weight on Zyprexa. This, along with a propensity to cause diabetes, is a common side effect of the drug, and one that its manufacturer, Eli Lilly, knew about all along but failed to disclose to the public. The truth came to light in early 2007, when the *New York Times* reported in a series of articles that Eli Lilly had agreed to pay hundreds of millions of dollars to settle thousands of lawsuits brought by people who had taken the drug.

Wisely, Casey had gone off Zyprexa on her own. But at Meriwether they were tossing her Seroquel instead.

Thankfully, Casey was only in for three days before her therapist either came to her senses or responded to pressure from Casey's family and friends. She showed up at Meriwether and corrected her mistake.

Casey left Meriwether as bitter, angry, and frightened as I had been my first time around in the bin, and she had learned the same lesson. No matter how bad you feel, never go to the bin. In fact, never confess enough to your therapist to give her even the slightest inclination to commit you to the bin, unless you know her well enough and trust her enough to know she'd never do such a thing.

Don't assume she'll be able to tell the difference between contained, nonspecific suicidal thoughts and real, imminent danger to self or others, because the truth is, more often than not, she'll probably commit you either way, just to cover her ass in case you do end up trying something.

Discernment can be hard to come by in psychiatrists. This has been my experience, anyway, and, obviously, it was Casey's as well. The human touch is not very often their strong suit. Nor is true empathy. Attend the annual American Psychiatric Association conference, as I did, and you'll see that the emphasis is far and away on the science, not the emotional intelligence.

As noted psychoanalyst Adam Phillips wrote in the *New York Times* ("A Mind Is a Terrible Thing to Measure," February 26, 2006), "Psychotherapists of various orientations find themselves under pressure to prove to themselves and to society that they are doing a hard-core science.... Given the prestige and trust the modern world gives to scientific standards, psychotherapists, who always have to measure themselves against the medical profession, are going to want to demonstrate that they, too, deal in the predictable; that they, too, can provide evidence for the value of what they do."

These people are thinking in categories, not only because that is how they are trained but because anything else is too vague, too absurdly metaphysical, to advance the cause of their credibility in medicine.

And yet, given what it is capable of doing, the brain is like no other organ, and does not submit, at least in the lived experience of the patient, to anatomy and chemistry alone. How can we treat it the way we treat, for example, a kidney? There is the brain, whose business is thought and feeling and judgment and even mystical experience. And then there is the kidney, whose business is piss.

I can heal your kidney, or your heart, or your bowel without empathy, though bedside manner never hurts. But can I heal your mind without empathy?

So much of psychiatry is perception, not just bodily function. And so, to be effective, mustn't a psychiatrist feel? Mustn't he, too, have experience? And by experience, I don't mean how many patients he has diagnosed, or how long he has been diagnosing them. I mean personal experience. How much he actually knows, or at least can vividly imagine, about what it's like to be mentally ill, or what it's like, day-to-day, to take drugs that alter your consciousness, or, finally, what it's like to be locked in a ward.

It might do wonders for the profession if all psych residents were required to spend ten days incognito as a patient in a locked ward. Or to be given antipsychotic medications to sleep. Or to have their intelligence insulted by someone who doesn't know what neurotransmitter that drug happens to work on. Then, at least, they would know a bit more whereof they committed, prescribed, and consulted, and they'd think twice before suggesting hospitalization as a means of putting the Caseys of the world to rights.

If you ask me, Casey and I fell into the same category: the overdiagnosed. Certainly we were or had been depressed. Behaviorally, anyway. That was clear.

The question is, were we what you might call naturally depressed by life and our prospects? Were we too hypersensitive? Were our expectations too high? Were we clobbered by life's disappointments, as everyone at some point is? Or were we clinically depressed, suffering, as they say, from a chemical imbalance? Was depression in our DNA? Were we mentally ill, or were we struggling through a bad patch?

Moreover, was medication, and lots of it, the answer? Was it the only, or even the best treatment?

Nobody has answers to these questions yet. But in the absence of such answers does it make sense to pound everyone with the same rubber mallet? Does it make sense to give powerful antipsychotics both to someone who thinks he is talking to God and to someone who is just having trouble falling alseep? Does it make sense to put someone like Casey away, and keep her away despite her assertion of the plain fact that being in the bin was making her feel worse, not better? Wasn't that kind of treatment just going to make her, and me, and a hell of a lot of other people, shy away from consulting psychiatrists at all, for fear of being dangerously overmedicated and incarcerated?

These were all the questions in my head as I watched Casey leave the ward, and as I sat waiting out my time, succumbing more and more to fear and depression, despite knowing that I was only likely to be there for a short time, and that I was actually just doing a job. It was hard to keep any kind of perspective. Almost impossible. The intimidation and lethargy of the institution hung on me and ripened like a stink, and I sat in that stink with worsening amnesia, as if I neither had nor knew of any other life outside the confines of Meriwether Hospital.

I realize that this sounds overblown. And sitting here now, back in my privileged life, mentally so far away from Meriwether and that time, it sounds that way to me, too. But then I remember that my roommate Ellen had been stuck in there for six months, and who knew what was going to happen to her.

I wasn't Ellen, of course. Far from it. I had access, if necessary, to a whole host of resources, legal and otherwise, that Ellen and most of the rest of my fellow patients didn't. That, after all, had been most of the reason why Casey had managed to get out so quickly. She had resources. Family, some money, and enough education, savvy, and middle-class wherewithal to apply pressure in the right places. Yet she, like me, had seen on her first trip to the bin that although she had committed no crime, her accustomed freedoms could be taken away more quickly than they had ever been before, or than she had imagined they ever could be, even if only temporarily.

This is something that we in the free world, especially Americans, are not used to. It has never happened to most of us. On the contrary, we're spoiled. We're used to saying what we like, and suffering few or no consequences as a result. We're used to knowing, as surely as we know our own names, that we have rights. And it's not that patients in places like Meriwether don't have rights. They do. It's just that—and I can't overemphasize this—it feels as if you don't have rights when something as simple as coming and going, or smoking a cigarette, or seeing the people you love is taken out of your control because your mind, whether it actually is or not, is thought to be diseased.

Being put away does a number on you very quickly, and very thoroughly, no matter who you are in the outside world.

Finally, after watching other people leave, after losing a sense of time, and after losing more and more perspective on the system and my own position within it, my day did come. I was going to get out.

I had been through the treatment, such as it was. I had been given eight Lamictals and ten vitamins. I had swallowed one each day but not the other. I had had roughly ten to fifteen minutes of therapy a day, either with Dr. Balkan or with Sarah. I had sat in on the absurd fifteen-minute morning community meetings, where those who were awake or could speak intelligibly had said their piece, been heard, and usually been told that what they wanted either couldn't be had or would be taken into "consideration."

We all knew what that meant.

I had been aiming for the ten-day mark as a release date. So when Sarah or Dr. Balkan asked me how I was doing each day, I steered my answers progressively toward the lighter side of disaster, going from "I'm not as bad as I was," to "Getting better, I think," to the unequivocal, "I'm ready to go now, please."

Dr. Balkan and I decided together about midweek that day 10, a Friday, would probably be the day. Of course I knew enough not to take this dangled freedom for granted until I was on the other side of the door, but I did allow myself just a whiff of elation.

I told Deborah as soon as I knew.

"It will be heartbreak for me when you leave," she said, looking up into my face with eyes that bore no trace of their former mischief.

Sweet must have overheard this, though I don't remember her being nearby at the time. But then, she had a way of floating in and out of rooms unnoticed. I walked by her in the hall later that day, and she showed me once and for all that it was a mistake to assume she wasn't paying attention, just because she was talking to herself most of the time.

I heard the swish of her trench coat, and then, clear as a bell, she said: "I'm going to miss you."

The others reached out, too, as expected. Clean wanted to give me his number at a halfway house, and did. Mother T told me which shelter she was likely to be staying at when she got out. Even Kid gave me a number.

My last night, I lay in bed awake for hours filled with what was by then an irrepressible excitement. Like the Yenta, I thought with relish and in detail about the first things I was going to do when I got out.

I pictured and tasted each course, each bite of the meal I was going to have at my favorite restaurant. The juicy steak, medium rare, marbled with fat, oozing in my mouth, the buttery whipped potatoes, the firm julienned vegetables, the lemon custard, the red wine swirling in the bulbous glass.

I thought about the taste and smell of the fresh winter air, and the feel of it cooling my lungs and my lips and my ears. I thought about what it would be like to talk to people who didn't have power over you or weren't hearing voices. Normal society seemed desirable for once. The beautiful, beautiful mundane. What a thing.

As I lay there with my eyes open, and with my eyes newly opened, I listened to the nurses talking and laughing down the hall. I thought about how strange it was that so many of them considered themselves to be superior to the patients they oversaw, when the patients knew enough to leave as soon as they could, and even the worst among them were eventually discharged. But the staff was there all the time. By choice. Actual choice. Not, in my sense of the word, by voluntary commission, and then no choice at all. No. They had decided completely and repeatedly, of their own accord, to be in that place.

It's bad enough to be committed to a mental hospital, and to spend your time unwillingly in the company of disturbed people. Even disturbed people know that. So why would anyone choose to work in such a place, choose to spend at least forty hours a week there, and never have enough sense to get out? If you ask me, that's a far more deranged, senseless person than any so-called lunatic.

Of course I know now that this is too harsh a judgment, coming, as it did, out of extreme resentment and trapped exhaustion. I feel certain, even in my still jaundiced mind, that some public hospital somewhere employs one person, hell, maybe a few, who actually give a shit, and try to do some good.

The point is, fair or not, informed or not, this is how I felt at the time. Meriwether skewed—maybe even took away—my judgment on these matters for a while. I cannot deny that, nor should I. That is what institutions do.

I slept restlessly for a few hours, and then in the morning I woke again to the sound of Mrs. Weston clacking into the room. This, too, vaguely amused me for the first time, because I could just about relish how good it was going to feel to write about her.

The docs signed my discharge papers at 9:25 a.m., but I didn't make it out of the hospital until 3:15 p.m.

Those were the worst six hours of my stay.

I sat all day in anticipation, watching the hours drag by, tasting my freedom, but anxiety-ridden at the prospect of it being somehow revoked, or worse, eroded by my paperwork's slow, careless passage through the clogged procedural channels of the hospital bureaucracy.

Time had come to mean everything. A visitor who arrived ten minutes late, for example, could never know how painful those ten minutes were to someone watching every tick of the clock, living for a friendly face.

Discharge was that much worse, because you sat there, after having been boxed in for too long at the mercy of a flyby doctor's will, finally

knowing that you were technically free at last, but having to wait nonetheless for the heel-dragging staff to make it happen.

The staff's blatant indifference was offensive enough in the daily
rounds, but it made you boil when one more day of your life was coming
rapidly to a close and your release papers were languishing on the table
while the nurses studiedly procrastinated.

After making numerous inquiries at the nurse's station, I learned that
we were waiting on the pharmacy, which had yet to fill my prescription.

"Can't you just write me one that I can fill outside?" I asked Dr. Balkan.

This was not hospital policy, she said. And so I waited for several more
hours.

At three o'clock, desperate, I cornered the unit chief on her hurried
way through the ward and managed the miracle of bent rules. She wrote
me a scrip, and I got the nod to go.

Finally, having spent the day convulsed by turns with rage and despair,
I stepped over the wide white line in front of the nurse's station, the one
that patients were forbidden to cross, and stood by the locked double
doors of Ward 20 for the last time.

As I waited for the nurse, with his jangle of keys, to unlock the door,
I looked back at Deborah and Clean and Mother T, who had gathered to
wave me off. I knew what they were feeling. I'd felt the same mixture of
pleasure and envy when I'd seen Casey and the Yenta discharged during
my stay. You couldn't help but share in the free person's joy and be happy
for them, but watching them leave, you also couldn't help but feel that
much worse about your inability to follow.

I left Meriwether hospital with my few belongings in a paper garbage bag
that I got from one of the janitors. It was the same kind of bag that I'd
been filling with desiccated orange peels and secreted candy wrappers for
ten days. They had lost my backpack somewhere between triage and the
ward, and I wasn't going to spend one extra minute in that place trying
to find it.

It had only been ten days, and I was supposedly just a journalist at work, but I was a wreck, a pathetic, quaking, permission-seeking, cowering nonperson in petrified thrall to the keepers of mental hygiene.

As I made my long, slow way out of Ward 20, as I heard the locked double doors click behind me, with me at last on the right side of them, the outside, as I rode all the way down in the elevator and scurried all the way down the labyrinthine halls of the main floor, even as I stood in line waiting to sign for my valuables, I really thought that some disembodied arm was going to reach out and grab me by the shoulder and say:

"Where the hell do you think you're going?"

And when I finally walked into the same vaulted lobby that I had come through ten days before, pushed my way through those so much more symbolic revolving doors back out onto the street, and took my first lungful of liberated air, all I could say—and I said it out loud, yes, talking to myself—was "Thank God. Thank God. Let it be true. Let it be true."

And then I ran. I ran for blocks, clasping my crumpled paper bag to my chest, still thinking I might be chased and dragged back screaming in futile protest for the brief taste of gorgeous, real life that I had been given.

But—and I said, "Thank God" again out loud—no one came for me. As I slowed to a walk, it felt glorious to be out of breath, to have a wallet, and shoelaces, and a meandering gait, and my own sweet, whimsical will again.

INTERIM

As expected, I learned a lot about madness at Meriwether. By madness I mean, of course, madness as we currently recognize and label it, or, more specifically, as I was able to observe it in Ward 20 at Meriwether Hospital. I can make no meaningful generalizations about madness per se. I don't think any of us really can. Even if madness as some definable entity can really be said to exist, which I don't think it can as yet, nonetheless, mad individuals are as singular as other individuals, even if they tend to have certain propensities in common (delusions, paranoia, despondency, mania, and so on).

Yet generalizations are unavoidable, and we all make them, usually in less than charitable ways. Like most people, I harbored strong prejudices, especially about psychotic people. But living in close quarters with Deborah, Sweet, Clean, Mother T, and the rest of them disabused me of many of those prejudices, even as it reinforced and engendered others.

For example, it may surprise you to know that I never felt unsafe in the ward.

Portrayals of "psycho killers" and stalkers in movies have conditioned most of us to believe that psychotic people are always violent, menacing, and dangerous. When a mentally ill person makes the news, it's usually because he has brained a pedestrian with a cement block or pushed someone in front of a subway train. Sick-flicks and tabloid cover stories have given us our picture of psychosis and made it a staple of our worst fears and nightmares.

Sometimes psychotic people will play into this warped preconception, simply as a means of ridiculing our ignorance or deflecting the sting of our gawking eyes. Deborah did this when she cruised me so blatantly that first time in the hallway. And I allowed myself to be frightened by it. Looking back on it now, my reaction was as absurd as flinching when a clown says, "Boo."

Otherwise my fears in Meriwether did not stem from my fellow patients, but rather from the hulking, glowering institution itself, and the power it had over me.

The psychotic people I knew and lived with were more confused and disoriented than anything else. This may have been due in large part to the effects of the medication, but whatever the case, even at their most paranoid and fluent, they were more scared than scary. When they were exercised, it was more out of annoyance that nobody seemed to be listening to them or taking their wishes into account. I never worried about being in rooms alone with them. I never lost sleep thinking they were going to creep into my room and get me, and this wasn't, I can assure you, because I thought the nurses would get there in time.

They were as human as everyone else, of course. As selfish and petty and generous and witty, and most often, just as run of the mill. They were just as much a reflection of their class and culture as the average person on the street. They liked MacDonald's, iPods, M&M's, and TV. They were fat and fond of the same poisons that we all buy on every corner or in bulk at Costco. They didn't like being told what was good for them, and they didn't like being told what to do. But when they fell, they wanted to be picked up. They wanted to be saved and provided for, but made the minimum effort on their own behalf. I'd say that made them pretty normal.

None of this is to say that I came away from Meriwether with a sense that the psychotic people I knew were, in every way, just like everybody else. They were psychotic. There's no getting away from it. And I had to adjust my approach to them accordingly. When I spoke to them, I wasn't speaking to someone who processed information in socially common or easily navigable ways. It was different, and often it was harder, more off-putting, and even unpleasant.

Still, something very strange happened in my mind as a result of these everyday interactions on the ward. This partial normalizing of crazy people in the bin had the opposite effect, too. It made normal people in the outside world seem crazier.

Instead of going back into the public sphere and luxuriating in all the confidence and like-mindedness that I could have and find in normal people, I actually approached strangers with a new reserve. I realized how stunningly naïve I had been to assume that most people I met were sane. Most of us do this. We presume people are sane until they prove otherwise. But, after Meriwether, it suddenly seemed a lot wiser to approach strangers as if they were nuts until they proved otherwise.

I was so struck by this reversal—by how sensible it seemed, and still does. I mean, really, what an astonishing trust we place in other drivers on the highway, in teachers and priests and parents and government officials, in the power of social norms. And how astonishingly often is that trust misplaced?

This will sound crazy, no doubt, but, after leaving Meriwether, it seemed patently clear to me that the vast majority of the crimes in the world are committed by normal people. Either that or insanity is a lot more prevalent and on the loose than we like to think.

Obviously, whether for good or ill, Meriwether bent my mind. Or the world. Or both. But it also taught me some interesting and rather more mundane things as well, things about the health-care system, and about health insurance in particular.

When I presented myself at Meriwether, I told them that I had no health insurance. I was there to conduct my research, after all, and not because I really needed to be hospitalized. I didn't want the cost of my stay to be billed to my insurance company. But as it happened, because I had listed myself as having no insurance, the billing people at Meriwether took the logical next step. They put in for Medicaid. That's when the computer did a search and kicked back the information that I did indeed have insurance coverage. When she relayed this information to me, I told the billing administrator that I didn't want a bill sent to my insurance company.

"Just bill me," I said.

Naturally, they didn't. Nobody who shows up in a public hospital is capable of paying the bill out of pocket. They sent the bill to my insurance company, and another copy to me.

For a ten-day stay at Meriwether, the grand total came to $14,276. That's $1,400 a day. You could get a king room at the Ritz-Carlton in New York City for that and still have plenty left over for exquisite food and a private nurse.

Soon after getting the bill I called my insurance company to explain the situation. I told them that I was writing a book about mental hospitals, that my recent billed visit constituted research, and that I wished to reimburse them for the full amount they had paid out.

I may actually be the first person in history to willingly attempt to reimburse an insurance company. You can imagine that the fine folks in the claims department didn't know what to do with me.

In fact, irony of ironies, they thought I was nuts. I'm not kidding. After making repeated calls to various departments, in an effort to make myself clear, I finally got a call back from a social worker. She explained, in the most delicate possible terms, that she had called expressly to determine if I was insane.

Apparently, it's not uncommon for genuinely compromised individuals to call their insurance companies and attempt to stop payment on claims. Such people don't offer to pay the claims themselves, but they attempt to dispute the claim, mostly because they adamantly deny that they needed to go to the hospital in the first place, but also because, having gone, they don't want their hospitalization to appear on their record. They don't think they're crazy, and they don't want other people thinking it either, or having evidence on paper to prove it.

Because I, too, had told the insurance company that I wasn't legitimately ill, I fell immediately into the "I didn't need to go to the hospital, even though they dragged me off ranting and raving" category.

It only made matters worse when I claimed to be a writer who was under contract to write a book. I offered to have the social worker call my publisher. I even said, "Just Google me, and you'll see." But this didn't seem to fly, and I can see why. You try not to sound like you're having delusions of grandeur when you tell people that you were on the *New York Times* best-seller list and appeared on *The View*.

"No, really."

To date, I have heard nothing more from the social worker or anyone else at my insurance company. I guess they didn't believe me.

Overall, Meriwether as an institution made me think. I didn't come away with answers, but I came away with a lot of questions, which is at least a place to start.

Just as surely as I took on the mentality of the patient at Meriwether, I couldn't help taking on the mentality of the staff and the whole system as well. I saw why it was broken down and dysfunctional. I saw where the resignation and dislike began, and I saw where they ended.

I had gone, in an amazingly short period of time, from being one of the downtrodden to being the queen of social justice, and finally to being the laissez-faire absentee activist who says, "Not in my backyard." It was a predictable route, and one that left me unsure of how to effect or even propose lasting change, even though I knew that places like Meriwether needed to change.

To be sure, spending time in Meriwether had made me more sensitive to the plight of the indigent mentally ill. I knew what it was like to be treated like an inferior person whom no one cares about, a person who is never expected to get well, or even consistently better, and so doesn't.

I saw that taking people out of their lives, pumping them full of drugs, offering them no real psychotherapy, and then sending them out again to their old lives amounted to a revolving-door policy. They were bound, as so many of the patients I knew at Meriwether had been, to get arrested or committed again, and again.

But I also saw that working with people who behaved—I'm sorry to say this—like children could wear down your good intentions to a nub. What could you do with people who, when you tried to help them, often either tried to take advantage of you or allowed themselves to be infantilized by your efforts and made no effort to help themselves?

It wasn't Meriwether's fault, after all, if patients went off their meds or didn't go to follow-up appointments. I could understand why the meds were intolerable, and why these people's experiences with the mental health system hadn't left them wanting more, even on an outpatient basis. But I knew that these things were a recipe for relapse.

This is a classic public policy debate. What will work and what won't. The liberal will raise taxes to pay for places like Meriwether, assuage his conscience, and see the sorry results of inefficient bureaucracy and impersonal care. The conservative will ask the community, often the religious community, which is usually already in the business of dispensing charity, to take up the burden on its own, rather than fobbing off the unwanted on big government. But that is a burden that many do not want to take on: certainly not families and individuals. Charity may begin at home, or in the neighborhood, but that is where it can be hardest to sustain. As I had learned firsthand, developing relationships with people who are not only disturbed but quite often uncooperative, manipulative, and willfully irresponsible is a job that even people with an overabundance of fellow feeling often find too unrewarding, infuriating, and exhausting to perform.

Staying at Meriwether only inflamed this debate in my mind. I couldn't come down on either side. In a way, I had come down on both. But then I still had a lot more of the landscape to see before I would be in a position to make any sense of it.

I wanted to know, for example, if a private hospital would have more of value to offer a person in distress. I'd been to a private hospital before, my first time around in 2004, but that, too, had been a big-city hospital, and I'd had what I was still open-minded enough to think of as the misfortune of getting stuck with a lousy doc. I still held out hope for better consults—and maybe nicer staff, and better food, and cleaner bathrooms, and who knew what other luxuries.

Besides, I was looking for a totally different clientele. At Meriwether, I'd had the public, urban, indigent, mostly black and Hispanic psychotic experience. I wanted to find a rural, middle-class, whiter than white private clinic, where I suspected depression would be much more common than psychosis.

I was also curious about what I'd find in a state that had gotten bad marks for its treatment of the mentally ill. On its Web site, the National Alliance on Mental Illness (NAMI) posted the results of a report they conducted in 2006, in which they graded all the states in the union on their treatment of the mentally ill. Almost every state received a C or below. I wanted to go to an institution in a state that had been given an F. There were eight to choose from, and, conveniently enough for my purposes, all eight were in very white parts of the country.

To make it official, I consulted census data and found a place with a population that was both small and 95 percent white. I did a little more research on the Web to find a private hospital in the area, and then I had my target. I packed a bag and booked a ticket, and that was that. I was on to Phase 2.

Or sort of. Something unexpected happened around that time; unexpected at least as far as this project was concerned. It wasn't unexpected when you consider prior experience.

I fell into a depression.

And why? Because I went off my meds.

Over the course of several weeks, I adjusted the 20 milligrams a day of Prozac that I'd been taking when I went into Meriwether and brought the dose down to 15 milligrams. Then 10. Then zero. It took a few more months before I hit the really rough stuff: to be exact, the three months between when I got out of Meriwether and when I made my trip to the bin in the hinterlands. The timing was almost perfect. I started scraping bottom, and then I got on a plane to present myself at a hospital once more. This time I didn't really have to convince anyone that I was depressed. It was pretty clear, even to me.

There are really two reasons why I went off my meds. One good and one not so good.

The good reason was that, while doing some of the background research to write this book, I'd been doing a lot of reading about psychiatric drugs: how they were and are discovered or synthesized; how they're tested, marketed, and prescribed; and how little anybody really knows about what they're doing to our brains. The more I read, the angrier and more apprehensive I became about using them. Hence my reluctance to take anything at Meriwether.

I just didn't want to be dependent for the rest of my life on a drug whose effects neither I nor the professionals could understand or predict, and whose glowing reputation had been based almost entirely on the meticulous propaganda of the companies that were profiting hugely from its sale.

I wanted to find a way to do without drugs, and not to succumb without a fight to what I considered to be the drug company's and my doctor's less than disinterested suggestions that I needed them.

I thought that that was a pretty good reason to try to go off my meds. I still do.

The not so good reason was that I did it for the book. I did it because, as I have said before, my brand of journalism is immersive. You have to have the whole experience, or as much of it as you can. You can't just stand outside as an observer, the way I had in certain respects at Meriwether. The whole point is that you are not objective.

Besides, I had started this book because I went to the bin that first time for real. I had experience with mental illness, or distress, or whatever you want to call it. I was a subject, too. My own subject. I couldn't brush that aside or keep it discretely apart while I watched everyone else crawl through the tar pit.

But, without actually becoming depressed again, I couldn't really pull myself into the experience in retrospect. That's the thing about depression, I have found, and this is a great mercy under normal circumstances. When you're over it, when you're not depressed, it's really hard to remember exactly what it felt like when you were depressed. You can remember it as an idea. You can describe it analytically. You know you felt terrible, and you know you don't want to feel that way again. But you don't really remember the details, the quality of the suffering. But I wanted to be able to reexperience that, and then render that in real time, as it was happening, not after it had passed.

I know, I know. Stupid. But there it is.

And, for what it's worth, here it is.

So turn the page.

ASYLUM

St. Luke's

It began with dread in the morning. I woke with a feeling of dread. The first conscious thought. *Something is terribly wrong with my life, with life in general, how it works, how it goes. It's too much. I can't face it. I am frightened. I am too small and impotent to handle this.*

This was only an inkling at first, like the vestige of a bad dream. I could not even remember what I was dreaming about, but I woke with this feeling that lingered well into the morning, well into my coffee making and shower.

I stood in front of the toaster and thought: *It is absurd to be this afraid of nothing. But I am. I am afraid of nothing.*

I looked for reasons, causes to assign, but they were irrelevant. That was the point. The fear. The dread came from nowhere. It did not correspond to the present or the prospects of the day in front of me. I was on firm ground. I had an enviable life. But it felt as though I was perched above the void. Blankness below. And my world crumbling around me.

My doctors might have explained it as an incommensurate stress reaction, a flight response on overload but with no discernable provocation, my brain thinking I was rappelling on a cliff face, dangling in danger. Adrenaline pouring in, but nothing so extreme had happened. I was just standing in my kitchen. The cliff, the void, was in my brain, in my dreams—and then it carried over into the morning when I woke.

This was disconcerting enough when it began. More so as it grew and extended itself throughout the day, through more and more days. Then I was genuinely concerned. Taking a moment to step outside the immediate storm, which had become so consuming, I thought: *This is not normal. I have never been normal, but this is diseased even for me. There is something really wrong.*

I thought this especially when somewhere around midday I crawled into the bathtub without running a bath. The fetal position, taking comfort in the cool, white porcelain pressing against my cheek, a substance both strong and smooth bending around my bent body, binding me, solid, firm, the bounds of a disintegrating self, the bucket that collects me, dissolving into a pool.

Who do I imagine I am? This was a pressing question suddenly. But unanswerable, of course.

I stood abruptly. Rushed to the mirror. I held my face close and stared, reminded of a friend who, after a traumatic brain injury, emerged from a coma, looked in the mirror, and did not know who she was looking at. Really did not know who that person was. Had never seen her before. Could not fathom identity.

That was happening to me, only it was happening in the way that simple everyday words like "because" and "hello" lose their meaning when you stare at them too long on a page, or are suddenly unsure how to spell them. It was a fundamental falling away of the most basic assumptions. The known suddenly somehow foreign.

Who the fuck are you? And what the hell are you doing in the bathroom?

This was a real question. I meant it. I really meant it.

I was in a bad way, and it was my own fault.

I wanted to go off the meds and so I did, tapering slowly, wisely, this time, or so I thought. I had coping mechanisms in place, exercise, meditation, work, experience. And for weeks I was fine flying solo, though fatigued and susceptible to cold, even gaining weight, such that I wondered whether my thyroid had been thrown out of whack by the serotonin, another of those effects no one seems to know about and can only guess at from the symptoms.

After a few more shaky weeks, I began waking in the morning with the dread. And then the bathtub and the mirror. And then the extension of the morning dread into the day, and a darkness being thrown over the world, and a solid belief in the untenability of my life. The infantilization. The curling up. The sense of being ill-equipped for everything, the conviction gathering speed that death was the only real option.

I cannot work. I am useless. I am taking up space. Consuming resources. I have no function. I am stupid. I will fail.

I had gotten out of Meriwether untrampled and I thought I was on my game. And then there I was thinking about where I could buy a gun.

A gun seems best. I am a maimed animal. Perhaps I can hire a hit man. I will tip him very well to take a clean shot.

Cowardice. You see?

I had been commissioned to write a book about loony bins. I had been to one already. I thought it was going to be a success story. Look at how I got off the meds and learned to make it on my own. But that is not how it worked out. I was going in again, this time with a wound in my side.

For research?

If you say so.

Pah. For real.

There was no need to pretend this time around. I cried in earnest in the admission interview. And why? Because that is another thing that happens when I stop the meds. I cry a lot. Big jags of tears over things like *Oprah,* which was what I was watching on a 52-inch plasma TV, waiting in the lobby of yet another hospital.

The intrepid reporter undercover.

I want someone to take me in. I want to pretend that I am doing my job, but I belong here. I am a pitch-perfect silent screamer, a forlorn lump.

Oprah. And I was crying in this tiny Catholic hospital—facility, really—more like a clinic, a specialty clinic for addicts and lunatics plunked down there in the middle of the plains where the freight trains passed through town outside the rain-bespeckled windows, moaning like whales under the broad gray sky.

I listened as I sat. Sometimes I walked to the window and looked, saw the red signal lights flashing on the gantries, the line of waiting cars with their echoing rows of red taillights blurring in the downpour.

In the corner of the room, next to the window, there was a life-size gilded statue of the clinic's presiding saint, Luke, standing over the four rough upholstered armchairs, one of which I was occupying.

There was a Fisher-Price play station at my feet, with ramps and tracks and obedient balls, a knee-high table and chairs, a box of toys half scattered in the corner. They treated children here, too.

What a place, I thought. What a place. So kind. So homey. Carpeted and warm. Quiet. There was only the TV, the volume low, and then only the sound of fingers softly typing, phones mutedly ringing, genteelly being answered.

It was late Friday afternoon. I had come for an appointment I had made by phone earlier in the week. I had called in supposed distress. Said I was on the road, about a hundred miles out of town. But I really made the call on my cell phone safe at home in New York.

Right. Safe.

As soon as I got the appointment, the so-called needs assessment appointment, I booked a flight.

The flight had been due to arrive more than an hour before the appointment. This, I thought, would give me plenty of time to take a taxi, even if the flight was late. It wasn't, and the airport was a joke. Two gates and two baggage carousels, like something on a Caribbean island. It had never seen a crowd. I had to call for a taxi, and the one cop on duty at the curb knew all the drivers by name. It took ten minutes to get from the airport to "downtown." It cost $13 including tip.

So there I was, early, flipping through magazines. Waiting alone in the lobby. A business reply mail card fell out of *Bon Appétit.* On it someone had repeatedly scrawled the word "Bored" in big letters. Other cards that fell out of other magazines, *Redbook, AARP, Popular Science,* had more messages embedded. Always the same. "Bored," "I'm bored," or "Boring."

A good joke, and for me, an unexpected smile I was thankful for. Solidarity left behind.

Been there, my friend. I have so been there.

The admitting staff was not pressed. Behind the long bulwark desk, with its glassed-in hutches and computer nooks, impeccably dusted, veneered, and generic as a floor display, two menopausal moms floated at their workstations, their fat fingers fluttering papers.

They multitasked smoothly, smiled patiently like women who had spent years darning mittens and cutting the crusts off sandwiches. They watched snatches of *Oprah,* admitted the odd visitor, touched up a database, caught the phone on the second ring.

This was restful. It calmed the fear—the extra added fear, even though I was convulsed by fear already—of having flown into a far-flung place to check myself into the bin. Yes, this was all of my own doing, of course, so whatever happened would be my own fault, perhaps even deserved. And yet. And yet.

It was not all bad. Not at all. I felt strangely young, sitting there, and new to the big world, guided by these ladies, as if this were Take Your Daughter to Work Day, instead of take yourself to the psych ward.

The harbingers of good care in the clinic above were in the furniture and the carpeting downstairs. The carpet was so impressive, so calming. Sage green. A luxury bespeaking control in the clientele. It meant they didn't expect anyone to vomit or shit himself or otherwise besmirch the premises.

Effort had been made, even in the three yellow gerbera daisies in a pot on the side table in the small consulting room where they asked me to wait for the needs assessment counselor. There were color photographs on the walls. The trunks of tall oaks growing clustered in luxurious stretches of green grass with shafts of mystical sunlight beaming through them. There was a box of tissues on the coffee table, thoughtfully placed, close to hand, an accoutrement of admission. Admission of instability, depression, suicidal urge, and admission to the hospital for same.

Like a ticket in my pocket. Admit one.

I waited in the room and looked at the pictures and the tissues, and allowed myself to be soothed by them a little, until the counselor came in.

The counselor, the girl—she was a girl to me, no older than twenty-five. Or at least she had the sprightly affect of that age, and the uncreased eyes, and the babyfatted mode of inquiry, and the eiderdown belief in what she did. The girl was very kind.

She had not yet felt the bludgeon of experience. She sat with her legs crossed at the knee, a clipboard in her lap. And on her feet—one bouncy foot dangling over the other—a pair of what I would call Mary Janes if you could hike in Mary Janes. Sassy schoolgirl upper. Bumper toe. Gripper sole. I liked her for those. They made me trust her.

And so a tear rolled out of my eye.

I was seized unaccountably by rue. I was ashamed, awed by the unspoiled attention of a girl assessing my needs, a girl who wrote down my answers so carefully in slow, looping script.

She seemed somehow outsized in her kindness, almost allegorical, the figure of Help in the pilgrim's regress. And I was in retrograde motion for sure, slipping out of the light, the line of waning day making its way across my face and leaving me in shadow, like a planet turning from the sun. She saw this and understood. It was not beyond her, though she herself had never known that kind of orbit.

She asked what I was doing in that town, because it is not a destination, barely a stopover, and even to the locals it was the middle of nowhere. I told her I had been hitchhiking across the country from New York, fleeing an unmanageable life.

"When I got here," I said, "I knew I was in trouble."

My voice caught in the lie. She noted this with her eyes, then noted it down with the pen. She was filling out a form, several forms, back and front, the first of many. They were positively German about this. Her forms, along with the others completed by the doc, the nurse, the social worker, and me, would end up in a three-ring binder with my name on it. And next to my name the initials MI.

"What does MI stand for?" I would ask.

"Mental illness."

"Ah. I see."

The other labels were CD, for chemical dependency, and DD for dual diagnosis, which meant that you were a loon and you did drugs. Technically that was me. DD. My file would say "history of cannabis dependence," but not, thankfully, "unhealthy preoccupation with bowel movements" or "mean drunk." It would also say, notably, "Patient is homosexual."

This was one of Mary Jane's many questions in the interview, slipped in nonchalant.

"Do you consider yourself to be heterosexual, bisexual, or homosexual?"

They asked this of everyone, I learned, though I feel sure that "patient is heterosexual" never appeared in anyone's chart.

There were other odd questions. Ones I hadn't heard before, designed, I presume, to see how cognitively impaired I was.

"I'm going to hand you a piece of paper with something written on it," she said. "I want you to read it aloud and then do what it says."

She handed me the paper. It said:

"Close your eyes."

"Close your eyes," I repeated, and did.

"What is this?" she said.

I opened my eyes. She was holding up her pen.

"A pen."

She pointed to the door.

"What is this?"

"English as a foreign language?" I ventured.

No smile.

"Sorry. A door."

She handed me another piece of paper with two interlocking squares drawn on it.

"Draw what's on this paper, then write a sentence. Then fold the paper and hand it back to me."

I drew the boxes and wrote pompously, "When does it begin?" I folded the paper and handed it back.

She unfolded it and glanced at what I had written.

If I had to guess, I'd say she thought, "Geek." But maybe it was "faker."

"Are those real?" I asked, pointing at the daisies.

"No. Are you having thoughts of self-harm?"

"Yes."

I didn't believe that I really was. Not right then. But I had been a few minutes before, hadn't I? Or was it hours? Or days? Still, I said it anyway, for the research, I told myself, because admission of danger to self, others, or property is pretty much guaranteed to put you in the bin, if not of your own will, then against it.

"Are you feeling anxious?"

"Very."

"What about?"

"Myself."

A pause.

"I don't feel safe."

This was gold. Safety is to be found in the hospital. Theoretically, anyway. It was a mission in this place. A point of pride, you could tell. She would check off "inpatient" after that for sure.

"Do you think you need to be admitted?"

"Yes."

"I do, too."

She left the room to telephone the on-call psychiatrist and tell him that I needed in.

I am pathetic. I have insurance. They won't refuse me.

After the Meriwether experience, I decided it would just be easier, and would certainly make me much less conspicuous, if I owned up to having insurance and presented my card right away. I had to do everything possible to make sure I got into St. Luke's without a hitch. I didn't want them shuttling me off to another public hospital. Besides, I still had to chase down my insurance company about reimbursing them for Meriwether, so I figured I could pay up for St. Luke's at the same time.

One of the menopausal mommies made a copy of my insurance card and called it in. Mary Jane came back into the room.

I was admitted to the hospital.

I had not been told what to expect, or what voluntarily committing myself would mean when I wanted to get out, though I signed the papers that told me these things if I had cared to read the fine print. I had not, however, seen an MD. But somehow it didn't seem to matter. It was like going into someone's home. You feel bad? Poor dear. Come in.

I had been formally admitted, but I was still waiting in the lobby some time later. They were ready to take me in, Mary Jane informed me, but someone upstairs was apparently "very upset," so I was waiting out the tantrum downstairs.

A voice on the loudspeaker, which was very tame and dulcet as loudspeakers go, said calmly,

"CIT second floor. CIT second floor."

I heard this designation again once or twice during my stay. Crisis Intervention Team. But it was for other floors, so I didn't see who came. I imagined they wore dark red or dark green blazers and ties, like offertory ushers in church.

Sitting there waiting, I began again, as I often did when the depression got to this point, to get stuck in a spiral of thought. There was nothing else to do, so I was asking myself all the kinds of confused philosophical questions I always asked myself when I felt done for.

How does a person get here? To the point of commission, I mean. Is it a failure of will? Of discipline? Or worse, a metaphysical lack?

I could not escape this prejudice, if it really was one. I still can't. In the culture of depression as chemical imbalance they assure you that it *is* a prejudice. Words like "will" and "failure" are not only unfair—signs of an unenlightened view of major depressive disorder or bipolar disorder, or whatever as yet theoretic ailment I am purported to have; they are also false terms. They do not apply. Or so we are given to understand.

This is my fault. My deficiency. My mistake.

Thinking back on it now, I remember one of the videos they screened in the dayroom at St. Luke's, a video produced and paid for (surprise surprise) by one of the major pharmaceutical companies that markets antidepressants.

"Depression is not your fault," it said.

The white words appeared on a black background, the letters jumping off the screen, moving toward the viewer, highlighted in a box, the narrator intoning, too, for emphasis.

"Depression is not your fault."

That is what the drug companies and the doctors and a whole lot of patients wanted you to know. If you contradict this idea or question it, it's merely the depression talking, or ignorance. But is it? Entirely?

"I'm diagnosed," said Teary Molly, one of the depressed patients I would meet in the ward upstairs. She was a cherubic plump twenty-two-year-old mother of two. Her face was always pink and smeared with fresh tears.

"I want my father to know that I am diagnosed," she told me. "He doesn't believe in depression."

"Neither do I," I had wanted to say, but I didn't quite mean it the way her father did. I believed in depression as a phenomenon all right. I believed in it then sitting there in the lobby. I believe in it now. The fact of it, surely, is incontrovertible for me. I had been in the tub. I had been reduced to a quivering mass.

And yet still there was an argument going on in my head.

I am here. Depression exists. As for cause? Disease? That is something else altogether. I am open to it. I suspect it. But there is no truth to this as yet. And there may well be will or partial fault involved nonetheless.

There must be.

The argument goes on now, in much the same way as it did then: What is the role of will?

After all, even established, testable diseases and conditions, like heart disease or the famous depressive corollary, diabetes, can be and usually are exacerbated by human choices, lifestyle choices, hamburgers, sweets, cholesterol, laziness. Should depression be excepted from this list because it comes from the brain? And does it come from the brain, or is that just another effect? An effect of some as yet undiscovered virus, say, or simply the old culprit, stress?

Unknown.

I hated—sometimes I still hate—Teary Molly the way I hated and sometimes still hate myself, and probably the way her father hated her, too. I hated what I saw as her mewling, self-sorry entitlement to the mantle of illness as identity, her overeager taking of refuge in "diagnosis," in the imprimatur of the medical establishment that absolves her of all responsibility.

I come back to this theme again and again. There are no diagnoses in psychiatry. Only umbrella terms for observed patterns of complaint, groupings of symptoms given names, and oversimplified, and assigned what are probably erroneous causes because those erroneous causes can be medicated. And then both the drug and the supposed disease are made legitimate, and thus the profession as well as the patient legitimized, too, by those magical words going hand in hand to the insurance company: "Diagnosis" and "It is not your fault."

But what if it is my fault? Or partly my fault. Or what if it is, at least, a deficiency of my own neglect?

Maybe this was just the depression talking. More self-hatred, self-blame. But that didn't mean I was altogether wrong either.

Suddenly I was aware again of the television, of the ladies typing behind the desk, of myself sitting in that armchair. I wondered if I was making too much noise.

I must stop this. Stop the train of thought, too long, too arduous, too loud.

Let it stop.

I begged myself, because there was no commanding at this stage.

Let the relentless ideas stop. Let the judges stop pronouncing their sentences on me. In every free moment, in the shower, walking to an appointment, in the appointment, harping in the background, harpies over-head, shrieking and circling, in bed, in my dreams, in my teeth grinding themselves blunt in the night, I am pulverizing myself raw.

You. You. You. You. The finger points at you. Who is right? Who is wrong? Am I making an argument? Are we having an argument? Can't we have this out another time?

FUUUUUCCCCCKKKK. Stop.

But it did not stop. It went on.

People say that depression is tears and lassitude and fear and self-loathing. But they do not say that it is a brain made of tacks, that it is a relentless passing of sentence.

Guilty. I am guilty.

And an equally relentless rumination and breaking down in response to it. Perhaps like autism, depression is a protective reaction to too much information. Too many thoughts.

In this context it's interesting to ask: Why can't a depressive get out of bed? Because if the minute you woke up, you thought of all the ways you could die or be injured or fail or cause death or failure or harm to others in any given day, you wouldn't get out of bed either. If you thought too long and hard about all the people who die in crosswalks, you would never cross the street. If you thought of all the people who die in car accidents, you would never get in a car. And those are only the simplest considerations.

Life is lived on ignorance, on not thinking about all the possibilities, about ignoring the most basic fact, that you are mortal and that it is unreasonable to expect a sentient, self-conscious creature to live with the idea that she is going to die.

Life is lived on denial. Denial of the obvious and awful. Healthy happiness is the careful adjustment of the veil of obliviousness, the very same gossamer veil that acts of God and terrorist attacks punch a hole in. But only for a moment. And time stops. Life stops while the hole gapes. Because it must stop. Life cannot be lived full face. And that is what grief is. The stopping of life and time in the face of knowing, seeing too much.

And that is what depression is as well. A stoppage, or, as Nobel laureate John Nash called it when speaking of his own schizophrenia, "a mind on strike."

And so I was pleading again with myself from underneath the pile of disputes:

MAKE IT STOP. Please make it stop.

And what would make it stop? What would expediently make it stop? Drugs. Wonderful, dreamy, ameliorating drugs. Legal drugs. Drugs that I could have because I, too, had been diagnosed, and because when it got that bad I didn't care about anything but silence.

The kiss of the unconscious.

I had secreted a Klonopin in the change pocket of my jeans. I slipped it into my mouth and sucked the pill like a mint. Then I chewed, hoping it would work faster that way.

And immediately it did. It worked. Not the pill, of course, but knowing I had taken it. Just the knowing that help was coming helped.

Help.

Just then a greasy-haired, puffy-faced blonde appeared in the armchair across from me.

Meet Bunny Wags.

Bunny Wags would teach me to play rummy in the ICU to pass the time in the evenings. She would tell me many stories about the system, because, though she was only twenty-nine, she had been through it like a lab rat who just wouldn't learn. Or maybe just wouldn't stop pressing the lever for the drug. She looked like a hundred and fifty pounds of chewed suet, sitting there pasty, slumped, defeated, with her white hospital band still on her wrist. She had come from the emergency room of another hospital, one that had those kinds of facilities.

St. Luke's didn't. They didn't get their hands dirty at St. Luke's. They didn't have an emergency room, or at least not the kind you'd find in a real hospital. They had an ICU unit, which was just another ward on the second floor, a ward just like the wards on the third and fourth floors, except that it wasn't permanent for most people. As at Meriwether, it was where everyone went first thing, in order to be processed and evaluated by an MD. You only stayed there if you were especially disruptive and needed to be watched or managed more carefully. Otherwise, in a day or two, you went up to the main ward on the fourth floor, which was shared by the addicts, on one side, and the mentals, on the other. If you were a kid, you went to the children's ward on the third floor and avoided all the rest.

St. Luke's wasn't like Meriwether. They didn't take people right off the street. They weren't on the front lines. They were a rehab clinic and small-time loony bin. All of it was coolly controlled. There was no triage in progress at St. Luke's. When I had called to make my needs assessment appointment and asked explicitly about their admissions policy, they told me that insurance was not a prerequisite for treatment, but I got the strong impression that if you didn't have insurance, they shipped you off pretty quickly.

That impression got a lot stronger later on when, while fantasizing aloud with a couple of other patients about how to escape or otherwise shorten our stays, a veteran of St. Luke's said:

"You wanna get out? I'll tell you how to get out in a hell of a hurry. Cancel your insurance."

St. Luke's was where they deposited you on the far end of a binge to dry out in clean quiet once they'd pumped your stomach or IVed your des-iccated carcass back from borderline malnutrition—once the life threat was over and you were breathing on your own.

Bunny looked like that, like a body brought back from the brink by tubes and technology and cursed by the genes of generations to be a drunk for the rest of her life.

I didn't say a word and neither did she. She was still a bit quivery from the treatment, and I was a pile of dirty laundry with legs, having a circu-lar argument with myself about "the will," so what the hell did I have to say to anybody?

Finally, Mary Jane came for me. Crisis over upstairs.

"They're ready for you now."

Did that sound deeply creepy to anybody else? I wondered. Like the thing the too-pleasant lady says in the slow-moving 1970s horror flick. The viewer's first inkling that the hero is really in hell and all the staff are really demons.

But they were not demons there. At first, this worried me, as much as it surprised me. Everyone was just way too nice. Scary nice. The guy at the metal detector who searched my bag and wanded my body was that way too. Polite and accommodating.

It took him less than a minute to go through my things, which he handled with care and respect. He was just checking for anything blatantly dangerous—a knife—or illegal—drugs. The staff upstairs would do a more thorough job, taking inventory to make sure nothing was lost. He zipped my bag, handed it back to me and smiled, as if I had done him a favor.

"Okay. You're all set."

Then Mary Jane and I were walking through empty, carpeted halls and going up in an empty elevator, coming out on an empty floor, going through two sets of locked doors, passing along the way whole quiet well-appointed exam rooms with long-handled sinks and boxes of rubber gloves. We passed activity rooms and meeting rooms, too, all with intact tables and chairs neatly arranged. All perfect, clean, empty, new.

And then finally there was the third set of locked doors. The ward. The ICU.

Mary Jane turned the key in the lock, gestured me in, and followed.

The door shut behind us.

Click.

The unit was small, only six rooms, some double occupancy, all opening onto an octagonal dayroom at the center. The nurse's station was on one side of the octagon, so every room and the dayroom was visible from within it. Off to the side there was a kitchen, and a dining area with three round tables, each of which could comfortably seat five.

There was a full-size fridge stocked with bagels, cream cheese, bread, butter, cold cuts, bags of raw vegetables, broccoli spears and baby carrots, and various single-serving juices (grape, apple, prune, orange, cranberry).

The cupboards were stocked with Styrofoam cups, disposable plates and bowls, small boxes of cereal, raisin bran, cornflakes, frosted flakes, Cheerios, bags of microwave popcorn, bags of trail mix, graham crackers, pretzels, animal crackers, instant oatmeal, instant hot chocolate, tea bags, sugar, mayo, mustard, barbecue sauce, and almost any other condiment you could think of. In the freezer there were individual cartons of vanilla ice cream and orange sherbet, and more bagels, bread, and cold cuts.

Jesus. This is camp.

"Have you had supper?" they asked, they being the two ward nurses on duty who had introduced themselves, shaken my hand, and smiled.

Supper? This kindness was too quaint. I felt corrupt in the presence of the word, so anachronistic, so innocent.

Have you had supper?

"No."

"Well, let's show you around the kitchen and you can make yourself whatever you like."

And so I did. Amazed. I put some of the raw broccoli in a bowl with a half-inch of water, covered it with another bowl and steamed it in the microwave. I melted a pat of butter over the top of it and salted it. I toasted a bagel (whole wheat; 4 grams of fiber) and slathered it with cream cheese. I took a Granny Smith apple and a banana from one of the bowls of fresh fruit that had been placed at the center of each table. There were individual servings of peanut butter in the cupboards. I spread some of it on each bite of the banana.

This and raisin bran was most of what I ended up eating while at St. Luke's. Lunches and dinners were egregious, catered unwholesomely by the same company that served a local college. Often entrées were some form of semicongealed mash casserole consisting of hamburger, corn pone, peas, and potatoes. It was either that or macaroni and ham and viscous, ersatz cheese all served with an ice-cream scooper. Starch was the staple. At times even the vegetables were adulterated by it. One side dish of glazed carrots had soggy bits of bread mixed in.

But snacks! Snacks. God, how civilized. How good.

Of course there were always people for whom too much idle time in the octagon and too much access to the kitchen weren't a particularly healthy combination, people like the 350-plus-pound, six-foot, four-inch mulatto whom I unoriginally nicknamed Fridge, not just because of the famous football player of the same moniker, but because this guy spent way too much time gazing into, and dwarfing, that particular appliance.

He was twenty-one years old and seemingly still afflicted with the near demonic munchies of the growing boy. The siren song of the sandwich was so strong in him that the whole ward eventually took to joking about the fridge itself being haunted.

"It's calling to you, man."

And he was indeed a comical figure standing there huge as a door himself, gripping the handles of both fridge and freezer, swinging them rhythmically as he rocked back and forth on his size twenty feet.

Fridge was MI. Some undifferentiated mood disorder that made him prone to attacks of rage. He was the one who had been "very upset" while I was waiting downstairs. He got upset fairly frequently, and when he did, he often kicked open the magnetic doors that were supposed to keep us all locked in. There were three sets of them. He never got past the second. Not that he would ever have made a run for it. I doubt if he could have run: his size alone hobbled him. But he also had an understandable tendency to trip over his own feet.

Fridge had been in St. Luke's about ten times before, ostensibly to have his meds adjusted. He seemed to have some problem taking them when at home, or at least doing so consistently. He lived with his grandmother and was subsisting on welfare or disability or both. He said he was the victim of fetal alcohol syndrome, and that at least a good portion of his emotional difficulties were attributable to that.

When he wasn't in a rage Fridge was a lapdog, friendly and sweet, always amenable to teasing. He did remarkably well for a large man confined in a small space.

As I sat there in the kitchen munching my bright green buttered broccoli, he was standing with a sandwich in one hand, head in the fridge looking for more. He said a chewing hello. I nodded and smiled.

Soon there was a parade of others coming into the kitchen, like Fridge, for a snack and a gander at me, the new meat.

There was Clay, a fifty-one-year-old father of four. He wandered in sighing, wearing scrubs and socks. St. Luke's distributed scrubs to patients instead of pajamas, if they wanted them, though this was mostly just for the ICU, where people were more likely to have shown up without a change of clothes.

After a long look at me, Clay said quizzically,

"What are you doing here? You look great."

"Appearances can be deceiving," I said.

"I don't know," he countered. "You look like you work here."

He wandered over to a chair and fell into it, grunting painfully.

He was paying what for him was attention, but he was not altogether there. His eyes were at half-mast, and he was swaying ever so slightly on his feet, as if he were standing on a boat. He was one of the addicts. Chemical dependency. CD. He was detoxing hard from a spree.

He had lost his job a few months back, just before Christmas. Then on Christmas day he'd had a terrible fight with his wife and stormed out of the house. He'd spent the next three months in what he called "the rubber room," which meant that he'd holed up in a cheap motel on the edge of town, a place infamous for being a drug den, and had gone on a protracted 24/7 bender, drinking beer and shooting coke all day and night, bouncing off the walls until they had to scrape him off the floor, near dead, with a needle stuck in his arm.

You can have a mighty good evening on a couple of grams of coke. When they found him, Clay had done an ounce. An ounce is 28 grams.

They took him to the emergency room. Then, once stabilized, they transferred him to St. Luke's. Now they were giving him 10 milligrams of Klonopin a day (1 milligram will make a novice woozy), plus trazodone (an antidepressant that everyone at St. Luke's said made them feel like a wet noodle), Ativan (another benzodiazepine, or "benzo," like Klonopin), and the famous sleep aid, Ambien. All this just so that he could cope, and pass out for a while at night.

Coming to see me in the kitchen was a feat at that hour, around seven. He'd had his evening meds, which is why he had the sea legs. Usually at that time, he was sitting on the couch in the octagon, his knees bouncing like they had a jolt in them, his face flushed, his eyes darting, his whole nervous system in overdrive.

I would see him in this condition fairly often over the next few days, but just as often he would be on the opposite pole. He tended to alternate between these two states. The one when he was on the edge of a panic attack, the coke making its hair-trigger way through his system, or the silly semistuporous one he got into about half an hour after he'd had his meds. Then, like now, he just smiled a lot, stated the obvious, and cheated very poorly at cards.

Clay, like Bunny, was still wearing a wristband. Seeing it, and having the same squeamish reaction to it that I had had with Bunny in the lobby, I was thankful that St. Luke's didn't use wristbands. To patients they are indicative of anonymity and neglect, and the doctors who owned St. Luke's seemed keyed into that, or so I imagined, understanding on some level that being tagged is a gross insult to your dignity. It makes you feel like property, or a corpse, a body not a person, the implication of the tag—maybe the need for it—being that if you passed out in the hall, they'd know who the hell you were.

By the time the introductions with Fridge and Clay were over, Bunny had made her way into the unit as well. I looked over and saw her slumped in a lounger in the octagon.

She was as wrecked as Clay, but alcohol was her drug. As she told me later, she was only recently out of prison, where she had done a six-month sentence on her third drunk-driving conviction. Depending on the state, the legal limit for blood alcohol content (BAC) is either 0.08 or 0.1 percent. When Bunny was admitted to the hospital, her BAC (or so she said) was 0.59, a poisonous, quite possibly fatal amount.

Though obviously an alcoholic, Bunny was, by her own admission, primarily depressed and self-medicating. Her mother had died a few months back, and that was most of what had precipitated her recent binge.

She was a bright woman and had spent her life in this dinky prairie town going mostly nowhere. There was nowhere to go but out and away, very far away. But she never had, and so, like so many of the other addicts and depressives I met at St. Luke's, she sank, and then did drugs and drank to pass the time, or obliterate it.

That part of the world would depress anyone—anyone with imagination or ambition. It was easy to see how it would happen, how slowly, over the course of years and many dull days, the landscape would destroy you.

The people were a mirror of that landscape. Flat, simple, but existentially in pain. They spoke plainly but liltingly, their vowels all attached to an *e*, as if transcribed from the Greek—*ae, oe, ie.* They were eager to help, and easy. Not southern sluggish, but in no particular hurry or busy snit either.

They were real, and rudeness was rare, but they would not let you into their hearts. They would not even let themselves. They were kind on the surface, but, as on the farms so plentiful in the region, the soil underneath was black. Not the black of cruelty, but of despair. The thing that nearly everyone around me was in the hospital for.

And the prognosis was not good. Not good at all. Because even if these people landed in St. Luke's or places like it, there would be no lasting remedy for the disease—the disease of their lives. Even if you cleaned a person up and dusted him off and stanched the flow of immediate tears with a rub on the back and a pat on the head, there would still be the same world out there to confront when the treatment was over.

There were still the hours to fill and the lack of opportunities or hope. These people would still go home to an empty apartment or a family fight, all the same stressors still in place, and they would have no means of lessening them, because their will, if they had amassed any in their time away, was still weak and always a quick casualty. No match for the horror of lost chances.

That's why they all landed back in here. They came in zonked. Got sober. Went home, and the minute they put their keys down on the counter, took their first real breath, and the smell of all they were running from got way up in their nostrils, they reached for the same solution, and did it all over again.

That's why, when Clay was on the phone talking to his mother or his cousin, he said, "Yeah, that guy who kicks in the doors is here again. Remember him? And that lady with the red hair, too."

He was talking about April, another depressive alcoholic repeat who may have set some kind of record for rebounds. This time around she had been in St. Luke's half a dozen times in as many months. She was fifty-eight years old and divorced, living off the settlement and boozing her way through it, drinking 1.75-liter bottles of liquor in two days with no food. Now she was on a boatload of tranquilizers too. Five milligrams of Klonopin a day, trazodone, and Lunesta for sleep.

Living alone with no occupation was the killer for her, and the reason why she relapsed so fast, usually within hours of release. It usually took her a few weeks to work her way into such a state of acute malnutrition that she had to come back to the hospital, but she always did it. A terrible, common cycle.

Of course, not everybody was a repeat. Chloe was a first-timer. I met her, too, that first night.

She was a nineteen-year-old student at the local college who had come in for suicidal ideation. She was yet another one of those hapless people— there always seemed to be one, usually a woman—who, in an unguarded moment, confessed to feeling suicidal or inclined to self-harm and got shuttled off to the psych ward.

The door had locked behind her before she had gotten her bearings enough to know that she couldn't just walk out, and she was stuck here at the mercy of a total stranger's judgment about her own internal life.

I found this bitterly amusing, and so indicative of the state of psychiatry today. They admit a person to the hospital based solely on what she tells them about how she's feeling. They diagnose her on that basis, too. Yet once she's in the hospital her word is no longer good enough. She has been magically diagnosed, and that diagnosis supersedes her testimony. Suddenly the doctor knows better, even though he knows only what you have told him.

Does the word match the disease? Does the disease exist at all? The doc is dealing in shadows. Yet we all speak with such conviction, as if diseases were made entirely of ideas, floating in judgment between doctor and patient, and then somehow locked down, the person locked in and trapped by the doors and the diagnosis.

When I first saw her that night, Chloe was talking on the pay phone, crying. The trap had done its work. She was frightened and feeling worse, looking around at all the rest of us downhearts and drowsers and thinking, "What the hell have I done?"

She was a tall, broad-shouldered, athletic girl with medium-length dirty blond hair, which she often wore in a ponytail. She was wearing jeans and a jean jacket over a T-shirt, the jeans and the jacket both fitted and faded to the same ice blue.

She moved and held herself upright and square-shouldered, with the command of someone whose body is an instrument, efficient and well trained. Her face was covered with shiny pink pimples, which she picked unself-consciously, often until they bled. This, combined with an air of insouciance that somehow coexisted with her depression and self-loathing, had the effect of making her seem even younger than she was, and more exuberant, as if her youth could not help bursting through all the worldly woes that had gotten her here.

She was filled with determination and energy. Nothing like the other depressives I met at St. Luke's. But then this was part of her problem. It was what drove her to self-harm and a suicide attempt.

She told me that when she was a child her father used to give her a sheet of paper every morning and tell her to use it to make out a schedule, dividing the day into fifteen-minute increments. She was then required to write down exactly what she had done during each of those fifteen-minute periods, everything from brushing her teeth to saying her prayers. At the end of the day her father would read over her schedule and tell her whether or not she had had a good day.

Her life was a drive. One long drive to be good enough, to achieve, to use time, not to fail. She was a good athlete, she said, basketball and soccer, and a good student, though not a natural one. She had been on antidepressants for two years, and had been cutting herself for longer than that, just trying to find some relief from the expectation.

"I don't feel that I will be loved if I'm not the best at everything," she said.

Nonetheless, she had her head screwed on pretty straight. She had enough perspective to say that her father meant well, as no doubt he did, even as he hammered her into shape. He wanted her to succeed, wanted to teach her to order her world, a skill that she knew had served her well in many respects, even as it had drummed home the message that love was to be earned, not freely given. She knew that medication was not a hale holy panacea, and that she would have to build her emotional well-being out of effort and vigilance as much as the almighty chemical fillip.

She waited in the ward thinking what I had thought in the same circumstances, that this was not a place much designed to help people like us, the semitalented, sometime wayward overachievers who got a little carried away with the X-ACTO knife when we got a bad grade, or otherwise tripped on the ladder to betterment.

Having a doctor tell you how it was when you bloody well knew how it was, and had told him; having to be paternalistically shut in for your own good despite your protestations that no good was to be had in the shutting; this was not the stuff of recoveries. She shared this sentiment, especially since it was the weekend—her goddamn weekend—earmarked for some well-earned play.

Incongruously laughing now after her phone call, scribbling furiously in a coloring book at the adjacent table, she said, "I'm a kid. It's my job to play."

And so we played. All of us. Me and Clay and Bunny and Fridge. Per her invitation and instructions, we played Indian poker.

"What the hell is Indian poker?" I asked.

She held a card up to her forehead, face out.

"Like this."

It stuck to the grease on her face like a cartoon feather, and she smiled, lowering her hand. She dealt us each a single card.

"Don't look at your card. Just put it up," she said.

We did.

"Now," she ordered expertly, "you bet based on what everyone else has, but not knowing what you have."

"What are we betting with?" asked Clay.

Nobody had money. Valuables were locked in the nurse's station.

"Skittles," she said, producing a large bag and doling out piles to each. She popped a few loose ones into her mouth,

"Okay. Aces are high. Left of me bets first."

That was me. I looked around the circle. New faces that I seemed to know already. Eased into a game together on this Friday night in lockup. How strange. How somehow easy and almost normal.

Clay had a king. Fridge had a jack. Chloe had a five and Bunny had a ten. It wasn't looking good.

"Fuck me," I said, throwing down my card, "I fold."

I had an ace, which provoked a chorus of near miss "Ohhh"s from the others.

"Damn," I said, "my deal."

And so I dealt and we played well into the night. I was coasting by then on my own popped Klonopin, nearly forgetting where I was and what I was, until one of the more officious members of the staff, who saw that we were betting (albeit with candy, but betting nonetheless), stopped us.

"Gambling is not appropriate in an addiction recovery facility."

Lights out.

No one woke me rudely in the morning. It was Saturday, so no one woke me at all. Another human luxury. Another piece of myself handed back, left to my discretion. As was breakfast, which I wandered into the kitchen around ten to prepare.

On each table, thermal pots of coffee had magically appeared. It was bilge, of course, but I doctored a cup with creamer and sugar and drank it anyway, out of pure gratitude for the option.

Clay stumbled in looking stupefied by the night, as if sleep for him was a beating, or hard labor he needed respite from. Then there was Herbie, whom I hadn't met the night before.

Herbie was a ninety-two-year-old former night watchman who fought in the Second World War and was now living a strange, reclusive life with his ninety-four-year-old wife of thirty years. Like so many of the rest of us, Herbie was in for depression.

"I don't have anything to do anymore," he said by way of explanation for why he cut open one of his arms in what was either a botched suicide attempt or a stab at self-mutilation. But for an extremely old and ostensibly depressed person Herbie was oddly upbeat and on his game.

He used a walker to get around, though he could navigate short distances without it. He often did laps around the octagon, the walker's wheels squeaking intermittently and wobbling at the base like a busted grocery cart. He liked to play games of chicken with whichever one of the other patients happened to be making the loop in the opposite direction, or he'd make a mock show of running us down as we crossed his path.

Herbie was always full of sly humor. I asked him why he was in St. Luke's.

"I signed the wrong papers," he said.

People had taken to Herbie and took care of him, making sure he was eating enough, toasting him a bagel or whatever else he wanted for breakfast, and bringing it to him at the table.

"Do you want some kiwi, Herbie? I know how you like it."

They'd had kiwi the night before as dessert with dinner and Herbie had never had it before. He'd loved it, and everyone had noticed, saving the leftovers in the fridge for him to pick at over the next few days.

Herbie had hit it off especially well with one of the other patients, Karen, the most high-functioning psychotic I have ever met. She was another repeat. She came in every now and again—via ambulance from a hundred miles away—to have her meds adjusted and chill out from an episode.

She knew enough about the course of her condition to know when she was losing touch with reality, and she had a very helpful circle of psychotic friends with whom she had what she called regular "reality checks." This meant that, because their delusions were all different, she could call one of them and say, "I think the CIA is watching me," and they'd be able to set her straight, confirming that, in fact, no, no one was lurking in the bushes outside her house or listening to her phone calls. Similarly, when they called her to ask if aliens were landing in the park down the street, or check whether the computer chip in their molar was actually picking up signals from police radios, she could assure them that they were, in all likelihood, mistaken.

Karen also went to group meetings, which functioned as a similar corrective if she was slipping into delusions.

Karen had a delightful sense of humor about herself. She said of one such group meeting, "Yeah, I was sitting in one of those meetings and I said, 'Am I God?' and everyone shouted, 'Noooo.' Now there's a reality check for you."

Like Herbie, Karen was extremely well liked around the ward. People appreciated how easygoing she was, especially since they knew that she managed to be that way even while she was hearing voices and seeing shadowy figures skulking in the corners of the room. People would say, "How's it going Karen?" and she'd point to her head and say, "Getting louder in here."

Karen was a good example of what a support system could do for you when you were seriously mentally ill, and how much of a difference a social network could make in how functional you were. The people at Meriwether were largely without resources, and most of them lived on the street. As a result, they didn't get regular reality checks. They had no friends to speak of, certainly no psychotic friends who were functional enough to help anyone. And no "normal" person was going to serve as a touchstone in their world. Normal people gave them a wide berth and looked away as they walked past.

It's not hard to imagine that a sane person living on the street for a few weeks, frightened, isolated, and scorned, would start to lose touch with reality. It happens to any of us when we spend too much time alone in our homes. But then factor in the chaos of the street, the dangers, the drugs and alcohol that make beggardom bearable, the dejection and extreme loneliness of being an outcast, and you have a very bad situation for anyone's mental health. Throw voices and delusions into that mix, and you're guaranteed to get someone who is barely reachable.

Karen was getting the benefit of both friends and nurturing asylum because she was middle-class. She had insurance. She had resources, both social and financial, and she got the benefit of effortful care in a hospital that was not overcrowded, overburdened, poorly managed, and resentfully staffed. In stark contrast to the patients at Meriwether, when Karen came into the hospital during an episode, not only was she greeted by nurses who treated her respectfully, but, most important, she found herself among other people like herself, people who were not the products of the ghetto or life on the street. This meant that they could almost all, in some measure, take care of each other, offer an ear, advice, laughter, and companionship in distress, even if only in a game of cards.

These are the luxuries of the relatively healthy and at least marginally grounded. Being such a person, I am learning, has a lot to do with your present economic station in life, as well as the one in which you were raised.

Karen was not the sole example of this type. I met four diagnosed schizophrenics during my time at St. Luke's, and all of them were like Karen, highly functional, capable of discussing their illnesses and taking part in group sessions where they could both give and receive at least some counseling. At Meriwether, you were lucky if you could keep order in a ten-minute meeting. Perspective and co-counseling were unheard of. Impossible. People were too drugged or too incoherent from their life on the streets to do much but slump or babble.

Of all the psychotics at St. Luke's, I got to know Karen best—or got her to say the most intimate things about herself—when we were on smoke breaks.

Among the many ways in which St. Luke's far outstripped Meriwether—allowing the patients to smoke and get some fresh air was one of the best.

Seven times a day—twice in the morning, twice in the afternoon, and three times in the evening—one of the nurses took us outside (there was no limit to the number who could go) to a small fenced-in garden area just off the ground floor. It wasn't much, and since I didn't smoke, I spent a lot more time inhaling the other residents' furious puffs than I did breathing actual air. But still, it was outdoors, and if the weather was fine and I found which way the wind was blowing, I could steer clear of the smog, and even get a little sun on my face. It was glorious, even when it was cloudy or raining. It got me through, knowing that I always had a break to look forward to.

People stood around in groups, having procured from the nurses their two allotted cigarettes, chain-smoking and catching up with people they knew from the main ward upstairs.

The main warders took their smoke breaks at the same time as we did, and this was usually when repeat offenders like Clay and Bunny reunited with other addicts whom they had met during previous stays at St. Luke's.

Slapping each other's shoulders and laughing, they'd say, "Still a class A fuckup, I see."

"Oh yeah. Always."

"How'd they get you this time?"

"Oh, ya know. Dog ran out of the house. Got hit by a car. Caused an accident, and the cops came. I came running out after him so coked out of my gourd that I forgot I was carrying an armful of the stuff. Busted right there."

"Wow. Sucks. Dog okay?"

"Oh yeah. He's fine. Ducked right under the chassis. No scratch."

"Lucky fucker."

"Yeah. I could kill him."

The dog owner was Fenske. He'd been in repeatedly, like so many others, for drug rehab. I noticed him right away because he looked like a New Yorker, a college-educated bohemian East Village type, who'd somehow been airlifted to this desolate place and left to languish among the drab, doltish natives. He had luxurious wavy shoulder-length blond hair and a pale freckled complexion. He wore horn-rimmed glasses, jeans, red Puma Clyde sneakers, and a beat-up black leather blazer.

He made an impression on me right away, as I must have on him, because going up in the elevator after one of the breaks he looked across the group of us, all crammed in like cattle, focused on me, and said,

"You," he pointed thoughtfully. "You're some kind of emotional parasite, aren't you?"

"A spy, actually," I murmured.

"Thought so."

"Nah. Just an emotional cripple like the rest of us. Wrist-slasher, oven-header, that sort of thing."

"Oh, okay. Gotcha."

He said this like I was telling him what I did for a living at a barbecue, which is what we all learned to do in there when we heard even the most extreme stories.

I found myself doing it when I made the mistake of asking the shaved-headed handlebar-mustachioed guy in the Marines sweatshirt what he was in for.

"Drinking. Drugs."

"Were you in Iraq?"

"First time around. Got discharged."

Post-traumatic stress, I presumed, but feigned ignorance.

"Why?"

"Liked it."

"Liked what?"

"Killing."

"Oh, right."

"Volunteered for one too many missions and they were on to me."

I remembered reading a recent article about sociopaths flying under the radar in the military and then surfacing as the henchmen of some civilian massacre or Abu Ghraib-type fiasco.

We crowded into the elevator right after he told me this. I was standing close enough to practically lick the scorpion tattooed on his scalp.

"Uh-huh," I said, pretend-thoughtfully. "Gotcha."

In the ICU, I had a room to myself. It was a double, but I didn't have a roommate. It was just me and the empty bed next to mine, and the deliriously clean tiled bathroom.

I was in love with that bathroom. I sat in there a lot with the light out and the door shut, like a kid playing fort in a closet. I forgot myself in there, where there was only the thick enveloping dark and the band of light around the door frame, and the close, cool quiet. I was whole in it, unseen and unseeing, crept away in a cleared place so perfect in remove, like a pod gliding in space.

Sometimes when I sat in there I thought about odd things, more of those depressive thought patterns I had come to recognize. I thought, for example, about the woman who cleaned my bathroom. Like everyone else here, Fridge excepted, she was white. Scandinavian white and chirpy cheerful even as she mopped. I imagined she baked pies on the weekends for her extended family and smiled at the weather from the porch, where she rocked away her aching back and what I thought must be her quiet desperation. For all I knew she was happy. But I couldn't imagine that. I inhabited her bland life as I saw it, and grew sadder.

As with everyone else I encountered when I was depressed, I went way too deep too fast. I was like a sponge, or a medium, soaking up the pain and dissatisfaction of strangers. The minute my eyes took them in, I took them in. This was another aspect of my disease, my problem, or my way of being in the world, whatever tag you want to put on it. It was a habit of mind that had no filter, no shell or thick skin that separated me and my pain from everyone else's. Call it depression as a form of extreme empathy, and then overstimulation, as if every person I met or passed in the street was a loud radio blaring.

This was why I hid in the bathroom or in the tub or on the couch curled up in a ball, because even to leave the house was like stepping into some relentless Russian play. I was overwhelmed immediately—by the postman whose shorts were his humiliation, and the dog walker whose acting career was not going so well, and the cashier at the drugstore whose life happened behind a counter, and even the filthy rich lady sitting alone at the bar at Bergdorf's at noon in her kelly green broad-brimmed hat that said "Notice me."

Pain. Too much pain. Loneliness, frustration, loss, the broadcast of each striving mind, the malaise of a failed attempt, so common, or the vortex of one never made, commoner still.

And me sitting in the bathroom in the dark thinking about it.

The truth was, I was spending too much time alone. The thoughts were too heavy again. Besides, I thought I should have been working. Or spying, I guess, so I wandered into the kitchen to join another game of cards.

Bunny was playing bullshit with Bard, Clay, and Fridge. Bard was a nineteen-year-old Ritalin wastoid committed by the state for ninety days. He dropped out of school in the eighth grade, after having done the grade twice, moved into an apartment with his father, worked at a thrift store, and sat around doing "hot rails" (crystal meth inhaled through a super-heated glass straw) for the rest of his adolescence. When he was eighteen he came home one day to find that his father had left him, just took the furniture and moved without a word.

They had him on the antipsychotic Zyprexa, but true to form in that joint, he was as clear as a bell. He admitted to paranoid moments in the past, but to see him you would have thought he was just like any other jacked-up parapubescent vandal with too many muscles and nothing to do with them.

He was small, but built and wired to do damage, with a buzz cut, black wife beater, and a bulbous pair of ever susurrating headphones, which the nurses had lent him as a pacifier. He looked and acted like he was raised backstage at a rock concert, weaned on noise and petty crime, like a mascot of dystopia. He was singing along with the radio as he put down his cards.

"If you want to undo my sweater . . ."

"Five jacks," he blurted.

"Buuuuulll shiiiiiittt," shouted Bunny.

Bard flipped the cards. There were indeed five jacks.

"Suck on that, bitch."

Bunny laughed, and so did the rest of us.

In bullshit you use two or three decks, depending on the number of players. The decks are dealt evenly among the players, so it's possible to have as many as eight to twelve of any suit. The object of the game is to be the first to get rid of all your cards, so fibbing about what you've discarded, and catching other players in their fibs is the sole object. Hence the name of the game.

These games of cards were another gold mine for me. People will talk about almost anything if their conscious minds are otherwise engaged, and they don't have to look you in the eye. That was part of what was so relaxing about a game of cards in there. It functioned as a form of group therapy, but for my purposes, far better, because people would spill everything they wouldn't dream of saying in front of the staff.

Bard, for example, who was peevish and monosyllabic in social work group or activity therapy or any of the other meetings that formed the backbone of the treatment at St. Luke's, was positively chatty in a game of bullshit. He even produced his commitment papers, which Bunny had asked to see, because she had once worked as a paralegal, and because she'd been committed enough times to at least claim to know the minutiae of state law on mental hygiene.

I was peering over her shoulder as she read.

"So you were committed initially for two weeks," she said, perusing the document, "and then at the end of that time you were recommitted for ninety days. I assume you had a lawyer?"

"Yeah," said Bard, "but he was insane himself." Stretching out an exaggeratedly shaking hand to mime the action, he added, "He signed the papers like this."

Bunny flipped through the pages of the order. "Yeah, you're pretty screwed."

"So I should elope?"

"Well, you could. I've done it. They'll put out a bench warrant for you, but if you leave the state until the commitment expires, and don't get pulled over for speeding in the meantime, you should be fine."

"What do you mean?"

"Well, if they pull you over for a violation, they'll call in your license and find out about the bench warrant and drag your ass in. Do you have a plan?"

"Yeah. I can have my sister waiting outside in the car, and just slip out on smoke break."

Unlike at Meriwether, elopement at St. Luke's would have been easy. I had slipped away from the group unnoticed once already, on the way back from a smoke break earlier in the day. I had found a bathroom in the hallway with a lock on the door and a glass mirror. For a suicide risk this is a bad combo. I sat in there for ten minutes just to see if anyone would come for me, but no one did. Granted, that bathroom was still inside one of the three locked doors, so I couldn't have gone anywhere had I wanted to, but I could have done a lot of damage to myself.

On smoke breaks they lead us past all three locked internal doors and within twenty feet of an unlocked outside door. A person could have turned off and been long gone before they caught on. This was Bard's plan.

Bard was not doing well at St. Luke's. Cooped up and resentful, he lashed out unwisely at the staff, some of whom could be too prissy and petty to deal with a blunt adolescent whose usual form of protest was

"Bitch." The way he said it, it sounded like a punch in the face, especially when paired with his other favorite epithet, "Fuck."

"She's a fucking bitch," he would say. Or, "Fuck that bitch."

I could feel his frustration bursting out through the words.

He said it right then during the game of bullshit. He was talking about Nurse Grace, a plump, vaguely officious type who took the bait every time Bard threw it.

"Grace is a fucking bitch," he said, putting down his cards. "Four kings."

"Bullshit."

Nurse Tally, another plump tattletale, was spying, lurking by the door with her arms crossed. At this, she stalked out, off to inform to Nurse Grace.

Sure enough, five minutes later, Bard was called to the nurse's station.

Nurse Grace: "Tally tells me you called me a bitch."

Bard: "Then I must have."

NG: "I would like an apology."

Bard: "Forget it, fatty."

NG: "Well, you may want to think about that for a minute while we consider taking away your smoking privileges."

Silence.

Bard (*sighing heavily*): "Fine. I'm sorry."

NG: "Sorry for what?"

Bard: "Calling you a bitch."

NG: "A what?"

Bard: "A fucking bitch."

NG: "Thank you, Bard. Now, I would like you to go and apologize to the other patients."

Bard: "What?!!! For what?"

NG: "For poisoning the therapeutic atmosphere."
Bard: "You're fucking kidding me."
NG: "Eh, eh, language."

And so it went.

Scoffing, I told Bard to shove his superfluous apologies and resumed the game.

I spent the rest of that weekend in the ICU plugging people for information—their stories, their diagnoses, their meds. I compiled a chart with all this information on it. I suppose it was then that it really began to strike me how many of the people who were in St. Luke's for detox were really depressed or, in one case, psychotic. That was why St. Luke's used the label DD, dual diagnosis. It was the gray area between illness and abuse.

Obviously, it wasn't an accident that St. Luke's catered to the addicted and the mentally ill. There was, I was beginning to see, considerable overlap between the two.

Of course it would be hard for anyone to say for certain whether it was the mental condition, the depression, the anxiety, the aggression, or even the psychosis that had brought on and worsened the substance abuse, or the other way around.

We've all heard stories about teenagers who were fine until they got a bag of bad pot dusted with PCP, or they overdid it their first time experimenting with LSD, mushrooms, or methamphetamine and then just never came back, were never the same again.

But it's really impossible to know in so many cases if that kid went for the drugs in the first place because he was depressed, or trying to manage anxiety or mania or incipient psychosis and then went into orbit after using these drugs because his brain was already compromised to begin with. Clearly, the drugs didn't help.

Bard was a perfect example of this, it seemed to me. Perhaps his childhood hyperactivity had ended, or been managed by Ritalin, but, to hear him tell it, that's also where his subsequent drug abuse had begun.

"Meth made me feel calm," he said. He said he'd gotten to the point where the Ritalin just didn't do it anymore. He needed something stronger. Another form of speed to slow him down. Would he have gone for the meth if he'd never had the Ritalin? Maybe. Did the meth tip him over into psychosis? Or what looked like psychosis, but was really an effect of the drug? Or would he have been psychotic anyway? Who knows. It was all a big mess at this point, but it was certainly possible that the doctor who prescribed his Ritalin had set him on the course that ended here, with Zyprexa and a ninety-day commitment. Not that Bard was innocent, mind you. But he was certainly dually diagnosed.

All in all, however it began, in many of the people I met at St. Luke's there was a mutually reinforcing and destructive correlation between MI and CD. Almost everyone, whether they were categorized that way formally or not, was DD. The depressives had abused alcohol, and the alcoholics were depressed. The meth-heads had heard voices, and the psychotics had abused meth, and coke, and alcohol, too.

Chicken or egg? It was anybody's guess.

I had a speech prepared. It was Monday at last, and I was going to meet my doc. I had been told his name already, but had forgotten it, but it didn't matter. I had only one thought anyway. I was sure he was going to be a dick and a pusher, so I'd worked up a preemptive rant about my unwillingness to take drugs, except maybe Klonny or Ambien, if I just want to blunt out the world at 10 p.m., like slamming the door on the day.

Forget reporting. Forget guinea-pigging myself and submitting to whatever they might or might not see fit to prescribe me. I was in full-on patient mode. I was being stubborn because I knew that I would probably have to go back on some drug to dig myself out of this hole. But for now it was on principle that I refused. I wanted to do it when *I* was ready, not when the "for your own good" brigade decided.

I had met with the on-call doc over the weekend, a cursory Turk who finished my sentences and scribbled his two cents in my binder. MI. Yep. Sure enough. *Depresso domesticus.* Run-of-the-mill.

"You want something to sleep?" he said.

"Sure," I'd said. "Why the hell not."

But today, I was meeting my keeper/king of the hill, the guy who had power. That was how it usually worked in these places, at least the ones I'd been to. The MD psychiatrist sat at the top of a pyramid and delegated everything down.

Beneath him (at St. Luke's anyway, where there were such luxuries) were the psychologists, the PhDs accorded the respect of their educations, though they were largely symbolic and without real pull. They did give you therapy, however, three times a week for fifty minutes. Actual one-on-one talk about your problems, believe it or not.

Then there were the social workers, the nurses, and finally the psych techs. Psych techs were babysitters. They had no degrees, no real qualifications but youth and optimism. They took you on smoke breaks, they led formality wrap-up discussion groups at the end of the day, and they told you to stop gambling with Skittles.

But the doc was the man. Everyone else was really a peon with pretensions. Everything you wanted came through him. To every significant question the stock response was: "You'll have to ask your doctor about that." So, if your doctor was a dick, you were screwed.

Still, I was going to fight like with like, if need be, and get myself an hour pass to leave the hospital, even if it meant sucking up to his expertise and burying fathoms deep my resentment that my life had been reduced to a file under his arm.

But as it turned out, there was no need.

Hello. My doctor was not a dick.

He was like the dad on a sitcom, extra large, warm, even cuddly, six-foot-four, bald and bearded, roomy and soft in the middle, big paws, and a smile that got into your veins like homemade gin.

I could tell in the first exchange—"So how are you?" for example—that he really wanted to know, and didn't think he already knew the answer. He was so wholesomely paternal that I wanted to crawl into his lap and talk about my investments. I was so pleasantly surprised I could have shit myself right there and happily sat in it. He was a keeper.

I said this right out.

"Wow, you're actually intelligent and not arrogant. How'd you manage that?"

He told me he was dyslexic and thought that maybe that was why he was humble. He knew what he didn't know. I admitted that I couldn't spell, and often made homonym errors. We bonded over the grammar school challenges of language that still somehow persisted. He submitted that English is really backward, and I added that, yes, wasn't it interesting how, for example, in German, the verb came at the end of the sentence.

He agreed.

"Yes. Instead of 'He fell down the stairs,' it should be, 'He down the stairs fell.' "

This was going well.

It got better. I told him I didn't want drugs. I rattled on a bit about this, as planned, expecting that once I'd nixed the SSRIs as being too mania-inducing, the favored Lamictal would come floating into the conversation like a bellwether balloon, and the phrase "no side effects aside from the rare but serious rash" would follow hard upon, like a bandwagon.

But no. To my great and glorious surprise, when I finished—he had actually let me finish—he looked at me respectfully and, without a spark of hesitation, said:

"Okay."

Okay?

This shut my smart mouth effectively and melted my sassy little heart. Had the doctor just rolled on his back? Doctors I knew didn't say okay, except maybe to themselves, and then only as the coup de grace. As in, "Okay, we're gonna take off this limb."

But this guy had just used it in context to actually mean what it said. Okay. You got it. Your call.

Now I was quite possibly in love.

And then the capper. I told him I needed exercise if I was going to get back on the stick. He nodded knowingly. Got it.

"I need an hour pass to go running in the park," I said.

I expected I would have to lobby for this each day, but he shocked me again.

"I'll put an order in your chart for an hour pass every afternoon. Will that work?"

That works nicely. Very nicely.

He was trusting me with freedom, giving me back a piece of my will with faith, believing that I could handle it, or if I couldn't, believing that the failure would help me to measure where I was.

Wisely, he said this when I again expressed amazement at his willingness to grant the request.

"Day passes are a useful tool. They tell both you and me whether or not you're ready to go back into the world, or to what degree you're not ready. If, for example, you go out and find yourself totally overwhelmed in an hour, then you know you need more time."

He was making me part of the process, giving my mind its necessary role in healing itself. He was listening to me when I told him what I needed, and giving it to me, because, unlike so many of the other deadheads in his profession, he could make a distinction between someone who said exercise would do her good and someone who said a ritual murder or a hit off the crack pipe was just what she needed to get back into the swing. He saw that I knew what I needed, or at least I knew in part; what's more, he saw that I was right. He had the power to make it happen and did, because he also knew that the simple act of giving me what I asked for, when it was reasonable, made me feel enfranchised and heard, a partner in the treatment plan, not its bound-and-gagged recipient.

He was a wizard of common sense.

Our meeting was short, as short as the meetings at Meriwether had been, about fifteen minutes all told. But it served its purpose. He knew his role. He wasn't there for therapy. The psychologist was for that. He wasn't simply there for himself either, to impose his smarmy better judgment, or, per his job description, to assess and "treat" me. He was there responding to me. He was empowered to make things happen, and he used that power beneficently without personal agenda.

We shook hands and parted laughing, he, because I'd said how nice it was to meet a doc who was smart enough to know that he was stupid, and I, because he'd said that maybe the only good doctor was a dyslexic one.

―――

Per Magic Doc's suggestion, I went up to the main ward that day.

My good-byes to Clay, Bunny, Bard, Fridge, Chloe, and the others were abrupt and strange, as abrupt and strange as the immediacy of our acquaintance, which went deep and narrow very fast, like a vein of precious metal in rock, and died that way too, a dead end, deep in drilled recesses, greedily mined and abandoned.

The hellos and good-byes were redundant, they always were, more pleasantries of the outside world dispensed with in there because what was encountered within those walls was already known and as quickly forgotten, but assimilated somehow nonetheless, like knowledge of a prior life. Like all the characters in the Jungian dream, everyone was you and you they, manifestations, internalizations, combined, recombined, recycled, made superficially to appear as another, but all the while simply more of you.

But you, reader, are the sane person reading this now, and you are thinking that these people on this page are not you. By no means are they you. They are the other, put away, out of sight—and yes I, too, laugh at this expression newly now—out of mind.

It is a significant expression in this context—out of sight, out of mind. But out of whose mind? Who is out of whose mind? The lunatic is out of his mind and so we put him out of sight—not because being out of sight is necessarily good for someone who is out of his mind, but because when the lunatic is out of sight he is out of our minds. We can forget him, forget his resemblance to us, forget that he is a member of the family. Thus he is made into not just "an," but "the" other.

That is what pathology means. Other. Over there. Not me. Not mine. Another path diverging in the wood, going off, erring, deviating from the main. The road not taken, the path to wrack and ruin. Keep to the road, the main road, the mainstream. Stay out of the woods, the bracken, the mire, and most of all, forget. Forget that I am one of yours and that you know me.

In much the same way, I had known them, and then I forgot them. I saw them on smoke breaks a few times in the next couple of days, but we had less and less to say to each other. Bunny got out a few days later. Her first night home she called me. I took the call on the pay phone in the main ward. She was drunk and going on and on about how she and Clay and Bard had had some kind of weird love triangle going on in the ICU. She said she missed everybody and didn't know what to do. I didn't know what to tell her, so I just listened until she tired herself out.

Then we hung up, and I felt terrible.

Clay made it up to the main ward on the addict's side a couple of days before I left, but again, the magic intimacy of our time in the ICU was gone. He was still shaky, and he didn't know what he was going to do when he got out. He was still unemployed, and to make matters worse, he'd had a call from his mother who'd told him that his cousin had robbed his apartment while he'd been locked up. He'd taken Clay's TV and a few other things to sell for drugs. Clay's mother had called the cops and had him arrested. It was all in the family.

I thought, sadly, that given what he'd be facing when he left, it wouldn't be too long before Clay was back in here, or in jail along with his cousin.

I heard that Karen left in much better condition. She'd rested. She'd adjusted her meds, and she seemed to have tamed the worst of her flare-up. I held out hope for her success. Fridge left, too, presumably to go home to his grandmother and stop taking his meds. But maybe this time he'd stay away longer. One could always hope. Bard, of course, was stuck for a while. They kept him in the ICU because he was disruptive and because, or so he said, they were working on transferring him somewhere else to sit out the rest of his time. He was still in the ICU when I left.

Chloe's parents came and got her the day I went up to the main ward. She went back to school, as far as I know, and went on as before, overachieving and probably cutting, though maybe doing so less obviously, so that she wouldn't end up in St. Luke's or someplace like it again. Still, I didn't worry about her. Of all the people I met at St. Luke's, I thought she was the most likely to recover, stay out of trouble, and go on to have a productive and mostly fulfilled life. She had never belonged at St. Luke's in the first place. All she needed was a good therapist and some time to put a little distance between herself and her father's expectations. She was going to be fine.

A depressive ward has a very different feel from a psychotic one. They don't confiscate your pens, for one. Though I had come prepared, with felt-tips and retractable Sharpies, I needn't have troubled. Never mind ballpoints, there were enough sharpened pencils in the dayroom to riddle yourself like St. Sebastian if you were so inspired. But nobody in here had that much energy or imagination. They hardly spoke.

I felt it the minute I walked in. Heaviness in the air, like some kind of spiritual humidity bearing down on my bones. When I stepped through the ward's main magnetically locked doors, I came into a short T-shaped hallway. To the right, twenty or so yards down, there was an octagon exactly like the one in the ICU, though its set of locking double doors was propped open. This was the MI side. To the left, again, twenty or so yards down, there was another octagon, also with its doors propped open. This was the CD side. A short hall ran between the octagons, and, though the doors were almost always left open, we were not supposed to cross back and forth, so the wings were like two docked spaceships, with separate species looking warily across at each other.

The addicts' side, though filled with people who were primarily depressed and only secondarily addicted, had a lighter feel than the depressive tank I was in. It had the levity of creative self-destruction, and the people had the charm of self-hatred. The addicts were people fighting their natures, clobbering their malaise with a high, and laughing over their resultant lost limbs, whereas at my end of the hall, there was no fight at all, no bite, just the occasional whimper of the unwashed or the glassy eye of the defunct.

Gerald was the worst case on the ward, by far. Even among the cave dwellers, he was unique. A person utterly destroyed. Psychic pain taken to the point of psychic absence. His eyes were dead. They did not fill with tears or recognition or response. He spoke only when spoken to, and then only in Bard-style monosyllables: Yes. No. Don't know. Unlike Teary Molly and me, and a lot of the other depressives I would meet in this ward, he was not stubborn or childish, or self-indulgent, or complaining, or sorry for himself. Those are remnants of dissent. He simply wasn't there.

He wore the same clothes every day, a pair of black jeans and a plaid button-down shirt. He was grossly overweight and shuffled along the walls half-bent at the waist. He was about sixty, and his hair was turning from dirty blond to gray, though he never bathed, so it was hard to tell what was actual color and what was just oily buildup matted to his skull.

There is not much else to say about Gerald, because despite repeated efforts to engage him, he would not talk to me, or to anyone. I'd try a joke, but he'd never smile. He would not even look at me. He just said in his usual distancing monotone, "Yeah," and resumed his hollow contemplation of the carpet, or the walls, or whatever else wouldn't look back and ask for contact.

Aside from Gerald there was Teary Molly, of course. She was often to be found at the small table in the dayroom, drawing or coloring while she talked with another of the more taciturn patients about the overwhelming burdens of her life and tried to swallow yet more rising sobs.

There was Trevor, a tragically ugly, infantile man afflicted with bloodless, pale dry skin that fell in large flakes from his bald spot into the long, stringy grayish brown hair on the sides and back of his head and lodged in clumps in the waxy porches of his ears. His ungroomed mustache cringed stiffly above his startlingly red wet lips. When he spoke in group therapy meetings, he had the unfortunate habit of knitting his scaly, long-nailed clawlike fingers together, resting them on the table in front of him and looking down at them gravely, as if he were a trauma counselor delivering the bad news. Thus he displayed his unkemptness, all in a row, from the top of his head to the tips of his hands, and people in the circle averted their eyes.

In the feeble voice of a boy who still wets his bed, he spoke of having nightmares every night, filled with flying "demons and devil dogs," and he complained of having to leave the light on at night to banish them.

There was Josephine, who stomped around the ward wearing a permanent puss face. She was in her early twenties, but she whined at the nurses like a grounded fifteen-year-old who wanted to know why she was being punished for crashing Daddy's car. She was constantly eating and drinking, shoveling fistfuls of trail mix or Cheerios into her mouth from a bowlful she carried wherever she went, and gulping 24-ounce bottles of hypercaffeinated Vault soda, which she purchased at the mall when they let her out on a two-hour pass.

There was Delilah, a dumpling-shaped, impish sixty-five-year-old who, like Trevor, appeared to be functioning at the maturity level of a second-grader. In our daily group therapy sessions her contributions took the form of transparent attempts to tell the staff what they wanted to hear so that she could get out sooner. That or giggling interjections, as when she pointed at Gerald and said, "His zipper's down."

There was Celine, a small, quiet, feisty woman with a tart smile and a keen eye. She was in her late seventies and lived with her son's family. She had what Herbie had—the depression of old age, the accumulated despair of feeling useless and having nothing to do or look forward to, as well as the added humiliation of feeling like she was a burden on her family. Interestingly, like Herbie, she retained a sense of humor and perspective in her depression, contradictory as that sounds. She seemed resigned to waiting it out and enduring it as she had obviously waited out and endured so much else. She was one of the few people in the octagon, aside from Gerald, whose depression didn't manifest itself as a kind of prolonged childish snit, or a one-note chorus of "Woe is me."

At the sight of all this, you can imagine why I took to my room right away, and thanked Christ that I had a single. For others, especially those inclined to self-harm or night terrors, a room of one's own might not have been the best option, but for me, this private realm turned out to be the very best thing about St. Luke's.

Again I had my own bathroom, though there was no shower this time. Still, it was cleaner than clean. The communal shower was down the hall between the octagons, a tiled room with a locking door. Half the room was a changing space, with a chair to put your clean clothes on and hooks for your dirty ones, and the other half was a large open shower with powerful water pressure and a wonderously efficient drain.

My room was painted blue, each wall a different shade, sky to cerulean, and the walls were at odd angles, so that the bare-bulb night-light that was set in a glassed-in niche near the floor threw a strange light. Weak, diffuse, yet penetrating.

This private little room that money could buy—that money, or actually insurance, had bought—very quickly became a refuge and retreat for me, and I came to think of it as the best that any hospital could give you when your mind was what ailed you. I had control of my light. The night-light as well. And so on rainy days, which turned out to be most of them, I usually had the night-light on in the afternoon, like a beacon in the gloom. And the room, like the prow of a ship, seemed to seep through fog, like fog, to Patagonia or somewhere else mysterious, far away and lonely.

I sat in there often with the night-light, and I did it because I could, the benefit of privacy and cleanliness and a little trust. I could do it because the bathroom did not stink, and because I was not afraid to do yoga on the linoleum floor next to my bed. In fact, I liked it, the alone time, the V-shape of the room, tapering toward the entrance, holding me, helping me find the deep mystery of the world in a secret place.

At those times I was not afraid or depleted. I was full. I was sitting inside my brain, up behind my eyeballs, buzzing, washing the day's thoughts off my shoulders in waves.

The light came in from the dayroom, filtered to a calming glow by the frosted glass in the top of the wooden double doors. (The glass was shatterproof, with embedded chicken wire.) I was allowed to keep these doors closed, another luxury denied me at Meriwether. This made time alone in the room even more recuperative and cherished.

On the outside of the door the nurses had stuck a small white tag with my name on it, handwritten, not typed. We learned each other's names quickly that way, as did the nurses, and we were granted a small piece of property as our own. And so I could say to myself: *This is my room. My space. Tomorrow or next week it may be someone else's, but for now it is mine and I am safe in it. I am respected in it.*

It's hard to overestimate how much this meant, how much healing it actually allowed, and could potentially allow anyone in similar straits.

The room or partial room you occupy, if it is clean and quiet, and you are left to yourself when you want to be, if you can shut the door and turn off the light, or turn it on if that is your preference, if you can exist in this place in a suspended state, separate from the stressors of your life, alone, but knowing that just outside the door there are people who will talk to you, or play cards with you, or help you if you are shaking—if all of this is true, then that room becomes a type of sanctuary. In it you can get a version of what people get on religious or spiritual retreats, what fleeing emigrants of catastrophe and danger desperately seek. Asylum.

That is how things began to change for me a little. That is how I managed to get some actual benefit out of being in St. Luke's, even though I was supposedly only there as a journalist, getting the feel of a small, rural private hospital. I did, at times, achieve a state of vacancy that I could not have achieved at home, both in my person and in the space around me. Expectation fell away with the scenery. The familiar and often burdensome trappings of my apartment, my life, and my personality were at least intermittently replaced by a friendly, clean medicinal emptiness. Not the painful emptiness of exile or imprisonment or the shut-in's disheveled bed, but the paradoxically full emptiness of relinquished expectation.

I knew that I could hibernate in my room. But I also knew that I could walk out into the dayroom, and walk down the hall to the addicts' side (as I often did, despite the rules, because I found my fellow depressives' company too depressing), and chat, or watch TV with someone like Fenske, who didn't want anything from me. I had the option, and it was this luxury of choice between the easy fellowship of cheap distraction and the reprieve of a good, long, soulful gaze at the ceiling that began to give me some partial shelter from my despair.

Sister Pete appeared on the ward each night after dinner, wearing her generous brown habit and beige sneakers. Around her neck there hung a four-inch crucifix that glowed in the dark. When she talked to you, her soft brown eyes were always widened in surprise, her hand always moving to adjust the headband of her wimple, which jumped and slid as her scalp crinkled in response to whatever you were saying.

Though she was in her sixties, everything was news to Sister Pete, and a cause for wonder. She called me Norah Baby and sought me out wherever I was hiding, though I didn't hide from her explicitly. She was too good to pass up.

She was addicted to the Eucharist and went to mass three times a day to partake. In her theology, you were what you ate. Literally. The more of Christ's body you consumed, the more like his body your body would become, until, she said, you were thirty-three (and presumably bearded and olive skinned) forever.

It was notable how small a deviation this really was from received Catholic doctrine. The transubstantiation was orthodox. So was the cannibalism. It was only with the look-alike age regression that Sister Pete ran off the rails.

She grew up on a farm in a town about ninety miles from St. Luke's, and spent her childhood sitting in a tree house dreaming of God and the contemplative life. She entered a local convent at eighteen, and lived there for forty years, at which point she came to St. Luke's, took up residence in an efficiency apartment on the grounds, and became spiritual adviser to the patients. It was a job she loved and took very seriously, and by all accounts performed very well.

She was a kind of savant in this regard, giving mad solace to the mad, living every moment in the moment, happy and at peace, even if she was permanently out to lunch, or probably because of it.

This use of Sister Pete was the single greatest act of kindness and therapeutic intelligence that I saw among the institutionalized mentally ill. It had made Pete whole and beloved, given her a sense of usefulness, the guiding purpose that is the cornerstone of any person's emotional well-being.

I imagined how Mother T would have flourished in this kind of role. I thought of all the people I saw at Meriwether, and I wondered how their lives and conditions might have changed for the better if someone had made even the smallest provision for them, had given them a blithe sinecure to occupy their time, to make them feel useful. What might have been accomplished?

What might happen if we as a culture took even the most minor responsibility for the lost among us, rather than consigning them, and quite possibly ourselves, to the ravages of the system? The indifferent system.

Have we abandoned each other to "the professionals," pushed ever on by our definitive work ethic to perform or sink, to behave as though we do not live in bodies, do not have emotional lives, have no ties to community? If we are healthy, we get the benefits of family and a place in the social order, a place that reinforces our mental health, makes possible our continued ability to hold that place in the social order.

We are pack animals sustained by companionship, bonds, and our position in the web of human contact. But if we fall, if we fail, if we succumb to the breakneck pace and onerous demands of our lives—too much work, too much family, too many responsibilities and natural, normal fears—then we are cast out, shut away, ripped from the sustaining web, and expected, alone and abandoned, to recover.

What about a community that makes a place and takes personal responsibility for the impaired, accepts them as part of the larger civic body and takes the burden on itself, spreads it among the healthy to lighten the load? What about a community that says, "We will care for our own"? Instead there is the alienated demi-apocalyptic world that detaches signified from signifier, piece from whole, and sends the wounded off to languish in the psychic poorhouse.

It is the difference between public and private solutions, the cold grasp of the institution, and the warm fold of a refuge where people have names and not wristbands.

This reminded me of Meriwether again, and Mother T.

I remembered Mother T trying to say the word "psychosis." She never stumbled over other English words, but this one she did. Psychosis. She said it like she was trying to get her mouth around it, like it was too big a bite taken from a burger. She'd learned it from her doctors. Her diagnosis. Psychosis.

That's how Sister Pete said the word "kerygma," uncertainly, but with gusto nonetheless.

"What is that again, Sister? Kerygma?" I inquired.

"Yes, kerygma."

She was telling a joke about Jesus.

"Is that what you get when charisma meets enigma? Jesus as charismatic enigma?"

I liked my own bad joke. She did, too. She laughed.

"No no. Kerygma."

I asked her to write it down. The whole joke with the word in context. She produced a piece of scrap paper from a memo book she was carrying. The memo book was full of scraps, none of which was much bigger than a gum wrapper. Some were blank. Some had old jokes or reminders written on them.

She told the joke as she wrote.

"Jesus asks the modern-day apostle: 'Who do you say that I am?'

"Answer: 'You are the eschatological manifestation of the ground of

our existential being, the kerygma, in which we find the ultimate meaning of our interpersonal relationships, the pristine quintessence of Him
whose very essence is to be, the primordial sacrament exerting a tran-
scendental holding on our becoming.'"

She paused here before the punch line, her wimple rising.

"And Jesus said: 'Huh?'"

Her eyes went especially wide when she said the "Huh?" and then she
grinned and started in on a long lilting laugh.

"That's good, Sister," I beamed, charmed as always by the pure joy Pete
took in the smallest things. And I began to wonder whether true goodness
wasn't, in this fucked-up creation, a form of retardation. Not an avoidance
of vice but an ignorance of it, a lack of acquaintance with it that cannot be
willed after the fall, no matter how strong the intention.

The temptations the rest of us are forever trying to elude are things
that would never occur to Pete, wholly oblivious, in her tree house still,
listening to the birds and blissed out on God. This led me to thinking
something I had thought before, that perhaps mental illness is a form of
brain damage or brain trauma. Maybe the upside of that is that it functioned, as it appeared to in Sister Pete's case, like a protective coma that
kept the thinker from thinking too much.

And so in this vein, like a jackass, I said sophomorically:

"Sister. Don't you ever feel the burden of existence?"

She cocked her head to one side, brought up short from her laugh in
true puzzlement.

"The burden of existence?" she asked.

Touché, Sister. Touché.

Now that I was upstairs, the program began in earnest. First thing each morning, as soon as I emerged from my room, perhaps of my own accord, perhaps coaxed by the gentle sarcasm of Nurse Maggie, who chirped, "Good morning, Sunshine," or Nurse Candy, who wheeled in a blood pressure monitor and said, "May I?"

However it happened, first thing, when I sat myself down in a chair in the octagon or the kitchen, someone, a nurse or a psych tech, handed me my self-inventory form.

This form was used as the basis for the first group meeting of the day, which began at 10 a.m. and was variously called process group or goals group or social work group. In this group, all the patients on the unit met with a nurse or a social worker or a psych tech to take stock of our progress or lack thereof.

Question 1: Target behaviors

Depression

CHECK ONE.

Not at all ＿＿ Not much ＿＿ Somewhat ＿＿ A lot ＿＿ Extremely ＿＿

Anxiety

CHECK ONE.

Not at all ＿＿ Not much . . .

Suicidal ideation

CHECK ONE. . . .

166

Question 2: How is your relationship with your family?

Improving ___ The same ___ Getting worse ___

Question 3: How did you sleep?

Well ___ Fair ___ Poor ___ Required Medication ___

Question 4: My appetite is:

Good ___ Improving ___ Poor ___

And so on down the line. My energy level is . . . my ability to concentrate is. . . . Have you had suicidal thoughts today? (If yes, please tell staff immediately.) What are your goals for today? Did you meet yesterday's goals?

Goals and groups were the backbone of the day, both a way for staff to keep meticulous records about each patient and an opportunity for the patients to vocalize their feelings as well as make requests and complaints. Keeping us occupied and checking in was useful, even if sometimes it was a great heaving bore for anyone functioning above a murmur. Naturally, a lot of it was going through the motions, the staff asking the same questions over and over again—How are you feeling today? What's your goal for the day?—and the patients, depending on their moods, usually giving answers that were either long-winded and peevish or prudent and angled to expedite their release. Still, it was better than being babysat by TV, and it did force each of us to mark the days in some meaningful way, however small.

After Meriwether's malign neglect, I respected the attempt at care, even if I made fun of it sometimes. When they asked me, for example, if there was anything I needed or would like, I wrote, "A heart, a brain, courage." Or on the sleep question, after the last option, "Required medication," I penciled in my own worst case, "Required bludgeoning."

Every day was the same. Process/goals group ended at eleven, with me and the rest of the crew having stated our purpose for the day ahead and

condition of the night before. Then there was an hour before lunch during which most of us watched talk shows on TV, or doodled with the
array of colored pencils that were piled in an old tin on the table in the
octagon, or worked on a jigsaw puzzle that was spread accommodatingly
on this same table. At noon we were lining up for the chow cart. They
scooped the daily grub onto our outstretched paper plates and handed out
plastic utensils. (Other than at meals, plastic flatware could only be had
by special request.)

At one o'clock, sometimes there was social work group. There we met
with a social worker and bellyached about our prospects, or fidgeted about
what we were going to do when we got out.

If it wasn't social work group it was medication group, where we bellyached to a nurse about how stoned we were or weren't, what kind of nightmares the meds were giving us, how shaky or sweaty or constipated we
were, and so on, and she made notes to give to our docs.

Some days there was no group at one, in which case we all ensconced
ourselves in front of the TV, or resumed work on the pastoral scene with
skipping girl that we'd so assiduously been coloring. Or, as in Gerald's
case, we got back to counting the pile in the carpet.

At two it was either occupational therapy or activity therapy: OT or AT.
In OT we headed into the art room and got all crafty-creative with beads
and glue guns. For an hour, we made pieces of jewelry or wind chimes, or,
in my case, a mosaic tile trivet, while listening to soft rock on the radio—
"WDSM, the station everyone in the bin can agree on."

In AT, we either played a game like Scattergories or Cranium, or we
headed down to the activities room in the basement, where there was a
foosball table, a Ping-Pong table, an array of Nerf balls, a plastic Fisher-
Price basketball hoop, and semifoam, semiplastic bowling ball and pins.
There was also an Exercycle and a treadmill, though not the kind you
could break much of a sweat on, or a limb, which was the point. Everything in the room was sue-proof, or as near as they can make it.

OT or AT finished at three, and the rest of the day was ours, not that there was much you could do with it, unless you had a pass. I used my hour pass at this time, from just after three to just after four.

The days went slowly, and as much as I found solace in my room, and in the company of the addicts, I found that working so often in groups with emotionally destroyed people only worsened my depression. The addicts were following their own program, based on a twelve-step model, and we never mixed in group therapy, so I was left to founder with my own kind.

Looking around the circle in therapy meetings, I often found myself going back to my ugly round of thoughts.

These are the palest, most rumpled, useless, yet somehow proudly despondent sacks of meal I have ever had the misfortune to call myself one of. The entitlement in all of us is appalling. My, me, mine. I'm unhappy. Fix it. Happiness is my right as an American. Not its pursuit, but its persistence, like an arc over my life, cradle to grave, a sheltering bough, for spacious skies and fruited plains, the bounty of my country. America the beautiful. And happy. Except that the next verse of that song says, "Mend thine every flaw." Meaning make a fucking effort, you sloth.

Sloth. A deadly sin. I'll have to talk to Sister Pete about that. But sin is so unfashionable now anyway. Who needs it when you have the great exoneration of disease? Hell, that's better than nihilism. That is nihilism. Nihilism with a candy coat.

What's easier than, Everything is permitted? I'll tell you what. Everything is a disease. That's what.

I was not really making sense or being fair. I was pissed off, rage being just another form of negativity to indulge at these crumpled people's expense, and my own. Yet, how could they expect the group therapy model to work for depressives the way it appeared to work for the addicts? They shared their stories, as so many other addicts did in twelve-step groups, and seemed to gain insight and relief from their fellow patients' articulated pain and reciprocated understanding. I knew this, in part, because of things I overheard in the dayroom, or things they told me directly when I asked them. But I also knew it because, despite the usual separations, I did manage to sit in on one of the addicts' sessions, an open AA meeting that met once a week in the basement of the clinic.

There, among the resident addicts, as well as another forty or so outpatient former clients, people joked and laughed. They spoke seriously, too, of course, about their more sordid escapades and histories, and about the destruction they had brought to their own as well as others' lives. But even the hard ideas helped cement the bond of public confession and shared mistakes. There was a sense of forward motion and positivity even in the darkest stories. People were there to lance their boils and walk away relieved. They were not, as my fellow depressives and I seemed always to be, intent on stewing in their distemper.

Maybe it was just this particular crop of depressives—they were no one's dream team, to be sure, and neither was I—but I wasn't getting anything except more negativity and a heightened sense of alienation out of listening to Trevor talk about his devil dogs and watching Gerald become one with the wallpaper.

It wasn't that I couldn't see, in theory, how talking to other depressives might help me get some perspective on my own death spiral. It certainly had in the past, when I had spoken to depressive friends. But that had only been true when the depressives I had been talking to hadn't themselves been depressed.

Those conversations had helped me only because the person in question had recovered. They weren't in the hole anymore, which meant that (a) the hole hadn't swallowed them up, and so, by extension, it wasn't necessarily going to swallow me up either, and (b) they were standing aboveground and had some perspective on where they'd been and where I currently was. They could throw me a rope.

But these people on the ward were just as firmly in the hole as I was, so what rescue could they offer? To make things worse, it wasn't even the same hole. We were all in our own separate holes, so we couldn't even play blind patty-cake. The best we could do was overhear and cross-talk each other's pitiful wailing and griping. We were just blobs in sweatpants in dire need of dandruff shampoo. All those groups were just wasted time, as far as I was concerned. I got much more out of my individual therapy with my psychologist.

Not that that was transformative either. It was fine. It probably helped in the way that traditional psychotherapy is supposed to help, or at least in the way it has helped me in the past: by getting me to organize my thoughts through verbalizing them. But in the end it was just your basic three times a week for fifty minutes.

My stalwart therapist was very sympathetic, obviously thoughtful and caring. A practiced and expert listener. She always tilted her head to one side and slightly down, and tucked her long hair behind her ear. Her watery blue eyes looked up at me and blinked slowly at all the right times. She compressed her lips sorrowfully when I cried, or, as was more often the case, when I tried not to cry and failed, and licked the snot off my upper lip. When I choked on a word, she always waited for me to go on. She never spoke before I'd finished. She understood. She responded. She tried. She had all the right tools of the profession, except maybe that spark of the dark arts that therapists always have in the movies, and that I had always looked for in real-life therapists but never found. It was probably just as well that I hadn't, since the most appealing movie shrinks usually turned out to be serial killers anyway.

I don't mean in any way to denigrate her. I am grateful to her. She did well by me, such as doing well can be with bread and butter. She was the companion piece to my room. Another clear benefit of St. Luke's that I had not enjoyed elsewhere. A place to rest and confer with myself, a wall to bounce my riffs against, a small but true light to steer by. It wasn't her fault that I needed Hannibal Lecter as my therapist. Or thought I did.

But whatever the misfires of the treatment, the staff treated us with what I came to see as St. Luke's trademark kindness and concern, and sometimes staff members even made surprising and creative extra efforts to reach us.

On one occasion, for example, a psych tech named Mitch did something far more inventive and healing than I would have expected from anyone in a hospital setting. Just before wrap-up group one evening, he hid a remote-controlled fart machine under Teary Molly's chair. When it was her turn to blubber and whinge about her day, he hit her with a loud one. She looked puzzled. Didn't get it. The group, presuming she had lost control of her sphincter in her distress, decided to ignore it. But then very quickly he sent another. The machine was well designed, offering an inspired array of sounds from plappy to squeezed, and every permutation in between. This one was a percussive blurt, like a low note from a flügelhorn, followed by a long slow deflating wheeze. At this Sam could no longer keep a straight face. He dissolved in silent laughter. I, being me, took the helm on this one.

"Jesus, honey, do I need to move?"

Mitch sent another. A classic whoopee-cushion bubbler.

"Okay," I said, "you have my respect. Peace."

Now the whole circle was roaring.

Mitch had done the impossible. He had tickled the walking dead. Like the employment of Sister Pete, this struck me as an awe-inspiring act of kindness on Mitch's part, and I was impressed anew with the quality of person St. Luke's managed to employ. Not only had the nostrum of laughter as best medicine managed to survive the pharmaceutical age, but it came sliding into that circle of pathetics on the whim of a young man who had no degrees or pedigrees, just some old wives' wisdom about what was good for a soul in pain.

Sister Pete was holding a black Grave Digger Monster Truck, a stuffed toy that a kid on the children's ward had given her to mend. She was planning to sew up one of the wheels whose seam was ripped and return it tomorrow. But for now, sitting with me in my night-lighted blue-walled room after supper, she was holding the thing like a baby, fascinated as usual.

I, too, was interested in this artifact. Where else but on a children's mental ward would you find a stuffed truck? No hard edges allowed, even in toys, which could be and no doubt were thrown. The children's ward was above us, and I had already heard loud pounding coming through the ceiling in the octagon on the addicts' side, where I had been spending most of my social time.

"What the hell is that?" I had asked Fenske, who was watching the Lakers game with me on TV.

"Another kid flipping out," he said casually, as I wondered whether that strangely soft thumping was someone's head drumming the floor.

Aside from the monster truck, Sister Pete was also carrying something she called "the hem of Christ's garment." She carried this wherever she went, but this was the first time I had seen it, a conspicuously laundered-looking relic that she housed in a Ziploc bag. I couldn't quite tell whether she thought the tidy white swatch was two thousand years old, but still suitable for dry-cleaning or she just liked having something talismanic to place on people's heads while she stood over them and said her blessings.

She said she pressed the hem against the tabernacle for hours, praying feverishly to imbue it with, or replenish, its healing power, which I can imagine was sorely drained after a night on the ward. As I'm sure she was.

It must have taken a lot of energy to pump so much spirit into three wards full of people, especially when a third of them were kids. I actually wondered what she ate to make herself so round, when she claimed to eat a fairly healthy diet. There must have been some doughnuts and potato chips in there somewhere.

She said she ate her food mostly raw. Veggies for sure. Potatoes too. If she ate animal protein, it was usually at some public event, like the Lenten Friday fish fry at the community center, where clergy ate for free. She was living on a tiny budget, I'm sure, and so she was duly frugal. She could rattle off the price of celery at three different markets. Usually, when I was talking with her in the kitchen of an evening—say, about depression and the sin of despair—she would investigate the fruit bowls for brown bananas.

"They just throw them away," she'd say, slinging them like pistols into the hip pockets of her habit.

I was talking about despair with Pete because it was the theologian's version of depression, and I had been thinking about what they taught us in catechism as a child. Why is despair a sin—a mortal sin? I used to ask this of my teachers, it seeming unfair to damn a person for feeling bad.

But as I watched so many of the patients at St. Luke's, myself most of all, indulging in depression as a form of bratty rebellion, and as I had fought with myself about volition, about how much of depression is a willful resignation rather than an actual absence of will, I had begun to understand why despair could be characterized as vice. It occurred to me first because so many of the patients around me were fat. Clinically obese, actually.

I thought again of the favored diabetes analogy. "Would you begrudge a diabetic his insulin?" they say. "So, then, why begrudge a depressive his Prozac?"

But I began to think of the link between diabetes and obesity, one exacerbating the other, one biological, the other behavioral, and I began to see how fault and will could come into it. I thought of how eager we are, a society in which corpulence is an epidemic, to absolve ourselves of our own bad eating habits, how eager we are to locate obesity in the genes or blame it on a virus. Take this pill and be thin, says Big Pharma (how rich will the first company be that can really say that?) and we'll make billions telling you what you want to hear. Obesity is not your fault.

And so I was back to depression and Catholicism. Gluttony, like sloth, was one of the seven deadly sins, I recalled, and then it seemed clear. Despair was a mortal sin in the catechism, because despair was a gluttony of sadness and a form of spiritual sloth. An overindulgence of an appetite or propensity. The people in St. Luke's, and I was just as guilty of this, consumed their depression, rolled in it like pigs. We were all so eager to decline responsibility for everything, to recline in the arms of a disease and quit, to take our failures, our gloomy, angry view of the world and make it into a fortress against that world. A defense.

That is what quitting is. It is not a passive state. It is, to return to John Nash's analogy, a very active resistance, a work stoppage, a throwing down of the spade in the face of adversity. Despair, in this sense, is not a giving up, but rather a taking up, a forceful "No" that says "I will not participate."

This, in theology, is the rebellion of the fallen angel who says, *Non serviam.* I will not serve. This is the soul that sets up a rival good to God's and makes negation his creed, the soul who will not struggle, the king of pain, the emperor of resentment gorging himself on sour grapes.

Depression is hell. Indeed. But perhaps a participatory one, I thought. After all, the fallen angels didn't really fall. Like every high-rise successful suicide, they jumped.

Again it was the ugly train of thought at work. Convincing, to me at least. But right or wrong? I didn't know.

And so what? What did it matter? The better question was: What now?

What was I going to do with my own gluttony of sadness, my own spiritual sloth, the nihilism with the candy coat that I was gobbling as greedily
as Josephine devoured her trail mix, or Chloe her Skittles?

I was either going to have to convert some of this shoestring theology
into action, or I was going to have to stop grinding the ringer. Either these
thoughts led somewhere or they didn't. And if they didn't, I was better off
medicating myself back to some sort of functional retardation than I was
sitting with the Don Quixote of nuns over a bowl of brown bananas finding cosmic truth in the last words of Lucifer.

I was becoming annoyed with myself. And this was a good sign. An
impatience with thought. A dialing down of the navel gazing, and the
first mild rejection of all my Cracker Jack college education running at the
mouth. The first rays of perspective breaking through.

After I made my first trip out on an hour pass, I found that one hour wasn't quite enough time to exercise and walk into town to get a little something to eat, so I requested two hours, figuring that it would be turned down. But Magic Doc stepped up and gave me a two-hour pass every day from then on.

My run in the park across the street hadn't gone all that well on the first day, partly because it was a very small park, and running laps around it made me feel like a hamster, plus doing so in my white socks and brown loafers, the only shoes I had brought (because they don't have laces) made the young mothers in the playground pull their children closer.

There was a YMCA just up the road, and I could get a day pass for $12. For the rest of my stay I spent the first hour on pass working out on the StairMaster. Then I walked the ten minutes into town—I had to time this perfectly so as to be back on the dot of 5:06 or 5:08 or whatever minute was exactly two hours after the time I left.

In town I stopped at a brewhouse for a real meal of grilled salmon, sautéed veggies, and two beers. I only ate at the brewhouse because it was on the near side of the freight tracks, and I knew from experience that a train could take ten minutes to pass, blocking my return to the hospital when every minute counted.

The beer tasted like God's brew, especially since I was not supposed to have it, so cold and smooth first thing after a workout, a quenching buzz rushing to my brain, pumped express by an elevated pulse. There was a little joy in my loins, with the sweat and the blood and the delirious high of temporary freedom, which was at least as potent as any drug, the power of sitting at a barstool of my own accord, almost like a person.

Yet I felt like a criminal, sitting there incognito, the loon on the lam. Or did everybody know? Did the waiters all have jokes about this? A game? Spot the tuner on furlough? Shoes with no laces must have been a dead giveaway. I was grateful again for no wristband, but I couldn't help feeling marked nonetheless, like yet another kind of queer, like the dyke whose sartorial misstep or too rugged swagger gives her away as a weird sister, a genetic mistake faking it poorly.

"I mean really," says the normal, "who does she think she's fooling?"

Am I? Fooling? Or am I the fool? Like Lear's fool, all-wise in jocularity, my barbed jests cutting to the truths that kings will heed from no one else. Or am I, like every preening brooder, the self-styled Hamlet? Mad north-northwest, but knowing a hawk from a handsaw?

Are the mad so easily recognizable? Or are they only craftily off-kilter? Their screws not loose but loosened, like the hinge on a practical joke or the dousing bucket cleverly balanced over the door. What role does the madman play? And does he play it straight?

I was sipping my beer thinking all of this. Again. Did they know? Did I want them to know? Did I know? Did my being who I was serve a purpose for them? Did I play this role, rather than simply live it? Was it my job, like being the village idiot? Did they need me to be this way so that they could safely be that way? What was normal, after all, without contrast, without aberration? The extremes define the center. Not that I flattered myself that I was on the extremes. More just somewhere nondescript on the tapering of the curve.

As I paid and finished, I sent a few quick text messages on my phone (which I would have to surrender at the nurse's station when I got back). I did this just to let a few friends and family know that I was not in a Turkish prison having the bottoms of my feet pounded by a fat man with a length of pipe. On the contrary, I said, all was well. This was an enlightened penitentiary, where they (or at least my doc) understood the benefits of exercise and fresh air and private vices.

They had rules, like any locked facility, but I didn't have the sense that they expended much energy on the details. If I had been fifteen minutes or even a half hour late getting back, for example, I doubt if anyone would have noticed, much less said or done anything. I didn't test this, though, because my freedom meant too much to me. Likewise, I don't know what they would have done if they had smelled beer on my breath. But since I wasn't there for addiction, I wasn't on any medication, contraindicated or otherwise, and I wasn't getting drunk, it might not have mattered. At most, they would have revoked my passes. But no one smelled my breath. The security guard downstairs put me through the metal detector and checked my bag every time I reentered the building, but he didn't pat me down or make me empty my pockets, so smuggling wouldn't have been hard. Still, what was I going to smuggle in that town? Library books?

For obvious reasons, the addicts only went on passes accompanied by family or friends, and the involuntary MI people, especially the less cooperative ones, didn't go on passes at all, for equally obvious reasons. But several of my vanilla fellow depressives, like Josephine and Teary Molly, did take advantage of the breaks and leave the grounds for an hour or two of an afternoon.

I was going to meet with Magic Doc when I got back and this put a little pace in my walk as I crossed the minigrid of sparsely populated downtown streets and passed through empty lots overhung by billboards advertising hotlines for the pregnant and the drug addicted.

As I turned a corner, I was surprised to see someone I knew.

Fridge was lurking in front of a shop with a friend. I said a booming hello, but he was less than enthusiastic, not eager to acknowledge a fellow St. Luke's alum, especially in front of a friend who hadn't been there. Unlike prison, there's no pride in doing time in the bin.

I passed on, skirting the skateboard park where bored ruffians of

Bard's approximate age and type were caroming off curbs and railings, honing a legal outlet for their rage.

Finally, I was back through the doors, through the metal detector, up in the cattle-car elevator, and back in the sanctum sanitorium.

As I was walking down the hall to the ward I heard a nurse announce over the loudspeaker:

"Please take a moment of quiet reflection this evening. The thought for the day is: The essence of prayer is seeing everything through its life-filled dimension."

I just had the chance to shower and change before doc time.

As soon as I sat down, Magic Doc delivered some bad news. Or what would have been bad news to a normal patient, but which turned out to be of interest in my case.

"I have to apologize to you," he said. "It seems your insurance company is not going to cover any more of your stay here."

"Really?" I said. It wasn't clear to me why this was, or why it was his fault. "I don't understand."

"Well, they gave two reasons. One is that you're not taking medication. The other is that you've been going on two-hour passes every day."

"They think I don't need to be here?"

"Right."

"Because I'm getting fresh air and exercise?"

"Well, their reasoning is that if you're well enough to leave the hospital for two hours a day, then you're well enough to be at home. I don't agree at all, but that's the way a lot of insurance companies see it. I didn't realize that you had out-of-state insurance. If I had, I wouldn't have given you the pass and risked this cancellation. Around here, most local insurance providers won't stop coverage because somebody is going on a pass, so it's usually fine. But a lot of carriers in other states will. Obviously, yours is one."

"It's amazing. I do something that will actually speed my recovery, and they penalize me for it," I said, shaking my head. Then I added, "You know, that reminds me, not that I haven't been immensely grateful for the passes, for all kinds of reasons, because I have been, but I've been meaning to ask you this anyway. Why don't you have a gym right here in the hospital, or an outdoor track or something? That way people could work out and not have to leave for two hours to get it all in."

"I agree," he said. "I've tried. I lobbied for a lap pool and all kinds of things, but the liability insurance costs are just too high to have exercise facilities here. It's just easier to give you a pass so that you can go across the street to the Y."

"Ridiculous."

"I know. I know."

"And the meds are the same story?"

"It was probably both things, the pass and the lack of meds, but again, attitudes on meds are different in this state. That's, in fact, why I came here. I'm not from here, and, as you can imagine, I wouldn't have chosen this town for lifestyle reasons, but it happens to be one of the few places in the country where the insurance companies don't make it impossible to practice real psychiatry."

"You mean psychiatry without meds?"

"Yes, or at least the option not to use them."

"What happened with that back in your home state?"

"I was practicing child psychiatry, but I didn't want to prescribe Ritalin to kids. First thing I did when I got a new patient was take them off the drugs. I wanted to see who the person was."

"So you think the drugs really got in the way of therapy?" I asked.

"Oh yeah. And the kids end up taking much more than they should. What often happens is that the mothers give the kids the pill in the morning and it works great. But then when it wears off, the kids are worse than before, so they give them another pill in the afternoon, even though they're not supposed to."

I thought of Bard, and asked, "And do you think that this ends up predisposing them to taking street drugs like meth as they get older?"

"Sure. They're craving that high."

I thought of myself going off the Prozac and feeling worse than I'd ever felt before taking it. I wondered if I was hooked in much the same way, needing the drug just to feel normal. I told Magic Doc that I thought a lot of psychiatrists were prescribing too much medication to a lot of people and either not understanding or not disclosing the dangers of dependency.

He agreed.

"A lot of psychiatrists these days are not really practicing anymore. They're not listening. They're just prescribing meds. I don't know why most MDs even go into psychiatry."

"No shit. Most of them have got the emotional intelligence of sandstone. And I won't even get into the way too cozy relationship between doctors and pharmaceutical companies."

"Yeah, I had that out with the drug reps at one point. They wanted to sell me on Lexapro when it first came out. Lexapro is just half a Celexa molecule. The patent was running out on Celexa, so they needed a new drug that essentially did the same thing. They realized that they could get the same effect with half the molecule, so they created a 'new drug' by cutting an old drug in half. I told them that I'd prescribe Lexapro if they admitted that they'd released it when they did and in the way that they did because the patent was running out on Celexa. But of course I got no answer."

This jibed with critiques I had read in which it was asserted that when drugs go off patent and the pharmaceutical companies market their patented replacements, only then does the public learn about the original drugs' downsides or unknowns. It is either that or, as happened with Zyprexa, lawyers and the media got hold of suppressed information and blew the whistle.

I brought up Zyprexa, and mentioned how heavily I'd seen it being advertized in places like Meriwether. I told him about the pens and the clipboards that the nurses carried around.

"Yeah, I've seen that, too," he said. "I used to walk around the offices throwing away all that stuff—calendars, pens, clipboards. I used to say that if they want to pay us to advertise for them, fine. Otherwise the stuff was going in the garbage."

I was really impressed. What a find. This guy was a jewel, stuck out here in the boonies because it was one of the few places he could help people try to get better without drugs, and where he could give them access to a few healthy and genuinely recuperative options like fresh air and exercise. He was in the minority in his profession, it seemed. Maybe even fighting a losing battle in the system. I admired him even more for that and was grateful for having met him.

He saw to the greedy core of the pharmaceutical companies and refused to buy the line they were selling. Not that he never prescribed drugs. He obviously did. He was nondoctrinaire enough to realize that the meds on the market were, in some cases, probably better than nothing. But he was exercising his judgment, evaluating patients as people and not just opting for the prescription pad as a reflex.

As for the insurance problem, I told him that it was fine. I could cover whatever was left. I'd been in for a week already, so I figured I didn't have much longer to stay. We worked it out that he'd discharge me on day 10, and they'd bill me for whatever my insurance didn't cover.

As I left his office, laughing again and glowing with appreciation for his renegade style, I said, "Welcome to the lunatic fringe."

I spent my last two days at St. Luke's trying to avoid as much group therapy as I could, hiding on the addicts' side or in my bathroom until the session had already begun. I was bored and I had gotten the material I needed. I didn't see the point. The staff wasn't usually too strict about hunting you down or making you go to meetings if you really didn't feel like it, and, unlike at Meriwether, I didn't have any fear of jeopardizing my release if I didn't comply.

I tried to sneak my way into some of the addicts' meetings, just to get their stories, because I knew from people like Fenske that I was bound to hear some pretty entertaining stuff. But those meetings were very closed and carefully monitored, so I usually ended up going to one or another of the meetings I was supposed to be in, just because I felt it was part of my homework.

I went to occupational therapy and finished my tile trivet. I played Cranium and Worst-Case Scenario with Trevor and Delilah, Gerald and Molly, and the rest. I counted the minutes until three o'clock when I could pound it at the Y across the street and then pound a couple beers at the brewhouse thereafter.

I took long hot showers when I got back, and then washed my dirty workout clothes in the washing machine and dryer in the hallway between the octagons. I went on every smoke break, just to overhear things and breathe the air a little more. I started taking the offered Ambien at night to sleep, because it was just nice to turn off at ten or eleven when pretty much everybody else was dead to the world too, having taken their own

Ambien, and usually a whole boatload of other downers to stave off the
jitters or the withdrawal or whatever else was wrong with them. Pretty
much everybody was on Ambien. It was kind of a joke. We'd all be sitting
around the TV at nine thirty, and somebody would ask you:

"Have you taken yours yet?"

A few hours after dinner, a line always started to form outside the medication window. Then people would recongregate in front of the TV and
maybe have a bowl of raisin bran or a bag of microwave popcorn while
they waited for the dose to kick in. Bit by bit, people would peel off, and
you'd hear their doors closing softly behind them until there was nobody
in the dayroom but me and some other holdout. That's when I usually
made my way back to my night-light.

I loved that dependable sleep. No tossing. No going over the failures of
your life as you lay there clenching your jaw. Your head hit the pillow, you
closed your eyes, and you enjoyed those few aimless moments of knowing that you were coasting to the other side untouched. I knew the Ambien probably wasn't good for me, and I was as suspicious of it as I was of
every other drug, but at times like that I just didn't care.

On my last night, Sister Pete came to see me in my room, as usual,
where I was sitting with night-light. It was Palm Sunday, in fact, so she
had made me an elaborately woven little token out of palm leaves. She
gave it to me with a small card that had the Memorare printed on it. I
remembered this prayer from childhood, the special prayer of the distressed calling to the Virgin for help. It had always moved me. Rereading
it with Sister Pete, with her wide surprised eyes gazing into my still teary,
still uncertain ones, I couldn't help but be moved by it again, and hope in
some residually superstitious way that it could help me.

Remember, O most gracious Virgin Mary,
That never was it known
That anyone who fled to your protection,
Implored your help or sought your intercession,

Was left unaided.

Inspired with this confidence,

I fly to you, O Virgin of Virgins, my Mother;

To you do I come,

Before you I stand, sinful and sorrowful

O Mother of the Word Incarnate,

Despise not my petitions,

But in your mercy hear and answer me.

Amen.

I was better than I had been ten days before, but I wasn't firm. I was still weakened and half down. I was susceptible to the power of prayer, as I always was in the bleakest times, not necessarily because I believed in its ability to make things happen but because I believed in its ability to comfort.

I thought it so perfect, so quintessentially Sister Pete, that at the bottom of the Memorare card there was a hotline number and a Web site address.

I said good-bye to Sister Pete, grateful for all the things she had made me think about, even if a lot of them were things she had probably never wasted time thinking about herself. I hugged her long and hard in the doorway of my room. We wished each other well. She turned to go, and as I stepped back to close my door, she turned around to face me one last time.

"Trust till ya bust, Norah Baby. Trust till ya bust."

And then she laughed her lilting laugh.

"I'll try, Sister," I said, smiling, and closed my door.

As for other partings, Fenske caught the flu a couple of days before I left, so he spent most of the time in bed in his room, or occasionally wrapped in a blanket on the couch in the dayroom. The last I saw of him was a handwritten sign on his door that said: "Wake me ONLY for (a) smoke break, (b) a phone call, (c) food, (d) if Keith Richards is here to see me."

Josephine got out a few days before I did, still wearing the puss face. Delilah got her wish and left too, still impish and unchanged. The others were still there when I left: Gerald in his chair looking at the floor, Trevor sitting with his hands crossed formally in front of him, and Molly, coloring and crying.

I didn't say good-bye to most of them. I hadn't established enough of a connection. I hadn't wanted to—maybe because I saw in them too much of a reflection of myself, or maybe because I just didn't have the energy to make friends. It had taken all my resources just to pull myself out of my own funk, and in that process, the only company I was capable of entertaining was the touch-and-go, snack-and-mumble variety that I found with some of the addicts, most of whose names I can't even remember.

I saw Magic Doc one last time, just to say good-bye and get the formal approval on my discharge. Short and sweet. Five minutes tops. He was very busy and I wasn't technically his charge anymore, so there really wasn't much for me to say or do except shake hands and say thank you. He was gracious, as always, and thorough. He wanted to make sure that I had a safe way of getting home and someone to greet me when I got there. He urged me to follow up with my psychiatrist in New York, and I told him that I would. (Per discharge procedure, I had made an appointment for two days after I got home.) He wished me well and I wished him the same, and that was it.

The nurses expedited my paperwork because they knew I had a plane to catch. I had no prescriptions to delay matters, so I was walking out of the ward by just before noon. Nurse Maggie escorted me down to the lobby, chatting cheerfully the whole way, as though we were just two happy housewives at a Tupperware party who happened to have spent the past ten days behind locked doors together.

I waved to the security guard at the metal detector, and to the menopausal mommies, too, as I strolled through the sage green carpeted lobby, past the golden statue of St. Luke, the upholstered armchairs, and the 52-inch plasma TV.

Maggie had given me two taxi vouchers, one to get to town, where I planned to eat lunch, and one to get from town to the airport. I waited for the first taxi in front of the clinic, sitting on the curb of the small circular driveway. I texted a friend on my cell phone, which had been returned to me fully charged, and I checked my messages. The sun was out in earnest at last, and I turned my face up to it. I closed my eyes and breathed deeply, feeling the first warmth of spring on my eyelids and smelling the first hint of that rich black prairie soil coming to life again underneath me.

PENDULUM

If you had to go to a locked psych ward, you could do a lot worse than St. Luke's. It wasn't paradise, but it was a far cry from Meriwether, that's for sure. And, interestingly enough, for the same length of stay (ten days), the bill came to almost exactly the same amount: just under $14,700. When you consider how much more I got for that money at St. Luke's—as many snacks as I could eat, fifty minutes of therapy three times a week, a room to myself—it's pretty astounding. Granted, this difference can be accounted for, at least in part, by the fact that St. Luke's wasn't paying urban rents. But it may also be the case, and this is the fiscal conservative in me showing, that bureaucratic waste is often prevalent (some would say endemic) in the public sector, whereas privately run institutions, subject as they are to the corrective influences of competition and profit, are forced to bang more for the buck. Think of the difference between the U.S. Postal Service and Federal Express, and you will have a pretty good indication of the difference between Meriwether and St. Luke's.

Whatever the case, $14,700 is still a hell of a lot of money to spend (or for an insurance company to spend) when what I got out of my stay at St. Luke's could have been achieved by going on vacation. Clearly, pulling myself out of the context of my life, suspending myself in a neutral place where I had, by turns, privacy and company whenever I wanted them, was essential to regaining a sense of perspective. Theoretically, I could have done this at a resort or on a group vacation. I could even have found a therapist in the area and seen him or her on an outpatient basis as often as I saw my therapist in the hospital—or even more often. What's more, I would have had the same (or, if I got a recommendation, better) chances of finding someone good. In any case, this would have meant starting from zero with a stranger, which is what you always do with an assigned doctor in a ward.

But if you had no choice in the matter and you were forced to spend time in the hospital, a place like St. Luke's would do fairly well by you. If it didn't make you any better, at least it was unlikely to make you any worse.

And in some cases, at least, people I saw there did leave in better condition than when they arrived. Karen, for example, had gotten something similar to what I had gotten. She'd found a place where she could step off the merry-go-round and catch her breath for a minute. It wasn't a permanent solution to her psychosis—what was?—but it was the next best thing. It was a place to go and rest or reorient herself when things got too out of control. The good effects would wear off, and she'd be back in a few months or a year, but because of the time she spent at St. Luke's, she was able to keep going, to manage her disturbance and go on.

A lot of other people appeared to get a lot less out of the experience. If they were drunks or addicts, they dried out or cleaned up while they were there, which surely wasn't a bad thing, given that some of them, like Bunny and Clay, had been near death when they'd come in. But that was about the extent of it for them. Bunny, as I heard firsthand on the phone, got drunk the first night she got home. Given her recent track record, April was likely to do the same thing. Clay had unemployment, a dying marriage, and his cousin's crime spree to deal with when he got home, which didn't bode well for his abstinence.

Fenske had a better chance in my view, simply because he had his education, a good job in computer programming, a relationship, and a supportive family to fall back on. His father had come to see him at one point during his stay, and I had seen them together visiting in the dayroom. I had seen other patients and their visitors doing the same, Clay and his wife, for example, or Bard and his ragtag group of not quite immediate relatives. In those cases, the tension in the air was palpable, but with Fenske and his dad you could feel a genuine bond, a sense of caring and support that far outstripped obligation.

Fenske was a screwup, but he was smart and resourceful underneath. He'd had the benefit of being loved, and in my travels through the system I knew that having been loved, as well as still being loved, was one of the best predictors of success and life change after hospitalization. It would probably take him a few rounds to kick the poison, but I felt sure that he would do it.

I suppose that was one of the things that was becoming clearest to me about how people with mental health and substance abuse problems fared in the system. The quality of the institution—cleanliness, therapy, and kinder, more committed staff—made a difference, no question. The people who worked at St. Luke's had chosen to be there, not purely out of necessity, but usually out of some sense of vocation. It showed in how they performed their jobs, and that in turn showed in how their performance affected the patients in their care.

But community resources, family, jobs, prospects, good relationships, and education seemed to me to be far more important determining factors in how the patient would come out long-term. The people whose bonds with family were broken, or who had lost their jobs and had little hope of finding other or better jobs, people who were desperately lonely and without a sense of purpose or place in the community, these were the ones who had repeatedly slipped back into abuse or depression or both. People like Fenske, who was born and raised with it, or Sister Pete, who had been lucky enough to find mental health professionals who understood the importance of social bonds in recovery—these people were on the road. The institution gave them the kick-start or the break they needed, and they were on their way. Perhaps not quite always thriving in the best sense of the word, but making do and staying clean or clearheaded most of the time.

In the end, I don't think that the real difference between the quality of care my fellow patients and I received at St. Luke's had as much to do with money (private versus public) or even location (rural versus urban) as it had with a sense of mission. And I don't use this term in the religious sense, even though St. Luke's was a Catholic hospital. I use it to mean that the people who ran St. Luke's (unlike the people who ran and worked at Meriwether, or the people who operated the private hospital I stayed at my first time in the bin in 2004) believed in what they did and knew that the personal touch, however trite that may sound, went a lot further than drugs and diagnoses.

Many pundits and social theorists, from Robert Putnam (*Bowling Alone*) and Francis Fukuyama (*Trust*) to Marvin Olasky (*Renewing American Compassion*) and Christopher Jencks (*The Homeless*), have explored the importance of human bonds in the overall health and well-being of both the individual and the society. My experience at St. Luke's led me to similar conclusions.

We need each other. We do better with the support of other people who know and care about us than we do at the hands of indifferent professionals who squeeze our untidy empirical woes into theoretical abstractions and boil our lived experience down to chemistry. We do better when people listen to us, even if we are not making much sense. And, most of all, we do better when we are given respect.

I'm not offering this as a cure, but I think it is a better way through our challenges.

As for my own journey at St. Luke's, that was a slow-motion course of obstacles that took place largely in my head. My depression had its own logic, twisting every positive into another source of pain, every avenue of escape into a weak spot where the enemy could get in. I hunkered down in misery and brooded. I turned ideas on their heads and shackled myself with contradiction.

Take hope, for example. Even that became a devil in my brain.

To me, hope was an open wound. A form of vulnerability. Hope was waiting with the door ajar. Hope was looking for rescue. It was weak, because it was dependent. Dependent on the arrival of someone or something else. A savior, a miracle, a change.

But despair. Despair was strength. Despair was the scab and then the scar. The walled city in a time of plague. A closed fortification. A sure thing, because it was always safer, less painful to stop trying than it was to repeatedly try and fail. Failure—disappointment—was a poison in my blood. Despair was the antidote.

And so, in that sense, depression was not my disease, but rather a sign of health, my immune system's response to an assault. The assault of hope. Of contingency. Of chance.

In my little head downturned, my lidded eyes looked inward. I curled in a ball, my back to the world, knees up. Everything inside was known, accounted for. There were no variables there. To rid my world of disappointment, I had to rid it of luck and surprise. And so I chose despondency, because in it there was no relevant question. The answer was always no. The sweet consistency of negation in a word. A perfect answer, a loud, comforting, final, punctuating word. No. A muscular sound, like the bark of a guard dog. Keep out.

My thinking seemed clear on the matter. There could be no more loss in what was lost already, in what was thrown away. No more falling at the bottom of the well. Just the rock of isolation, the dark, the silence of no evil seen, heard, or spoken, and no good either. No contrast of shadows to make me long for the light. No gray to make me loathe ambivalence.

What was not admitted, not let in, was unknown, unmourned.

People say that darkness is a negation. An absence. The privation of light. But for me this was not true. Darkness was full. Robust. Complete. Privation was a substance, the way that black is a color. It sustained. It hid. It comforted. It excluded.

This was why my depression happened, why it worked. But it was also why it had to come to an end, at some point, or kill me. Because, of course, life cannot be lived permanently alone in the dark, any more than it can be lived in a coma, however restorative or protective that state may sometimes be. We are pack animals and heliotropes all, bending toward the light, the open, the air, dependent on it, even as we bemoan the constant flux and injury to which free will and society subject us.

It's a battering life. But it is the only life.

So at the end of my time at St. Luke's I began to emerge from the despair. I began to know, to risk hope again in all its variety. And use it. And allow myself to be used by it, understanding newly that it was an elixir with a kick, a bitter kick.

The most I could expect from a psych ward, even a good one like St. Luke's, was to walk out with revised definitions of my terms, more resigned to the grays, and with my veil of necessary illusion firmly replaced.

I was better when I left—not well, but better. And I would remain better until I wasn't, which was bound to happen. And happen again. And go on happening as long as I lived.

As long as I live.

That is why psychiatry is as bankable and recession-proof as prostitution. There's always a demand for it. I, and other people like me, will never be fine—that is, impervious. We will just be more or less balanced over, cripplingly aware of, or functionally oblivious to the abyss.

And how was this miracle, this overhauling of perspective, achieved for me at St. Luke's? Not by meds, that's certain, though meds would come back into the picture in small doses after I left. That, too, was certain.

But right then in St. Luke's, recovery happened because I began finally to use, to make progress on, some of those ideas that I had spent way too much time futilely indulging while in despair. Ideas and words.

Like hope.

And so, for me, hope came stubbornly back, with its helping hand on my back. But with all its false promises and mean little pinches, too, saying, "Go forward. But I'll get ya. But go forward anyway."

I began to unwind the loops my ideas came in and got stuck in, and

I began to internalize them in new ways. I took them with me like talismans or touchstones in my pockets.

Courage. There's another word. Another idea too big for its casing. It, too, means something new to me now. It means blind. And deaf. And dumb as a god who doesn't answer. It means put on your helmet and jump, or cross yourself and charge. Stop thinking so much and just do, because there is nothing else for it but a crazy, all-out, arms-flailing gumption and gusto that defies all logic and sense.

Normal life is nuts. It's a downhill deterioration to death no matter how you spice it along the way, and there's nothing you can do about it. Now, a sane person, when faced with that, would just plunk his ass down at the starting line, or wherever along the way this realization finally came to him, and say, "Are you kidding? I quit. I'll slide the rest the way or sit here and smoke."

It takes a true lunatic, or someone functioning with the critical apparatus of a worker bee, to keep scrabbling up that hill when he knows his destiny is dust.

But that is what is required. Go on.

It's not that my view of the world changed at St. Luke's. I just learned to stop obsessing about it so bleakly. Or, I should say, I learned this again. It wasn't new knowledge. Not entirely anyway. I had learned it, or implemented it in the past, through the wondrous circuit-breaking, cloud-busting effects of medication. That, in my view, is the great virtue of medication. It blocks thought, or filters it to a manageable glow.

But you can get some of the same results with your mind, too, if you work at it.

At St. Luke's I got it through the silence and calm and privacy of retreat in a room with a night-light, and I got it with the help of the kind of group therapy that you get in card games in a dayroom with drug addicts and other high-functioning kooks like me. I got it through announcing my troubles aloud to a good listener and by meeting a doctor I could believe in. I had my faith in the system restored a little at St. Luke's, and this can do wonders for your outlook on the world. Realizing that some people are good at what they do, that they care, that they want to make a difference, and do—all of this gives you back a little spark of belief.

And then we are back to words.

Yet another puffed-up word. Belief. That was really the big one for me. And, boy, was it redefined. Because when I say "belief" I really mean "make-belief," and by make-belief I mean pretend.

I learned to pretend. To pretend that I didn't know all the heavy things that I thought I knew. I learned to purposely forget.

Because—and here is Sister Pete having her say again—as Eve and then Adam found out, there is a whole hell of a lot of knowledge about the goddamned human condition that we are not ready for.

So when you happen on it—*it* being some kind of insight, which may or may not take the form of a really delicious apple—and *it* convinces you of a bunch of true, inescapable stuff that you really can't live with, the best advice I can give you is this: just hand the apple back. Just unknow. Because you can. That's one of the beauties of having fallen from grace. You can lie, especially to yourself. What's more you can lie to yourself about lying to yourself, and best of all, really believe it. That's denial. The real sinning graduate's prize. Lying in layers, glazing your eyes until the view is like a Monet. One pastel blur.

In my experience, going into the hospital for depression at a place like St. Luke's was a little bit like having a sit-and-spin, or performing that whirligigging motion you did barefoot in the grass in your backyard as a kid. The spiraling dizzied you, and then when you stopped and got your balance, for a second, you looked at your surroundings with new eyes, as if you had never seen them before.

That's the idea. To bring yourself back to ignorance, back to the empty center, because it's the only way through, or at least it was in my case at that time.

Asylum did that for me. Reset me to blank and sent me back into my life with the energy to pretend. It's the first game you master as a child—

pretend—and, for my money, it's one of the most helpful skills you can cultivate as an adult.

Magic Doc was right. The best doctor may very well be a dyslexic one, someone who sees the world a little backward and is kind enough to turn your head around, or, true to the slang of the profession, shrink it. Shrink your view, anyway. Resize the picture. Make the cosmic rinky-dink.

Bottom line? Definitely lose the forest for a tree, a branch, bark, a leaf, whatever your pathetic little mechanism can handle, because it certainly can't handle the whole show.

Is this a skill? Yes, but not one you learn in medical school. It's not learning at all. It's unlearning, which is why someone who thinks he knows everything can never teach it to you. I guess it sounds like I'm talking in circles. And I am, sort of. Because reason, of all things, is the enemy. An excess of sense is senseless. That way madness lies. Take refuge instead in the cupcake, the sugary sop morsel that gets you through. The digestible piece and no more.

And whatever you do, stop asking so many questions. It's true as advertised. Knock and the door will be opened to you.

So don't fucking knock.

Or do, because you're writing a goddamned book, and so you have to.

I had one more place to go.

I found this third facility, Mobius Group, on the Web. I was looking for a place that was offering a different approach from the locked-ward, often drug-riddled treatments I'd found in conventional hospitals like Meriwether and St. Luke's.

There weren't many. The first few I tracked down were outpatient facilities that were either defunct—not enough clients—or nearly defunct, struggling by with one or two stranglers and a mountain of crumbling goodwill.

These places presented themselves as being philosophically opposed to the use of psychiatric medications (deeming them addictive, dangerous, and purely cosmetic). They relied instead on intensive therapy, play, companionship, the human touch. I was sympathetic to the approach and eager to try it myself, but I didn't fancy being the only patient in the facility bouncing from shrink to paid playmate to art therapist like some overgrown special-needs child. I wanted to be among other people trying the same thing.

This kind of therapy is a lot of work. It's expensive and it takes time and effort. Most insurance won't cover it, so the clients need to be wealthy. They have to have weeks, if not months, to devote to therapy, and they have to be willing to fight their demons day in, day out, head-on. Most people would rather take—or are only offered—a pill. It's cheaper, faster, and easier.

But Mobius seemed to be up and running, prospering even. I suspected there were two reasons for this. First, while they catered (as advertised) to the mentally distressed, their primary client base was addicts in recovery. As I learned when I got there, a fair number of the people there were court-mandated to be in rehab, and as private, nonhospital rehab joints go, Mobius was quite a bargain. The program was often partially covered by insurance, depending on your plan, and even if it wasn't, it was only just over $6,000 for a two-week stay, less than half what it cost to stay at Meriwether or St. Luke's for ten days. And as for quality of service and environment, Mobius was a far cry from Meriwether and St. Luke's. It wasn't as cushy by a long stretch as some of the fancier private rehab facilities that celebrities and the obscenely rich frequent—these can easily cost $50,000 a month and up—but it was by no means uncomfortable. It was within reach of the middle class, and even possibly the working class, and gave you far more freedom than locked wards.

Second, and probably more important, Mobius allowed you to bring your own prescribed medications, which you then surrendered to the program nurse for proper dosing. They also had a psychiatrist on staff who could prescribe medications as needed. This meant that you could get the benefit of their intensive therapy without having to commit yourself to a potentially brutal withdrawal from your meds, or worse, and far longer lasting, a discontinuation rebound effect that could mean—and in my experience *had* meant—a worsening of your original symptoms, be they depressive, manic, or psychotic. Getting intensive therapy and discontinuing your meds are two separate things, both difficult. Doing them at the same time can be brutal and, as one doc at the near-defunct antimedication facility told me, really means setting aside three to six months of your life.

While locked away in Meriwether and St. Luke's, I often fantasized about the perfect therapeutic facility. I called it Therapy House and imagined building it from the ground up on spec with unlimited funds. I saw it as a kind of chalet, with a cathedral ceiling in the common room, big windows and lots of light, a working fireplace, sectional couches and reading chairs, and minimalist but cozy mountain retreat décor. Adjacent to the main room, I imagined a library with floor-to-ceiling bookshelves and a well-stocked assortment of periodicals, DVDs, CDs, and computers. Each client—say, the house could accommodate twelve—would have his or her own bedroom and en suite bathroom. There would be a large kitchen staffed by a full-time chef who would provide balanced, healthy, organic meals and snacks, which all the patients would eat together at one large table in the dining room. There would be an Olympic-size swimming pool, a fully equipped gym, a yoga and meditation studio and instructor, a spa with massage and body treatments, a large property with gardens and walking paths, bicycles, hammocks, climbing trees, and even tree houses. There would be a full-time staff of nurses, psychiatrists, psychologists, and social workers, and the patients would receive an hour of individual therapy every day, as well as several hours of various group therapies.

Sometimes I passed idle hours in Meriwether and St. Luke's dreaming this stuff up, furnishing the fantasy, even imagining which foundations I would apply to for the money. Best of all, I imagined making it accessible to people of all income levels so that anyone from Mother T to pill-popping upper-middle-class housewives could qualify for treatment.

Having imagined all this, I was astounded to find that the people at Mobius were offering something quite similar, albeit on a less extravagant scale and not all housed in one self-contained facility, though they were working on just such a plan.

Still, here was a place founded by a clinical psychologist, Dr. Franklin, and his wife, a place that had been up and running for six years, that was committed to the practice of healing the whole person—mind, body, spirit—and doing so without the use of restraints or locked wards.

Their Web site was very detailed, and by perusing it, I learned everything I needed to know about Mobius's facilities and program. Patients were housed in four three-bedroom apartments. Twelve was maximum capacity, a manageable group both logistically and therapeutically. Each client had a private bedroom, and shared two full baths, a living room with cable TV and wireless Internet access, and a fully equipped kitchen with small dining area. The apartments were all in a large apartment complex complete with a pool, a Jacuzzi, and a gym.

From 9 a.m. until 3:30 p.m. clients attended various group and individual therapy sessions at the Mobius offices. In the evenings, after class, clients did various things. Once a week they attended a yoga class; once a week they went to the bookstore for a few hours; once a week they did their grocery shopping (clients cooked all their own meals in the apartments); once a week they went to the movies; and three times a week they went to a spa, where they could book massages, pedicures, manicures, and facials (these were not included in the price of the stay, of course). They could work out in the gym, swim in the pool, or lounge in the hammocks out back on the shores of the bay. Not bad for three grand a week, and jubilantly close to my fantasy bin trip.

After St. Luke's, the idea of flying into a place I'd never been before and committing myself to a recovery facility sight unseen didn't seem quite so, well, crazy anymore. Besides, this was the last leg of the tour, I told myself. Get it over with.

So I did. I filled out the online application form and read all the material on the various criteria for admission. As far as I could tell, my admission to the program would not be denied or delayed for any of the reasons listed on the Web site. I wasn't suffering from acute drug withdrawal or undergoing drug detoxification. I didn't have a severe psychiatric disorder that required hospitalization. I did not have a severe sexual disorder (or at least I didn't think so, but it was unclear what this meant). I did not have any infectious, communicable, or contagious diseases, and I did not engage in disruptive or aggressive behaviors that would be incompatible with a small group living environment.

I would, however, have to consent to a criminal background check, as all clients did. Otherwise, the admission form was remarkably short and to the point. It asked me to list my mental disorders—clients could, apparently, be trusted to do this accurately—what medications I was taking, whether I used drugs or alcohol, and what search engine and key words I had used to find Mobius on the Web. Essentially, it was like any other commercial transaction: name, date of birth, address, and method of payment.

I booked a two-week stay for myself, booked a flight, and got on a plane.

SANCTUM

Mobius

Diggs, a well-dressed, whippet-thin boy of Indian descent, was sitting in the baggage claim area holding a paper sign with my name on it. The sign was perched on his crossed legs facing him, as if he'd half given up trying to find me. I had stopped in the main terminal for a Starbucks, assuming from past experience that it was going to be my last good cup of coffee for two weeks.

The line had been long, so by the time I got to the baggage claim area, it was largely deserted and my bag had been put in a pile to the side of the carousel. I passed Diggs once on my way to the pile and again on my way back. I saw the sign in his lap on the return.

"That's me," I said.

"I saw you before," he said, as he took the handle of my wheelie, "but I thought, No way is she forty."

A charmer. That's all he'd known about me. My name and approximate age. And presumably my diagnosis.

I wondered if they'd trained him to be this genial. Compliment the depressives right off. Women on their age. Men on their gadgets.

We walked the short distance from the terminal to the parking lot and Diggs heaved my bag into the Ford Expedition.

He was wearing pleated slacks, black loafers, and a pressed button-down shirt. Far better turned out than your average twenty-two-year-old psych major who is just out of college and makes his living shuttling fuck-ups to and from the airport.

He did more than that, actually, as I would soon learn. In the mornings, he shuttled clients to the Mobius group offices, where we underwent our therapy and took our daily instruction on how to stop being a danger to society and ourselves. While we were in therapy all day, Diggs did paperwork in the office, or took patients to the clinic for their blood work (state law mandated a test for syphilis), or made more runs to the airport for new arrivals. Then in the afternoon he shuttled us back to the nearby apartment complex.

He was dependable. Mature. A comely face to meet you in baggage claim when you'd bottomed out on substances, or sunk eyeball deep in the mood bog, or otherwise come undone enough to commit yourself to a place you'd only read about on the Web, and which you couldn't be at all sure wasn't a cult.

When you saw Diggs, though, your fears were allayed somewhat. You thought, "If this is the Moonies, they're *good*, because this guy seems totally normal."

And he was. Suavely normal. He knew not to ask anything intrusive, but he made pleasant reciprocal conversation that didn't sound like what a gofer says to a cripple, which is, by harsher accounts, what we were. However you sliced it, his job was to make a fairly shameful situation seem respectable, and he did it expertly. He smoothed. He handled damaged goods gingerly without appearing to do so, easing the last leg of a breakdown so that he could bring us in calm. He was the discreetest of valets.

As we rode along in the Expedition, I asked him about where he'd gone to school and where he was from, if he had any siblings, and so on. He tossed back softballs—"And where are you from originally?" He drove assertively but well within the speed limit, the way you do with your mother-in-law or other passengers who scare easily.

I never felt the burden of making conversation. It flowed through the predictable channels without effort, and the drive went by without incident. We drove directly to the Mobius offices for check-in.

Despite my good opinion of Diggs, I was still harboring a few thorny worries about the potential Moonie situation. I had read on the Web site, for example, about the program nurse, Jan, whom Diggs had said we were going to meet right away. I was expecting the worst, and for no other reason than that the term "program nurse" had given me the creeps. I'd been unable to stop myself from imagining some type A crypto-Nazi in starched white and squeaky shoes with a chinchilla hiding under her peaked paper hat.

But when Diggs led me into Jan's tidy windowed office, the first in a row of similar offices that all opened off a slim main hallway, I knew that I'd let my apprehensions run entirely away with me. Jan was barely five feet tall in her shoes and comfortably built, padded but not plump. Her dyed blond hair was styled in a grown-out pageboy and her blue eyes hid no subtext. She was wearing sandals, three-quarter-length trousers, and a short-sleeved button-down blouse, which is what she wore virtually every day, the default warm-weather business casual for a low-maintenance woman in her midforties. She was kind and efficient, remarkably cheerful about what was a fairly laborious routine that she was often required to perform several times a week with each new bumbling client.

Most of it was paper signing. I must have signed forty sheets— disclaimers and permissions for everything from the syphilis test, to a short-term lease agreement for the apartment complex, to a declaration of "patient's legal and human rights." But there was also the urine sampling, medication surrender, and bag inspection, as well as assorted sundry other smooth violations that constitute patient intake procedure in the bin. Jan, as anyone in such circumstances is required to do, took your dignity in one hand and your autonomy in the other, but unlike so many others, she did it like a den mother in the Cub Scouts, softening the blow of your demerit with a smile, even as she pinned the shaming badge on your sleeve. I half-expected to get a lollypop at the end.

I'd arrived in the late morning, so by the time I'd finished with Jan, it was time for lunch. Diggs went to the local Boston Market and got me a meal. I ate it at the table in Mobius's small kitchen, which was located just next door to Jan's office.

As I sat eating, Mobius staff and clients were breaking for lunch as well, so various people wandered in or lingered. That's when I met Sam, one of Mobius's three therapists and the instructor-in-chief.

Superficially, Sam looked like Little Richard. He had the same pencil-thin mustache and wild kinky hair, and even a hint of the impish sparkle in the eye. But the likeness ended there. Sam was not a flashy entertainer. He was wearing what looked to be the traditional black-belted gi, and he sat very poised in his chair, like a person who was used to treating his body as an extension of his soul. He was calm and centered, as his profession would suggest, open but not loose, deliberate but unmannered. He was just there without agenda, like something in nature, alive and present but seeming to occupy no space.

We sat at the kitchen table, he eating his habitual salad brought from home, and I eating my half chicken with sides. I asked him the usual background questions: Where are you from? How old are you? Are you married? Answers: New Jersey, fifty-three, and yes, two kids. None of this mattered much, though, when it came to knowing Sam. They were the wrong questions. There weren't any questions, really—just a sense that you got in his presence, the immediate sense of who a person is, because he knows himself.

Sam could teach me a lot, and would, not as my individual therapist— that job would go to another of the therapists on staff—but as a group therapist, and more so as our morning den chi bon instructor.

This was Sam's big gig. Every morning at Mobius the day's activities began with an hour and fifteen minutes of den chi bon, which I can best describe as a cross between tai chi, tai bo, and a séance.

At nine thirty we'd all gather in the activity room, which was at the far end of the long main hallway, at the opposite end from the kitchen. This was the room where all the group therapy and meetings took place throughout the day. It was the size of a small living room, piled with pillows and blankets, and people's art catharses were posted all over the walls.

Sam would start the class with yogic style stretches and deep breathing. We'd stand facing him with our feet positioned two to three feet apart. We'd spread our arms wide and swan-dive to touch our toes, and then we'd thrust our arms repeatedly from the prayer position at our heart centers, up and out to full extension above our heads, around to the sides, and back to center again. Soon these outward motions of the arms would grow more forceful and direct, like open-palmed punches, and the breathing would intensify accordingly, so that you looked as if you were parting a lead curtain over and over again, except that you were doing it gladly, as if mindless labor just made you happy and you gained energy and strength from the exertion. We'd do this for a long time, pulling and punching the air and stamping our feet, gesticulating more and more emphatically in ways that alternated between being voodooish and exaggeratedly masturbatory, and all the while breathing like we were about to give birth.

It was the kind of too earnest, misty-eyed exercise that I had trouble taking seriously, at least at first. Early on, I hovered at the back of the room, going through the motions, embarrassed, imagining all the people in my life watching me join the feel-good follow-along Dancercise of Mobius Inc. The therapeutic value of learning to make an ass of yourself.

But then, after a while, I thought: "Jesus, you self-important snot, just let go and have some fun. Nobody's watching."

And so I did. And then, before long, I started getting into it. Maybe a little too into it, actually.

The beauty of all that heavy breathing was that it got you high, an interesting concept for an addiction recovery program. Learn how to get high on your own. Oxygen is potent stuff, and concentrated gasping will make you feel pretty buzzed after a while if you do it right.

At the end of the air punching and limb flailing—the "air" and "fire" portions of the ritual—when we'd gotten around to holding hands in a circle and swinging our arms like skipping kids—the "water" portion of the ritual—I was usually smiling like an addict, my eyes closed, my head turned up and all loose and wobbly on my neck. At the close of the ritual, the "earth" portion, when we stood there swaying and humming along with the music, or declaring our sober guiding thoughts for the day, we were supposed to be coming back to ground, but I was usually floating somewhere around the ceiling.

By the second or third day, I was hooked on den chi bon. We all were. Sam always had great music to go with it, the cheesier the better. *The Phantom of the Opera* was much loved, as was the starting music, which was always the same: a tolling bell and an Indian man with a profound liquid caramel voice talking about the dharmal door being open, transcending the path of sorrow and death, and refreshing springs of compassionate water causing all suffering to cease. Fabulous stuff.

Sam was always so full of joy during the dance that sometimes he'd break into spontaneous laughter, and then several of the rest of us would, too, simply laughing at his laughter, and then laughing at our own laughter, and pretty soon we were crying with it, and the rest of the less game participants would look at us sideways wondering what demon had possessed us, and wondering whether they should break and run while they still could.

Laughter, like heavy breathing, is another one of those natural highs that can drastically improve your mood, even if you're laughing at nothing at all, because, as happened to us, pretty soon you're laughing at the fact that you're laughing at nothing, and how absurd that is, and yet how good it feels, and then you're on the giggle train and rolling, and spasming in earnest, and having all kinds of bodily functions. Tears are rolling down your face, phlegm is coming up from your lungs, your bladder is ready to betray you, or maybe does a little, and you might even be drooling. It's quite a heave, especially at the end of a vigorous dance when you're already drenched in sweat. It's like the happy version of vomiting, or the less profane version of coming, depending on your point of view. Your whole body gets into it and squirts, and it's so pure and spiritual, it's fun for the whole family.

This was the kind of release that Sam could bring about in you with the simplest, most elemental tools: earth, air, fire, water. Yes, you're smirking, those New Age medievalisms given a new spook. I know. Believe me, I know.

But there is a perfect sense to it that becomes pretty blisteringly obvious if you give it a chance. What are we made of, after all? Literally. Flesh, breath, heat, fluid. These are the most basic parts of us, and yet we have forgotten how to use them. Our mind drives us through the world, pushing us on, feverishly achieving, obsessing, looking for occupation and results. But it's the body that gets us there. The body that mechanizes the mind, and the elements that mechanize the body. How strange, then, that we could be so removed from our own breathing, our own movements, from what we eat and drink, and excrete, so alienated from our own basic functions that someone has to reteach us how to perform them.

We knew as children. But now not even breathing comes as easily as breathing, crying rarely comes at all, and laughter has literally galvanized to irony, a metal-hard mirth that tightens, never releases, whose only liquid is bile, passing through kidneys as stones. Who has ever pissed himself over irony? Pissed on, to be sure, with deliberation and scorn. Ever a critic. But the involuntary burst? No. We have medications for that, to correct it when it happens, keep the piss and the shit and the sweat and the tears under wraps, or expel them on our schedule, and all so we can forget that we have bodies. Is it any wonder, then, why we end up in rehab and therapy, dancing around with Little Richard and a crooning swami trying to put the pieces back together?

That's what they were trying to do at Mobius, to help you to put the pieces back together, however asunder they'd been torn by experience, neglect, bitterness, life. Mobius was all about process and change, learning to see and then go about your life differently.

They called it process therapy, and as it happened, I'd arrived just in time to get my first exposure to it. By the time I'd finished eating my lunch with Sam, it was two o'clock. Carol, a Gertrude Steinish-looking woman with a close-cropped graying cap of hair, was the second of the three staff therapists, and the one with whom I'd be conducting my private sessions several times a week. She specialized in process therapy, and she was gearing up to lead that day's group session on the topic. She asked me to join, and since there didn't seem to be anything else to do until I could get a ride to the apartment complex later that afternoon, I said yes.

Carol, like Sam, was a licensed mental health counselor, or LMHC, which is akin to being a licensed clinical social worker, meaning that she had completed a master's degree as well as at least two years of graduate-level clinical work and had passed a certification exam. In action, this meant that she knew the literature, but she wasn't bogged down by it, and tended to favor an experiential rather than an academic approach.

She was a connector. She connected with people emotionally. Her technique was interpersonal above all, but methodic, too. She warmed to you and led you out by the hand, if you would be led. But she also liked to draw charts and diagrams, or numbered lists and tables that could help you to organize your thoughts. She looked for patterns and sticking points, the layers of negativity and doubt that laced her clients' thinking and led them to despair or self-destruction.

As I filed into the activity room that afternoon with the five other resident clients (none of whom I'd met yet), Carol was already standing up at the white dry-erase board holding a smelly uncapped cobalt blue marker. She was writing the phrase: "I do not see things as they are. I see them as I am."

Then she turned and waited for us to settle, either sitting in the low L-shaped sling-back chairs that we unfolded and positioned in a semicircle around her or lying on our backs, heads propped up against a mound of pillows.

"True story," she said. "I was sitting in my office talking to a client." She paused here looking around the circle of six, scanning our faces for signs of attention, her eager eyes searching each deadpan slump for some shred of recognition. She went on.

"All of a sudden, we hear this scratching sound coming from behind the wall. We both stop talking, and I say, 'Do you hear that?' And he says, 'Yes. It's a rat.' 'What?' I said. 'It's a rat,' he said. 'You've got a rat in your wall.' Well, you can imagine this freaks me out, right? I hate rats. I can't bear the thought of them, and now I have to listen to one scratching behind the wall of my office all day while I'm trying to work."

She paused again.

Bobby, a hard-partying graduate student and alcoholic Xanax-head who'd been at Mobius for nearly two months per court order (three DUIs in a month), was already asleep in her sling-back. She'd heard the rat story ten times by now.

Carol looked at Bobby and frowned, but went on.

"So then, next day, I'm in with another client, and sure enough there's that scratching sound again. And I say, 'Hear that? I've got a rat in my wall.' He looked at me like I was nuts and said, 'What? Carol, that's a branch from a tree outside your window scratching against the wall in the wind.'"

Again, the dramatic pause.

"Now which explanation do you think I chose to believe?"

She looked around for the answer. Finally someone obliged and mumbled,

"The branch."

"Right. The branch. And why? Because I hate rats."

Bobby twitched awake.

Katie, another early-twenties Xanax-head, snapped a picture of herself with her camera phone. There was a loud click.

"Did you just take a picture of yourself?" Carol asked, whipping around.

"Yeah," Katie croaked. "Accident. Sorry."

Katie had been arrested seven times in the previous year. She, like Bobby, was at Mobius for DUIs. She'd done time in jail for them. She'd also had run-ins with the cops several times over domestic abuse. Giving, not receiving. She looked like the kind of blond buttercup whose primary task in life was working on her nails and her tan, so you can imagine my surprise when, sitting on the couch in our living room one night, she said of a recent assault:

"Yeah, Jamie [her boyfriend] said something stupid, so I punched him in the face. He's a pussy, so he called the cops on me."

With an audience peopled by the likes of Bobby and Katie, you could see why Carol must have developed a bit of a complex about her students. Were we there? Were we getting this at all?

Outright snoring and cell phone diversions abounded among the sling-backs.

Then there were the blank stares and the rude whispers, the skeptical blinks, the knowing sighs, and the more desperate harumphers who fooled Carol a bit as they leaned closer, not attentively, I'm sure, but hoping to catch a high off the fumes from her marker.

But Carol kept right on, shoveling learned optimism in our direction, watching it fall over sloping shoulders and accumulate in a heap. Maybe she thought of it as confetti. Most of it would sprinkle down and be tram-pled underfoot, but one or two pieces would stick on a few stubborn heads and somnolent lids, maybe on a shrugging scapula, unseen, and so undis-dainfully swiped away.

Of course Carol probably miscalculated, because in order to "think positive," as the T-shirt might say, you first have to be thinking at all, and there wasn't a whole lot of thinking going on in that room. That was the whole point of the drugs. To shut out thought.

People who pop Xanax—and I can say this from experience, it being a close relative of Klonopin—do it for the blank. Blank check. Blank out. Blank slate.

So, actually, the confetti idea wasn't even close. When it came to reach-ing most of us, Carol was clawing with quick-chewed fingernails on obsidian, smooth black volcanic glass, fired hard and unmarkable in the morass of mindless souls. She wasn't making a scratch.

But that's not entirely fair. There were, after all, a few night-lighters like me who, though we had popped our share of benzos in our time, were actually trying to learn and change.

I was even taking notes, and not just for the book.

Despite all the apathy and distractions, Carol launched into the ther-apy anyway, full of gusto and design.

She drew three columns on the board, the leftmost labeled Behavior, the middle one labeled Thought, and on the right Perception.

"Okay," she turned to face us, marker poised. "What's the behavior?"

The idea behind process therapy, a technique formulated by Dr. Frank-lin but akin to traditional cognitive behavioral therapy, was that most of us act before we think. The problem is the behavior, the undesirable behavior. That's what sends people into rehab or the bin. In the addict's case, it's pill popping, drinking, snorting, what have you. In the depres-sive's case it might be the same, drugging or drinking, or it might be self-abuse, cutting, burning, binging, or curling up in the bathtub and refusing to come out.

The fundamental idea of process therapy is that so-called disorders of the mind are not just inert conditions that exist; instead, they are patterns. They have behaviors that go along with them, behaviors that are attached to thoughts and feelings, all of which can be changed and redirected. Traditionally, the approach has been similar with addicts, which is part of the reason why addicts and mental cases so often end up in the same facilities, blurring the line between substance abuse and mental distress.

The treatment for both conditions generally operates according to a disease model. For example, the alcoholic, like the depressive, suffers from a disease, or so the common wisdom has it. It is not his fault. It is inherited, exacerbated by the chemistry he was born with, and accelerated by a fault in his system, some tic in his brain-body function, that doesn't seem to know when enough is enough. Now, once again, this is good news for the drug companies, who have marketed drugs like Antabuse that interfere with the body's ability to metabolize alcohol. Other drugs to come will target and block the cravings, and thereby thousands of drunks will be saved from oblivion by the newest miracle substance without ever having to do the hard work of changing their lives. The drug will do it for them.

Of course, no one operating within this disease model questions how it is that a drunk can stop drinking—and many have—without the use of inhibitory drugs. Yet, currently, abstinence is the cure. Pure and simple. Decide to stop drinking, and you do.

Now, as everyone knows, the recidivism rate for drunks is disturbingly high. This fuels the argument that alcoholism is a disease that cannot be cured by willpower alone. But again, few people seriously consider the idea that if the undesirable behavior, drinking, has a cause in your mind, comes about as the result of certain established patterns of thought and feeling, then you are far less likely to quit drinking over the long haul if you don't address and redirect those causative thoughts and feelings.

It isn't just a question of stopping the behavior—that is, quitting drinking, cold turkey—it's a question of finding out what motivated the behavior and addressing that source of distress so that the behavior will no longer seem necessary or, when the process works best, the behavior will no longer even seem appealing.

This, anyway, was the theory behind Dr. Franklin's approach. Change the perception, deal with the undesirable feelings in a different way, and a change in behavior will follow.

It was all a question of drawing maps, and the maps began with the behaviors and moved backward. Carol wanted to know what my problematic behavior was. She turned to me abruptly.

"Norah, what's the behavior?"

I was game for this. I was there to be real, to put it all out there for and as myself. I didn't hesitate. I said the first thing that came into my head.

"Affairs," I blurted.

"Affairs?"

"Yeah. I'd say sex, but I usually tend to convince myself that I'm in love, so let's just put it under affairs, short for affairs of the heart and loins."

Nobody blinked or even looked over to see the expression on my face. I couldn't tell whether this meant they weren't surprised, or they just weren't paying attention. Either way, it was good. I could work in that empty space.

"Okay," Carol said, and wrote it in the left-hand column. Affairs. "Now, what's the thought that goes with that?"

"I'm usually not thinking. That's the problem."

"Yes, but think about it now. Take it apart."

I thought about it. Then, again, I said the first thing that came to me.

"If I connect with someone I won't be alone."

Carol repeated this and wrote it in the middle column under Thought. "Now," she said, "what's the perception?"

"How is that different from the thought?"

"Take it a step further. How do you take that thought and convince yourself that having an affair is the right idea?"

"You mean how do I rationalize the behavior?"

"Yes."

"I tell myself I'm growing emotionally, sharing, fulfilling my emotional potential."

That got a response. Bobby peered over at me sideways, as if to say, "Wow. What a crock. Do you really buy that shit you're selling yourself?"

I looked back, turning down one side of my mouth and raising my eyebrows as if to say, "Yep. There it is. Pretty sad."

She smiled as if to reply, "We're all in the same stew, each one more full of shit than the next. Don't sweat it."

I looked back up at the board, where Carol had written out everything I'd said.

There it was all laid out.

Behavior: Affairs.

Thought: I won't be alone.

Perception: This is growth.

Yep. A crock for sure.

That's why they wrote it down. There's nothing like seeing your crap writ large in blue and white in front of a group of other top-shelf shit-crockers.

That'll wake you up.

"Now," said Carol, "what's the attachment? What's the thing you're holding on to that makes all of this come about?"

I screwed up my lips and sighed. This was going to take a minute.

The attachment. Hmm. What was I really trying to get out of the lovefest/fuckfest?

"Escape," I said, finally.

"Okay. Escape from what?" said Carol, right on my heels.

"Isolation, I guess."

"And . . . ?" Carol added leadingly.

No answer.

"Isolation is?" she said.

I thought again and the answer came.

"Myself."

"So, escape from yourself?"

"Yeah. Escape from myself."

She wrote this down under my three columns and underlined it.

There it was. The seed.

Carol moved to another part of the board and drew a stick figure.

"Okay. Let's take this now and turn it around."

She drew a thought bubble above the stick figure's head and wrote inside it, "I want to escape myself."

"That's your thought. Your real thought. Right?"

"Right."

"Good. Now," she drew a large heart shape over the stick figure's chest, "what's the feeling underneath that?"

"Loneliness."

"What else?"

"Terror."

"What else?"

"Inadequacy. Hurt. Pain."

She wrote each of these words in the heart. Loneliness. Terror. Inadequacy. Hurt. Pain. I thought of myself curled in the bathtub. Those feelings everywhere. And the thought. Escape. And the behavior. What is the behavior? Self-harm.

Carol drew an arrow pointing out from the stick figure.

"Now," she said, "you feel hurt, lonely, afraid. That's what's driving you to act. But the act, the affairs, don't make this go away. Don't get at it, right? At least not long-term. Short-term. And then it's just worse, right?"

"Right."

"So what can you do instead of having an affair? What's the new behavior?"

I had all kinds of seemingly good answers for this. Go to the gym. Clean the house. Call a friend. But the real answer, as the staff at Mobius would try to teach me, was to face it. Face yourself. Face the pain, the loneliness, the fear. Sit with it. Don't run. It was basic applied Buddhism. Be present and mindful. Focus.

My way of conceiving it was more pedestrian. Think of what's scary in a horror movie, I told myself. The unseen, the imagined, is always more frightening than what's graphically portrayed. The same holds true in your head. Face your fear, step into it, look at it head-on and it will diminish in stature, lose its hold on your imagination. But run, and it'll grow wings, breathe fire, and fly after you.

"So what can you do instead of having an affair?" Carol repeated.

"Stay with the discomfort," I said. "Face it."

"Good."

She wrote the word "STAY" on the board in caps. I said it to myself thoughtfully. Stay. It was a good word, especially when you weren't saying it pleadingly to someone else.

The thought is: I want to escape myself.

The feeling is: loneliness, hurt, fear.

The new behavior is: stay.

It made a somewhat confusing sort of sense. If I was lonely, if I was afraid of being alone, then why abandon myself? Why run to someone else looking to give myself the thing that only I could give? I wanted to escape myself because I felt empty, and the emptiness frightened me. But obviously, I was empty because I was always running out, running away. The only way to fill the emptiness was to remain, to take up residence in myself.

I wrote the word "STAY" in my notebook, also in caps, and underlined it. Carol was looking at me intently with her eyebrows raised inquisitively, as if to say, "You got all that?"

"Okay?" she said, her hand poised to erase the board.

I nodded.

That, in a nutshell, was process therapy. Stop, map, redirect. Learning the mechanism wasn't hard. I did that the first day. But putting it into practice in real life in the face of temptation, that was something else alto-gether. That would take time. Time and a lot of energy.

We went around the room, all six of us doing our charts and stick fig-ures. Aside from Katie and Bobby there was Petunia, a twenty-five-year-old imposing stack of man meat who looked like he'd completed Navy SEAL training. He had been shaving himself bald since the age of twelve, and had a diamond-embedded gold hoop in each ear, which only added to the menacing effect he had on you at first sight. He wore thick black rubber Michael Jordan ID bands on each wrist: one said "Baller," and the other said, "I own the guy guarding me." He smoked Black & Mild cigars, the kind you can buy in the drugstore, and often sported them, white plastic filter and all, perched behind one of his ears. He was at Mobius because he'd tried to kill himself by taking an overdose of Seroquel and alcohol. He'd nearly succeeded and had spent a week in intensive care. This last detail didn't surprise me in the least because, despite his appearance, Petunia was a tender reed, sensitive, and, like his cigars, mild. Hence the nickname.

Then there was Cook, a thirty-nine-year-old former coke and pot dealer, who'd been in the business deep enough to fly the stuff himself from the Caribbean. He had just done a ten-month stint in prison. Not for drug trafficking, of course. If he'd been caught for that he'd have been away a lot longer. They got him for passing a bad check or something, but it was generally understood to be in lieu of the real crimes that they couldn't quite catch him for.

Finally, there was Gary, another coke and pot aficionado, forty years old. He owned and operated a computer gaming Web site. He was a perfect mix between a high-strung secular Jewish computer nerd and a burned-out California surfer dude. He wore board shorts and brightly colored T-shirts and walked around barefoot, but he could argue God with you like a Yeshiva student.

He'd been at Mobius three times in the last four months, always of his own accord, taking, as he said, many steps forward but also a few too many back. He was even more into den chi bon than I was. He made these loud moaning and hissing sounds when he breathed in and out, and you were always guaranteed to get a good sweaty fire circle going when he was in it. Gary was a person you could be weird with and he wasn't threatened by it, but you could also be serious and tell him your problems. Like me, he was there to learn, and he didn't have any trouble letting go of his rational inhibitions.

As you can imagine, escape was a big attachment for everyone in that room.

Get out in a hell of a hurry.

That kind of escape.

Up, down, sideways. Didn't matter which drug. Just out. Out of the present. Out of the mind. Out of pain.

Again, the drug was a means. The real problem was the same as mine. Just the loud ouch of being alone and inadequate, and your thoughts like the Promethean eagle, pecking out your liver every day.

So for all of us it was the same cure, the long haul of learning to be present. Learning to face. All this, and I hadn't yet been there a day. That was Mobius for you. Roll up your sleeves and operate, elbow deep in the guts first thing. I liked it.

Our process therapy session broke up for the day at three thirty, and we all piled into the white van that they used to shuttle us around in, and which we quickly nicknamed the short bus. Diggs drove us to the apartments for the hour or so of late afternoon downtime we always had between classes and the evening's activity. Monday night was bookstore night, but the night tech on duty (Diggs finished at four o'clock) took me to the grocery store instead to buy my week's provisions.

I filled my half of the apartment fridge with foods I like, and like to think are healthy. Naturally, I still had to have one of my drugs. I bought lots of makings for coffee: grounds, sweetener, cream, filters. Mirabile dictu, there were two coffeemakers in the apartment and one in the kitchen at the offices.

The apartment was very comfortable, carpeted wall to wall, central heating and air, washer, dryer, dishwasher, microwave, and two full bathrooms. My roommate and I each had our own bathroom. My room had a single bed, a walk-in closet, a night table, a bedside lamp, a dresser, and a ceiling fan. My roommate was a TV junkie and a late-nighter, so I spent most of my postdinner time in my room with the door closed, reading or writing in my notebook.

A tech, whoever was on duty on the night shift, always woke us gently in the morning at around 7:45 to give us our medication, if we needed any. A couple of months after leaving St. Luke's, when the fear and downward thought spirals, though less intense, still hadn't gone away, I decided that trying to go without meds while in the middle of a book project wasn't the greatest idea. I went back on 20 milligrams of Prozac, the lowest maintenance dose. By the time I got to Mobius, I was holding steady. While I was there, I took my pill first thing at breakfast.

There were always two techs on duty in the evenings. During the night they'd make the rounds of the four apartments every few hours and peek into our bedrooms to make sure we were there. Most of the techs were either recent college grads like Diggs, interested in pursuing a career in mental health, or just doing an easy, relatively well-paid nonjob (they got $12 an hour) until they figured out what they wanted to do with their lives. The rest were youngish parents with two jobs trying to make ends meet, or slackers who couldn't handle more commitment in a job than a night shift with nutters.

The shifts went from 8:00 a.m to 4:00 p.m. (Diggs's time), 4.00 p.m. to midnight, and midnight to 8:00 a.m. It was all just glorified babysitting, shuttling us from place to place, or running errands, picking up laundry soap or bug spray or whatever else, if we needed it. They had to inspect our bags at the grocery store and gather receipts for what we bought, that sort of thing, but they never made a big show of being our keepers. Sometimes they sat on the couch with us at night and watched TV, or they sat at the dining table and did paperwork or read. There was also a small loft room above the kitchen in our apartment that had been made into an office for the techs, so they could use the computer or get on the Internet.

The techs were cool. They had the keys to the apartment, but the door was never locked except when we all went to the offices during the day or out for our activities in the evenings. They left us alone, even as they watched over us, or listened over us as they worked in the office above. They chatted with us if we wanted to, and they catered to our needs willingly, even if it meant driving to the store at odd hours.

We came and went pretty much as we liked, at least on the grounds of the apartment complex. It would have been quite easy to slip away and get high or drunk if you wanted to, or break the rules in other ways, including romantic encounters with other clients, as I learned that Bobby and Cook were doing virtually every night down at the Jacuzzi.

This was grounds for dismissal, but I didn't get the impression that the techs were making a particularly concerted effort to catch us in flagrante. If you shoved it in their faces, they'd have to report you, but otherwise the prevailing attitude at Mobius seemed to be that it was your cure, take it or not, and more often than not your money as well, so why sweat stolen kisses or other small infractions, if that was your game. Dr. Franklin's whole program revolved around his understanding of the will and its role in a person's mental convalescence. He wasn't going to give you the delusion of agency, only to shackle you with spies.

Dr. Franklin had an interesting relationship to his creation. Hands-on and hands-off. He was rarely in the offices, so I didn't actually meet him until several days into my stay. He was the presence behind, and the inventor of, everything that happened at Mobius, process therapy in particular, but you hardly ever saw him. Yet when you called the information number on Mobius's Web site, he was the person who answered the phone. It wasn't some hasty minion who couldn't give a shit, or some sleazy salesperson trying to part you from your money. It was Dr. Franklin taking cold calls. It was a smart way to keep his hand in, and it showed how personally invested he was. Everyone who came to Mobius had some relationship to Dr. Franklin from the start, since they had spoken to him on the phone and filled out his online application form to gain admittance. He had heard everyone's story, everyone's reasons for coming to Mobius. He had booked them in himself. He knew who was staying in his house, even if he wasn't there very often.

When I finally did meet him, it was like meeting Ronald McDonald or the Hamburglar or some other advertising mascot whose entire physical being and presence is dominated by a single exaggerated feature. In Dr. Franklin's case it was his bushy black mustache, which seemed to trumpet loud and clear: "I was a hippie back in the day, and now I drive a Lexus. But I vote green." And it was true. He did drive a Lexus, a sport utility no less. And I know this, because that's what he arrived in when he met me my first Saturday at Mobius at ten o'clock in the morning to play tennis on the courts at the apartment complex. He was a tennis nut, and when he found out that I played, he'd said, "You know, I don't usually do this with clients, but in your case I'll make an exception."

I knew he was environmentally conscious, too, up to a point, because he was wearing sweatbands on his wrists that were made entirely of bamboo fiber, and he said he was starting a whole line of green products, including, among other things, coffee mugs made of corn plastic. He even gave me a certificate asserting that a portion of my fee would go toward the planting of four hundred trees in my name in forests all around the world. He told me of his plans to move the Mobius offices to a new, "entirely green" building that he was designing with the help of an architect.

He was, as a hippie himself might say, a trip. He was way into the occult, talking about the mystic revelations of the Akashic records and the testimony of past life regressions, which he said he himself had performed many times. I asked him if he would try it on me, but he declined, saying he didn't do that kind of thing anymore. It was all a little hokey and strange. He was a little hokey and strange. An odd personality. An unusual combination of energetic and laid back, naïvely gung-ho and sagely hard-boiled. But I didn't care. To my mind, anybody who could think up and run a place like Mobius was a genius and a blessed shepherd of lost souls, even if he was a bit cracked. Maybe it took someone who was a bit cracked to even try it.

Besides, he was just too likable to dismiss. We smacked the ball around for an hour or so that morning, taking water breaks and talking about other treatment centers, mostly in Central America, where, in previous years, he'd established places like Mobius. He'd been in the alternative treatment business for a long time, establishing, refining, trying things out. At Mobius, it seemed, it had finally all come together. You could see that he was proud of his invention, and he had every right to be.

My first night at Mobius, I dreamed of a house by the sea. *I could live alone forever if I just had a view of the sea.* That is what I thought as I sat in the dream house at the wide wooden desk, in the large empty room, with the old unvarnished floorboards and the peeling white paint on walls as dry and bleached as driftwood, looking out through the large seamless windows at the sea. I thought: *I could live here forever.* And then I thought: *This belongs to me. This is mine.*

This place. This mind. This pole of being. Here. At the center. In me. Of me. Just me. And here again. Redirect the attention. Here. This spot. This still point. Consciousness conscious of itself. A being just being, each moment following upon the next, fully felt, fully found.

How many times have I heard the injunction "Know thyself"? But how? How to find oneself when the seeker is the thing sought? The dog is chasing his own tail, the snake is swallowing his.

In the dream, my house looks empty to me, because the person who lives there is outside looking through the windows, or she is inside looking out at the sea, but never inside looking in at herself.

How can she? How do I see myself but in a mirror? And why is the image so hollow? I search the glass for clues to the person behind the eyes, but there is nothing. The meaning is more elusive the longer I look, the eyes more two-dimensional, the more I stare. This is not the way. So what is the real mirror of the soul?

This is work for conjurers. How strange. I cannot be with the person who is right here, here all the time and yet not here, because I do not know her, cannot see her. I have never seen her. She is a ghost heard tell of. We are never in the same place at the same time, because we are the same person. I try to talk to her, and our conversations go like this:

Her: Knock knock.
Me: Who's there?
Her: Who.
Me: Who?
Her: Who.
Me: Who is who?
Her: Exactly.

My time at Mobius was full of dreams, dreams I woke up remembering and then drew in bright color the next day so that I could hang on to what they were telling me, imprint the pictures they showed me, and bask in the feeling they gave me. Calm and centered. Full.

I spent a lot of time there sitting with myself asking: How do you feel? And then listening carefully to the answer.

In the dream of the house by the sea I saw the metaphor of myself. I had a house, to which I had the keys, but I did not live there. Now and again I'd go into the house to empty the trash or do some other chore, but I always ran in and out as quickly as possible, full of anxiety, the way you might if you were the caretaker of a house you knew to be haunted.

But then one day, while I was in the house, I stopped in the room with the sea view and stood at the windows looking out. I was struck suddenly by the thought that this view was spectacular, and that it made the property, despite its disheveled condition, quite valuable. It occurred to me that I might stay, even take up residence. And that is when I began to consider the problem of identity, of how to both be and be with myself.

As my tutelage at Mobius went on, both alone in therapy with Carol and in process therapy with the group, it became clearer and clearer that the problem was very simple, and always the same.

Me.

Every behavior was a form of escape, evasion, or cover. I kept picturing myself sitting in a chair in the middle of an empty room. Every few moments, it seemed, I'd get up and check the clock, or fiddle with something at the window, or go for the door. I couldn't sit still. I couldn't just stay in the chair. And that, in the larger real-world sense, was what doing drugs and having affairs was all about, getting up from the chair, not doing the work, not sitting through the discomfort.

Carol did a lot of this work with me, pushing me by the shoulders into the chair and making me sit there with whatever came up, turning my head to face it again and again.

That is where I got the most traction at first, and learned to stop spinning my wheels.

During my first private session with Carol, she drew another stick figure on the board and said, as she had in group, "What's the thought?"

This time I wasn't going to varnish my answer.

"Do I want to fuck you?" I said.

She turned and furrowed her brow. When she saw my face, she said, "You're serious, aren't you?"

"Yes," I said, "I'm not messing around. That's what's in my head."

She needed confirmation.

"Every time you meet someone you consider whether or not you want to have sex with them?"

"Pretty much. I mean I usually discard the idea pretty quickly, but it crosses my mind."

She let out a big breath.

"Okay."

She wrote it down in the thought bubble above the stick figure's head: "Do I want to fuck you?"

She stepped back and looked at it for a moment, then reapproached the board. Again, as she had done before, she drew the heart over the stick figure's chest. She turned back to me.

"What's the feeling?"

Again, I didn't hesitate.

"Same as before. Loneliness, isolation."

She wrote these down inside the heart. Turning again she asked, "Anything else?"

"Emptiness."

She wrote this. Paused.

"Anything else?"

I listened for what would come through, trying to go deeper, trying to let a very old part of my brain speak to me, translate some hidden code into a concept and then corral it into a word. Then it came. Hard. Unexpectedly hard. I spat the word rudely, surprising myself.

"Hate."

She made an expression of interest, and then wrote that word in caps, larger than the rest.

HATE.

I felt a prick of rage, hot and pointed in my chest, and then a wave spreading from the point of entry.

"You know the drill," Carol said, drawing arrows out from the heart. "Now what's the behavior?"

The behavior that comes from loneliness? That was easy enough.

"Seduction," I said.

Pause. Then the behavior that comes from emptiness? Again, easy enough.

"Predation."

Pause. And the behavior that comes from hate? That was not going to be easy at all. Could I admit this? Could I own it? It was coming anyway. The channel was too open to stop it. Four letters. One syllable. Hate's other shoe dropping. Wait for it. Yes, yes, there it was, on the tongue, the tip of the tongue, then in the back of the mouth bursting forward, barking into the room.

"Rape."

There. Done. Criminal intent. On the board. In the open. Declared.

Carol took it well, considering, but I felt the need to clarify, so I added: "Men, not women."

As if this made it somehow better.

But it was true. I'd had pretty violent fantasies about raping men— always people who royally deserved it, mind you. Terrorists, rapists, child abusers, that sort of thing. In the fantasy I'm always a prisoner of theirs— usually in the terrorist fantasy—and they've had me for weeks, starving me, torturing me. At some point I break free or, more likely, I'm liberated in some trade or forced hostage relinquishment. There is always a big crowd of people waiting behind a fence when my captors bring me out, as if the transfer had been brokered and the meeting point revealed.

When one of the captors brings me out for the trade in front of the crowd, I turn on him with a hidden weapon, always a bat or a bludgeon of some kind. That, or I relieve him of his weapon in a stunning martial arts move right out of a Quentin Tarantino movie. I bang his head against the pavement a few times to subdue him, and then I tie his hands behind his back. Then I get him facedown on the ground, grab a fistful of his hair, and pull back his head so that I can spit my words right into his sweaty ugly face. Then I say something cringe-inducingly trite but satisfying, like:

"My friend, you picked the wrong girl on the wrong day."

Then I yank down his pants, still clutching his hair and pulling back his head as far as it will go, and then I shove my dry fist up his ass, or as much of it as will fit, and as I'm ripping up his insides I say:

"This is how rape feels."

The world is watching this, mind you. CNN and Fox have it live, even if they're blurring out the fisting, and the crowd is either roaring or stunned into silence, I can't decide which. Either way, this act is being seen. Recorded. Both on film and in the minds of every onlooker. It exists. It will be burned into memory and this man's flesh.

If a woman rapes a man in a clearing and everyone's there to hear it, see it, and taste it, does it make a sound, a sight, a meal? Does it register? Does it constitute payback for every private, silent, secret rape in the world? I don't know. Maybe it's just payback for one. And that's enough.

And there you have it. The subconscious at work, plucking scenes from bad movies and making a dream world of retribution. The poorly written script of my fantasy that plays over and over in my head, and has been for as long as I can remember, usually when I'm listening to raucous music on my iPod while I'm riding on the StairMaster at the gym or when I'm gritting my teeth to the cracking point in my sleep.

This was the rage wound up inside me like a tapeworm after years and years of feeding it and wondering why I always still felt hungry, and why I think about whether I want to fuck everyone I meet, making them into meat in my mind's eye and wondering how tender or tough they'd be, or how they'd smell, of clay and onion or maybe scalp oil and a musty old couch, or seaweed and the rotting sea. And I think about what they'd secrete, creamy or clear, salty or sweet. And then I'd force myself to think of drinking it, lapping it up and gagging, angrier still, but angriest with myself.

This is punishment. But whose? His, whoever he is or was, and mine. Mostly mine.

Punish me for my transgression. Because the transgression is mine. I fantasize about hurting the perpetrator, some perpetrator, any perpetrator, but the vector of revenge always turns back on me in real life, mostly because it is unacceptable to rape anybody, but also because the sickness lives in me, and that's where it has to die, be cut out, excised, exorcised.

I had said none of this to Carol. She was still with the thought bubble, the hate, and my last word, rape.

"Talk to me about this," Carol said, breaking my foul reverie. "How does it go in your head?"

I wasn't going to get into it, so I said what I'd said to therapists many times before.

"I was molested as a kid. I had a venereal disease before I was ten."

She was ready for this, of course. Had put it together from the moment I'd said the words "Do I want to fuck you?" and "rape."

"Molested kids are often hypersexualized as adults, you know."

"Yeah, I know."

She knelt down next to my chair. I wasn't ready for this kind of sympathy. Didn't want it. The molestation bit hadn't been a confession. It was old material. Really old. I'd talked it to death in the past, or at least what little I could remember of it. The doctor's office. The medical facts pointing to events I couldn't, still can't, recall except in comparatively innocent snippets. The virus suggests more. But what more? Who knows? Who cared? Yeah, yeah, I always thought, so somebody got to me in some way. So what? It happens all the time. Move on. I don't need you to hold my hand.

But she did. She took my hands, both of them, in hers, looked me long and hard in the eyes, waiting for me to meet her gaze and hold it. I couldn't. I looked at the potted fern behind her on the floor, occasionally glancing back at her eyes, which were searching my face for recognition. When our eyes did meet for longer than an instant, she gripped my hands a little tighter.

"Stay here. Look at me," she said.

Then she added, slowly and emphatically, "There is nothing wrong with you."

I guffawed.

"Uh, clearly there is. A lot."

"No. All of this," she swiped her hand across the board where we had written all my thoughts, feelings, and contemplated behaviors: hate, rape, fuck. "All of this is typical. A normal response to a very traumatic experience. Something very bad happened to you, and you reacted the way anyone would, the way most people have. That's all."

I shrugged my shoulders.

"Maybe."

"No. Really."

She clutched me by the upper arms this time and said the phrase again. I needed to hear it, and this time it got through.

"There's nothing wrong with you."

I heard the words and began to internalize their meaning. These were the words of the wellness model, not the accustomed disease model of so many psychiatrists I had known, the ones who were so eager to slap diagnoses and pathologies onto me in piles. Depressive, manic depressive, posttraumatic stress. These were all the things that were wrong with me. The troubles. But what if Carol was right? What if I was as healthy as the next person responding to an insult?

Kick me and I will bruise. Starve me and I will weaken and grow frail. Stab me and I will bleed. Are these not normal reactions to injury? A bruise, even a scar, is not a pathology. It is a sign of proper function, a sign of the healthy, *normal* body doing its job, coming to the rescue after the war.

All of this began to penetrate as I sat there, Carol holding my hands again in hers.

There's nothing wrong with me? I thought. Really? I'm not broken? Unfit? Weird?

And that, dismissive as I had been, was when I broke. I started to cry. Suddenly, urgently, big, hot, fat drops rolling down my cheeks. Silently, against my will.

I wasn't crying about the "trauma." I didn't care about that. I could barely remember it. It had never mattered consciously. It had never made me cry. It was this that mattered. The stigma, the malfunction, and the shame. The taint. Was there really nothing wrong with me after all? Was I not broken?

I cried harder.

I couldn't explain this to Carol. Not then anyway. The session was up, for one thing. For another, the shame, like the hate, was just one piece. Part of a chain, or a spiral of linked emotions that had yet to uncoil, each in turn. This was just the beginning.

Carol could sense I didn't want her to hug me, so, wisely, she didn't. She waited for me to gather myself, watching carefully with large, sympathetic eyes.

"Time's up, right?" I said, wiping my cheeks.

"Yes," Carol said, turning up the corner of her mouth as if to say, "I'm sorry the timing's so poor."

But it wasn't really. I wanted to go. Needed to. I didn't want to feel her eyes searching my face anymore. I didn't want to have to respond externally to what we'd discussed. I hadn't even come to Mobius thinking that therapy would happen to me, and yet, boom, it had. What had started as a crass willingness to play along, and to take notes about the process of therapy, had penetrated into real memory, real emotional content, coiled and waiting to spring. It had taken only the slightest touch to explode.

I wanted to regain some composure. Some remove. I wanted to stare out a window and let this tearful dousing sink in, and then leach through, like rainwater in soil. And then I wanted to close my eyes on the day and forget. I wanted to go back to being a journalist just doing her job.

Tuesdays were rebirthing days. Rebirthing sounds hokier than it was, though, I admit, it did have its moments. It was another one of those Mobius trademark activities, like den chi bon, that required a suspension of disbelief, or at least scoffing laughter, if you were going to get anything out of it. And it was possible to get quite a lot out of it, even if you didn't have visions, or weep copiously, or transport yourself back to the womb. Rebirthing, like a lot of other things they did at Mobius, was designed to access your subconscious, to function like a back door to your brain so that you could sneak in while the rest of you wasn't looking and grab a few fresh clues to what was really going on in there. It was a way around your defenses. That's all. Not, as I had worried, some form of devil worship or half-baked yankified shamanism all decked out in fake blood and feathers. As it turned out, it was really just meditation with a lot of deep breathing thrown in—again, for the oxygenated high, and the hoped-for partial dream state that might ensue if you caught that high while you were supine under a blanket and your eyes were closed.

Sam and Carol stood over us, guiding us into the trance, encouraging us to breathe deeply and energetically, and instructing us to say aloud a quick punctuated "Ahh" on the exhale, almost as if you were dropping the breath like a heavy bag.

Heeeeww. Ah. Heeeeww. Ah.

I had just come out of my therapy session with Carol, full of charted sexual rage, which then disgorged itself inside of me silently, splattering against the walls of my mind as I lay there huffing as instructed.

Hate, too. Hate was there in force, not just a word abstracted and splayed, written on the board in caps, but a bellyful, a meal of it rotting its way through me to shit.

Digestion. A metaphor. Yes. I considered this. Lying there. Breathing.

Emotion like a meal, always to the same end. I went with this train of thought. How marvelous to take every tasted morsel, from the lowly comfort food to the most refined and perfected dish, all of it made into shit. The same shit. Or different? Does the shit of a gourmet meal taste better to the dog that eats it than the leavings of a greasy spoon? And if so, is his palate more refined? It would seem so. To taste the chef's art or the fry cook's lowly labor in ordure, to suss out the progenitor in a potato, tell the coddled fingerling from the frozen shoestring, the Yukon from the Idaho.

Breathe. Heeeeww. Ah. Heeeeww Ah.

That is the psychologist's skill, to find the meal that made the shit you're sitting in. It being always shit in the end, one must work backward to differentiate the source, to know the ingredients of this particular pile.

Hate. What made the hate?

I knew what had made the hate. Sex had made the hate. And then hate had made the sex. And now there was just a whole hell of a lot of it going around in the bowels of my head.

I wondered what Carol and Sam would do if I crapped my pants right there or, better yet, stood up, dropped trou, and curled one out on the floor. Would that challenge their boundaries? Would it count as release?

"Let go," they kept saying.

Yeah, I'll let go. Here. Take that. A nice Cleveland steamer for show-and-tell. We could all gather around it and hold hands and talk about how it "speaks to us."

They say that smell is the sense most tied to memory.

I was gritting my teeth, breathing in hisses and cold whistles that made my fillings ache. The others were lying around me doing the same, watching their own show inside their heads, or maybe just checking out as usual. Everyone was breathing loudly, everyone except Bobby, who had again fallen asleep.

As the exercise drew to a close, Carol and Sam talked us down, but I was still rigid. When the lights came up I lay there unmoving, rude. I wasn't going to look at anybody and smile or exchange some glancing relief at the shared experience.

They shuttled us all into the art room next door and sat us around a large glass table. They brought out various crayons and markers and pastels and gave us each a piece of paper to draw on. The idea was to have an artistic reaction to the rebirthing experience.

I drew an unsurprisingly histrionic picture of an extreme close-up of my face, one enormous green eye in each top corner of the page, with a glaring black pupil at the center, as dark as I could make it. The whites of my eyes were bloodshot, and a trickle of blue X's fell down each cheek, the symbolic tears. I drew two rows of brown boxes in the two bottom corners of the page, my gritted teeth. Where my lips should have been I wrote in large black letters the word "No."

A little over the top, admittedly, but at least I hadn't shat on the floor.

When everyone had finished drawing we gathered back in the main room, sat in a circle, placed our drawings on the floor in front of us, and talked about what the drawings had meant to us and how they reflected both our rebirthing experience and our therapeutic progress to date.

When it was my turn I talked about the rage, or tried to. I wasn't going to really get into it in the circle, not then anyway, that was for later. But I did say that I thought that the rage was huge, insurmountable, standing between me and compassion for myself, a boulder that had formed itself around a liquid center, and the only way to get at the healing liquor was to melt or split the rock. I didn't see how that was possible.

In discussing the picture I suggested another way of looking at it. I had drawn my face. But I, like everyone else, was on the outside looking in, and the sign on the door said "No." I had not drawn my face at all, but a mask that was meant to scare the natives.

It was very like my dream of the house by the sea. I was outside looking through the windows of my own dwelling. The rage, which had grown up in me as a form of protection against invasion, specifically the invasion of unwanted adult hands and tongues and other organs, had done its job too well. I was locked out, too. My self-protection had been taken to such an extreme that it had become self-alienation. I didn't trust anyone, not even myself, and the result was that I had made myself a vagrant. I did not, could not, live in my own house. I was, in fact, afraid to live there, and so I spent all of my time looking for shelter elsewhere. Having affairs.

This was the very question of identity, again. How does one exist as a self, as a discrete person in the world, and yet not inhabit one's own self? This was my puzzle. I could not feel myself. I knew that I was standing there, or sitting there, or talking. I could hear my voice. Other people could hear my voice and had judged me to be a person. Why not? The hologram looked real enough. I moved from place to place and had ideas and bodily functions, and a past, and relatives, and a handful of friends who knew me, had known me over time and could identify my body if it came to that.

But the center was empty. I did not live there. I cannot emphasize this enough, nor can I adequately express the strangeness of this state. How can one not feel oneself? And then, having discovered that particular numbness, that confusing absence, how can one begin to remedy it? It is like trying to get to the North Pole when you are standing on it. Every direction is south.

After rebirthing I went away still full of the rage and the feeling of being locked out of myself. I sat there silently in the white van with Katie and Bobby, Cook, Gary, and Petunia, and as we drove and I stared out the window, watching the drably repetitive suburban landscape pass by, I became aware of a shift beginning. The rage was becoming something else, a close cousin but distinctly different. A loud song came on the radio, a song by a band I didn't know, an awful banging screaming song that made me feel old for hating it. Bobby asked Diggs to turn it up and he did. Way up. Bobby and Katie sang along and the van filled with young, careless energy. The inane lyrics and childishly simple rhythms of the song, sung and beat out so enthusiastically by the listeners, seemed to mirror, while ineffectually covering, the empty aimlessness of people in their twenties who were already disillusioned enough with life to have drunk themselves into jail.

I began to feel horribly alien sitting there, not knowing the song, hating everything it stood for, feeling touched by the terrible void we were all trying to fill or escape from. I had that feeling for the whole drive. I sat in it. Sank into it. By the time we got to the apartments it was all I could do to walk into my room and shut the door. I lay on the bed staring at the ceiling fan, slowly tilling, and I sank deeper into the alienation, watching it slide into the familiar feeling of isolation that the company of others can so often elicit.

I thought of the day's session with Carol. I thought of the taint. The feeling, for so long harbored in me, that I was abnormal, that there was something terribly wrong with me. This was the same feeling. Alienation, isolation. You are not like the others. You do not like or sing or know the same songs. You are not normal. Carol is wrong. You were sitting in the van and you did not know the song or like it, and you were surrounded by people and scenery that is all of a piece, all part of the same kit, the ground laid for the houses they build on it, the houses built all alike for the people, all alike, who live in them, the people who like the same songs and sing them loudly and feel familiar in their familiar world that is made for them.

You are not part of it. You are the touched other. Touched by damage, by madness, disease. For shame.

I began to cry again. I curled up on the bed, as in the tub, fetally, and sobbed.

In therapy with Carol the next morning I knew I would be able to map out the previous night's mood. I wasn't scheduled to see Carol that day, but this was one of the great luxuries of Mobius. You could walk in first thing in the morning, go to your therapist, and say, "I had a really rough night. I need to talk," and she'd make time for you right then and there while it was fresh. In fact, Carol had made it clear that I could call her anytime during my stay. The previous night I hadn't made use of the phone number she'd given me, because it had felt too intrusive to do so, and I suppose I'd felt too unworthy to deserve help. But after a night's sleep, I felt ready to talk, and I burst through Carol's open office door asking if she had time for me.

Therapy on demand wasn't really just a luxury of Mobius, though it's true that Dr. Franklin had fostered the creation of a flexible responsive atmosphere and had chosen to hire staff whose therapeutic styles could accommodate these needs. But each therapist formed his or her own relationship with each client.

Carol brought a tremendous amount of dedication and self-sacrifice to her work, and if you opened yourself to her, she would open herself to you in matching style. She was the antithesis of clinically detached. When you did therapy with her, you felt as though you were talking to a very insightful and selfless old friend, and while this might not have been an approach that worked for everyone, it was exactly what I needed. I'd had my share of intellectualized, rubber-gloved sessions with doctors, and I found them sorely lacking when it came to plunging deep into the muck of my emotional catastrophe. Even the best psychiatrists I've seen have always been too categorical for my taste, too trained in scientific method to follow the twisted routes of the battered human heart.

In my experience, going to a psychiatrist to get at your feelings had always been a bit like going to a gynecologist expecting to make love, and always with the same unsatisfying result. It wasn't that nothing useful could ever be gained from the encounter, but you were far more likely to be talking pathology than anything else. A quick poke and your anatomy would check out fine, but your culture would read abnormal, and you'd leave with a prescription in hand. If you talked, you talked abstractly, with the doc standing back making notes, or umm-humming while you fought off the devil on the floor.

Mobius's staff psychiatrist and I had had a joke about this very thing, in fact. He came in once a week, and I'd seen him for maybe fifteen minutes the previous day, per Mobius intake procedure. He'd asked me all the usual doctorly questions about psychiatric history, family medical history, which medications I was taking, and which ones I might be inclined to need while at Mobius.

"You know," I'd said, "I could be dying right now, riddled with disease, and you'd never know it. I could keel over right here and you wouldn't even notice."

"I know," he laughed. "I'd be too busy taking notes."

I respected him for that. He appreciated both the absurdity and the necessity of his position. Pharmaceutical gatekeeper.

The business of real therapy was for Carol and Sam and Josie. Josie was the third therapist on staff, a social worker who came in two days a week.

For them it was a form of art, especially for Josie, who was the most intuitively gifted of the three, and the best at removing her ego from the therapeutic encounter. She was alive with expectation, but only in the sense of wanting very much to know you, and for you to know yourself, as the person that you were. She had no categories. Guiding principles, yes. A practiced way of being in the world, certainly. But she was more interested in following your lead than imposing her vision. She listened more actively than anyone I have ever met, not straining to show interest (which is always so obvious in professionals), but rather genuinely wanting to know what you were going to say next. She was in the business of emotional suffering. She saw it every day and faced it anew in each person. In her healing, she observed no precedent, consulted no patented manual that told her what your symptoms meant, or junked you in with like and likely minds that were not like you at all.

There was no one like you. That was the point. Of course this didn't mean that we weren't all human, all facing similar fears and pains, joys and temptations, all processing experience with similar equipment, and therefore all likely to benefit from the application of a few tried-and-true coping skills that had helped many people of various constitutions and experience along the way.

Josie taught me one especially important skill for dealing with what often felt like the overwhelming intensity of my emotional life. She taught all of us this same skill, emphasizing it and reemphasizing it in subtly different ways until we began to take it in, each in our own time and apply it to our experience as it was happening.

The idea was this: emotional experience tends to feel repetitive and cumulative. This had certainly often been my experience with depression. My bouts of despondency had usually felt huge and insurmountable and vastly out of proportion to whatever was happening in my life at the time, and that is what had made them so puzzling and seemingly unconquerable. It was as if my brain didn't see what was happening as an isolated incident, but rather as an incident very like something it had seen before, in fact, many times before, and so it rolled the new experience in with all the others not just in kind but in quantity.

I was always asking myself why. Why am I feeling this? Thinking that if I knew the cause I could find the cure. But of course there was no reasonable why, at least not in the present. I was awash in an accumulation of past feelings and future dreads, all similar, at least as far as my brain was concerned, and so, lumped together as one. But nobody can handle a lifetime of experience in one moment. That's why depression crushes you.

So Josie taught me, and all of us, to stop trying to figure it out or account for it, to stop letting it seep into the past and the future. She taught us not to get lost in our brain's deceptive shorthand, in the accumulation. She taught us to stop asking the question why, and instead to ask what. "What am I feeling?" The idea was to stay with the feeling as it was happening, not to analyze it, but to experience it, to look at its contours, the way you would look at the contours of a landscape, to take it in with your senses, not your critical mind.

She would say, "Put a light around it, and separate it from the past and the future. From cause and effect. Just let it be what it is now, which is all that it really is anyway—the rest is an illusion."

Naturally, because all of us were experts at avoidance, none of us had actually tried this before. We'd always seen this seemingly huge tidal wave of feeling coming at us, and we'd run for the nearest distraction as soon as possible. But if you tried doing what Josie said, putting a light around it, or, if that was too airy-fairy a formulation for your taste, putting a fence around it, or a moat, or whatever worked, then you'd find that the feeling was more than likely manageable after all. Not only that, but rather than soaking you in misery for hours on end, it was likely to resolve itself quickly and drain away. Again, this was the idea that turning toward the thing that frightens you often diminishes it, the real and concrete being far less frightening than the imagined.

Sam explained this phenomenon in another way. His idea was that emotional discomfort was a kind of messenger. It was trying to tell you something, and if you turned away and didn't listen, it would just keep trying to get your attention in more and more inventive ways, intruding on your distractions, or your highs, so that it would take higher and higher doses to shut out the sound of the messenger's incessant knocking. Whereas, if you turned and listened, the way you might to an insistent child, the ruckus would die down quite quickly, and the message would come through in a manageable way. Of course this meant that you had to really listen, or as Josie had advised, pay attention to the what, to what was happening. But if you did, you often found that it was not nearly so bad, or huge, or terrifying as you had feared.

Carol and I did this in a less theoretical way in our one-on-one therapy together. The idea was the same. Break the emotion into its component parts, not just because it was snowballing and becoming far larger than it needed to be, but, per Dr. Franklin's theory in process therapy, because it was part of a chain reaction. If you could break the chain, you could stop the reaction, stop the undesirable end result.

As I began to pull apart my emotional responses with Carol, I began to see in practice why Dr. Franklin's method emphasized thought as well as feeling and behavior. The feeling and behavior parts made sense immediately, of course. The link between feelings and actions was clear. I feel bad, therefore I drink or I shoot up, or I cut myself, or I try to kill myself. But what hadn't been so clear was the idea that thoughts lie behind feelings. Thoughts give rise to feelings or, in a sense, feelings are made up of thoughts. In fact, there can be no emotion without thought. So to get at the feeling, you must first get at the thought. To break the reaction you must start farther up the chain.

Most of us tend to think that emotions and thoughts are separate entities running on separate tracks. It often feels this way in life. For example, you may know in your mind, your thoughts may be telling you, that your boyfriend is a jerk who treats you badly, and therefore you should dump him. But your heart just doesn't seem to get the message. You love him, and no amount of surety in your mind can seem to convince your heart that it's mistaken. Why, in this case, doesn't knowing something intellectually translate into feeling and then action? The thought is: My boyfriend is a jerk. Therefore the feeling should be; I hate him. And the behavior should be: I break up with him. Yet that's not usually how it works.

But when you spend enough time dismantling your thoughts and feelings, you begin to see that they are not separate. It seems that way merely because the links between the thoughts and the feelings are very old and very buried. As Josie had reminded us, thoughts are really thought patterns, a way that your brain has learned to process your experience. Breaking those links, and rerouting a thought pattern takes a lot of effort and concentration. It's a bit like learning a foreign language as an adult. Children pick up new languages effortlessly, organically, almost by osmosis, whereas adults have to do it the hard way, learning the grammar, memorizing the vocabulary, putting the sentences together word by word, or, as in my dream scenario, putting the house together brick by brick.

And that is what I did with Carol. I tore down my house brick by brick and rebuilt it again the same way. Or tried to. I can't say that my house is entirely rebuilt even now, but let's just say that I'm a lot more cognizant of the blueprints, so I know where the danger zones are. I know which walls are weak and likely to collapse, and I know which floorboards are loose and creaky.

I learned this by anatomizing my experience.

After spending the previous night curled up in a ball crying and contemplating hurting myself with one of the sharp knives in the kitchen, I went into Carol's office that next morning and drew a map of my mood, a record of the chain of thoughts, feelings, and intended behaviors that had conglomerated the night before.

In the previous day's therapy session I had reconnected with a familiar source, but in a more immediate way. The molestation. The fact of having been molested wasn't news to me, of course. Nor, really, was the idea that it had profoundly affected my emotional life and the way that I process experience. But I had never before seen so clearly exactly how the molestation, as the source, could set a chain reaction in motion, how it led me, if I let it, inexorably down a self-abusive and destructive path. I hadn't yet mapped the cycle on paper so that I could really see the process at work.

In the remote past, the molestation had triggered a sense of violation, unjust intrusion, and then, quite understandably and predictably, rage. That rage had persisted over the intervening years, and still lived very close to the surface, such that just speaking with Carol in one therapy session, having Carol ask the right open-ended questions and target the links between thought and feeling, had brought it up and out with a vengeance.

I had then carried that rage into rebirthing, and in the process of breathing and letting the emotional urgency come to the fore unfettered by my defenses, I had allowed myself to be consumed by it. I had visualized it as I had felt it coursing through me in the meditation. I had drawn the picture of it in the art room, the extreme close-up of my face, with the gritted teeth and bloodshot eyes, and the word "No" in place of a mouth. And finally, I had taken that feeling with me into the van.

Now, as I read back over my description of the ride home in the van, I can underline the words that serve as mile markers for the downward spiral of the mood from rage to self-harm. The word "rage" appears in the first sentence. "I went away full of the rage." By the next paragraph the rage has become alienation. "I began to feel horribly alien sitting there." By the end of the paragraph alienation becomes isolation. Then very quickly isolation becomes shame—the "taint." Finally, as I had done in Carol's office, in the face of the shame, I dissolve into a puddle and the description ends.

So the diagram looks like this:

Molestation → *Rage* → *Alienation* → *Shame*

Once the shame has taken hold, it's a short step from there to self-blame. Shame is essentially self-blame. From self-blame it's another short step to self-harm. You feel shame. You are, therefore, guilty. If you are guilty, then you must be punished. You must punish yourself. You must inflict pain, or perhaps even death. Obliterate the shame. Obliterate the self.

Now the full diagram looks like this:

Molestation → *Rage* → *Alienation* → *Shame* → *Guilt* → *Self-harm* → *Suicide*

And that is how the chain of thoughts becomes feelings becomes behavior. When you look at the whole diagram you can almost see the laws of physics applying themselves. For each act, in this case the act of molestation, there is an equal and opposite reaction, in this case rage. The rage then carries its momentum all the way through the chain until it emerges again on the other side as another act, self-harm.

It's very much like the toy on the executive's desk. The row of small metal balls all hanging next to each other on separate V-shaped strings. You pull back the ball at the far left and let it fly. It smashes into the row of other balls, and the ball at the far right end pops out in response to the blow. Conservation of momentum.

Molestation to self-harm, and the depression in between. All linked. All ingrained. A very old way of responding to an insult. A pattern always leading to the same place. A normal reaction, as normal, common, and predictable as a physical law.

This was a map of my depression and its source, as well as its propensity to repeat itself over and over again in response to a variety of stimuli, from work stress, to relationship stress, to any perceived violation or threat, all of which could set the process in motion in its accustomed way and dump me out at the far end in a heap.

This was my diagram of distress, or one of them anyway. There would be others. Other patterns. Other habits and modes. My depression is not one-dimensional. The molestation does not explain it wholly any more than drawing the map of its effects can heal all my ills going forward. It goes without saying that there are plenty of depressed and suicidal people in the world who were not molested as kids. They have their own triggering traumas, their own consequent patterns of emotion and thought, and the power of those patterns and traumas will not be magically expunged by this kind of charted uncovering.

As Carol would say, the diagrams and maps are coping skills, and they would not be drawn just once. They would be drawn again and again in different ways on different days when the feelings ran too high and were crippling. I would take apart my house brick by brick, and it would build itself up again when I was not looking. I would draw my maps and diagrams, and then I would promptly forget them in the storm of experience. And I would draw them again, and remind myself again to see that the feelings were not real, that they were just ghosts rattling their chains. And then, for a time, the feelings would seem less frightening, and I would move past them and go on. I would repocket the map or throw it out, thinking that I knew what it said and that I didn't need it anymore. And as I picked up my pace, and began even to walk with a little swagger in my step, I would succumb to the illusion that I was healed. And that comfortable, believable illusion would last for quite a while. Until the next time.

The days at Mobius ran according to a schedule. Each day was very much like the next, one floating into the other, blurring and passing by. But I never minded this. Time didn't drag me down and subdue me the way the empty days at Meriwether had, and it didn't feel stale and tedious like the well-meant, but mostly futile structured days at St. Luke's. My two weeks at Mobius were slow and pleasant.

We were spoiled. Everything worrisome was taken away, everything necessary provided or planned, such that you didn't really have to think about anything except the state of your soul or your liver, whatever the case might have been. And if you chose not to examine your life, which many of my fellow clients stubbornly did, then you just walked the short distance between sitting places, or rode the ten minutes in the van and then plopped yourself down again to zone out in another venue.

I liked the life there. It was easy and comfortable, and in certain ways it even helped me to practice for real life with training wheels on, which may sound infantile, but is not something to be overlooked when you've been depressed and found yourself in the humbling position of being unable to get out of bed.

So, for example, it was good for me to go to the supermarket and plan meals for the week and then cook each of those meals in the evening, or assemble and take the allotted lunch and snack provisions to the Mobius offices in the morning. It was good for me to do my dishes and my laundry, all in the safe confines of the playhouse.

I got used to the routines and found them comforting and stabilizing.

In the mornings I grew accustomed to waking immediately to the familiar sucking sound of the apartment's front door opening. I knew this meant that the night tech was there to give us our meds before he went off his shift.

Usually it was Roger. Roger was a father of two who worked part-time in construction when he wasn't working at Mobius, and he was one of the most polite people I have ever met. I hated the idea of putting the poor man in the awkward position of having to wake me in my room, where I was likely to be half out of the covers in my underwear or in some other unsightly state of disarray. So I had programmed myself to leap out of bed at the sound of the door, make myself vaguely presentable, then meet him in the kitchen, where he had taken to setting up his meds box on the table and waiting patiently for me to show. I didn't like to keep him waiting. Besides, he was a big fan of my coffee, which I always make very strong, and I liked to be able to offer him some before he had to go.

We usually sat there for twenty minutes or so over our cups, talking about some wounding lesson in manhood that he'd had to guide his son through that week or the progress of his latest construction project. He would often ask me how I was doing at Mobius, if I was getting something out of it, and what my plans were for getting back into my life. I always enjoyed those conversations. They were a homey segue into the day, and they kept me from doing the kind of unhealthy brooding that I tend to do when I first wake in the morning and lie there wishing I didn't have to get up.

When our twenty minutes were up, Roger would get up to go, thank me, wish me a good day, and I the same to him, and then I'd stand for a minute longer in the kitchen finishing my coffee and thinking over what we'd said. Then I'd wander over to Katie's door and give it a soft knock to let her know that we had about fifteen minutes before the van came. Usually she'd been up until four or so, still struggling with the Xanax withdrawal.

Cook, being a bit of a lady's man, always called in the mornings from his cell phone to say when the van was on its way. We'd chat for a minute, and give each other needless shit. He would flirt with me, even though he knew it would lead nowhere, and I would deflect his attempts sarcastically. Then we'd go on to other things. He'd been there in group process therapy, so he knew my private information. It was customary between us to rib each other on this score. He'd ask me if he was going to be my next affair, and I'd ask him if he liked it in the ass, because that was my thing. That usually ate up the couple of minutes until the van pulled into the parking area downstairs, and I'd throw my lunch and notebook into a bag in time to go.

Diggs would show up at the door and we'd take our seats in the van. On the drive to the office Cook and Gary, who both had houses on or very near the beach, would talk about power boats or deep-sea diving, or Cook and Katie, both of whom had been in jail, would advise Bobby on her upcoming incarceration and debate whether or not it was easier doing your time in the prison infirmary.

Petunia and I usually sat in the back row listening and looking sleepily out the windows. We always exchanged hearty greetings, but after that there wasn't much to say, which was fine with both of us. He was the kind of person who could hold a long silence well, and who had clearly come to the conclusion long ago that there was really very little that anyone needed to say to anyone else. I admired this economy of words, and thought it would behoove me to practice it.

When we got to the Mobius offices, we'd all put our packed lunches in the fridge and maybe grab a cup of the coffee that Sam or Carol had put on. Den chi bon didn't usually start until nine thirty, so we had forty-five minutes of loaf time when people who hadn't brought laptops and weren't availing themselves of the wireless service at the apartments could use one of the office computers and surf the net or check their e-mail.

The communal computer was on a desk in a sitting area across from the kitchen. There were also some armchairs, a large well-stocked bookshelf, and a table with a chessboard on top of it. The carved wooden chess pieces were usually positioned in various midgame arrays, but I never saw anyone playing. Katie usually commandeered the oversize leather armchair with ottoman and went back to sleep, impervious to all noise. I usually made notes in my notebook or read a bit over my third cup of coffee, unless it was a bad morning, in which case I'd sneak in to see Carol while she was trying to eat her bagel.

She was always welcoming. She wasn't the kind of therapist who didn't want you to know that she was human, so she didn't mind eating in front of you. In fact, she purposely asked me to stay in her office one morning while she made a phone call to Starbucks customer service in order to complain about rude treatment she'd received at a store that morning.

"I want you to hear this," she said.

She meant that she wanted me to know that she could be as petty as anybody else, and that the traditional transference process of falling in love with her, or making her into my spit-and-polish guru didn't have therapeutic value in her eyes.

And she was right. It didn't. She was a person as warty as anyone else and, as she reminded me, as defined by her past as I was, even at the age of fifty-one.

"This stuff doesn't go away, you know," she said. "I'm still doing all kinds of irrational things because of other things that happened to me when I was a kid. The number one characteristic of trauma is that it repeats itself."

She told me a story from her childhood about some freaked-out kid in grade school who had leapt on her from behind and tried to strangle her. It had taken four people to pull him off, and she still has a scar on her neck from the experience.

"Now whenever I go to the movies," she said, "I have to sit in the last row. I have to have my back to the wall. That's trauma. Old trauma repeating itself in my thoughts and actions even now, forty-some years later."

I'd never had a therapist who'd told me stories about herself, and our relationships had always, in my opinion, suffered as a result. I connected with Carol because she let me see that she was a person and that she was fighting the same fight, continually. She was an object lesson in perseverance and the sometimes bitter truth that no amount of mindfulness was going to renew you, or erase you, or make you into someone else. You were you. Stuck with you and, in a sense, stuck with your past, even if you could learn to navigate around it, or avoid falling entirely back into it. Patterns would repeat themselves, and the most you could do was be aware of and manage them. But you weren't ever going to be free, and there was no use in fooling yourself about it or, as Carol believed, fooling your clients about it either, catering to their dysfunction disinterestedly and impersonally like some kind of pie-eyed genie farted out of a jar.

Most mornings I left Carol's office and went right into den chi bon with Sam, which lasted for the next hour and fifteen minutes. Invariably I was calmer when we finished. Every day I got better at letting go and letting Sam lend me some of the immense positive creative energy he brought to work each morning. Every day I let the Indian man's liquid caramel voice penetrate a little deeper into my sour skepticism, and I let the strange thrusting motions of the exercises carry me away, until I was doing most of the session with my eyes closed, holding hands with Gary and Sam, and swaying to the sickly sweet swells of a Céline Dion song, with that same stupid contented smile plastered on my face.

What can I say? It worked for me. Hell, it was better than peeling oranges in the bathroom or playing board games with people depressed enough to make me look like Suzie Sparkle by comparison.

Anyway, it did more for me than coffee, and that's saying something.

After den chi bon, at eleven, it was back into perception therapy, where the rest of the clients weren't nearly as overeager and forthcoming about their twisted inner lives as I was, and usually mumbled whatever they thought they had to or could get away with in order to at least minimally satisfy Carol and get through the exercise.

And Carol wasn't forcing anything. She knew better, even if she was, at times, maybe a little too overly optimistic about the fact that she was often preaching to the deaf. But at bottom, she knew that the people who were there merely because they were court-mandated to be in some form of rehab, and had chosen Mobius as the lesser evil, weren't going to make much effort to get something out of the experience. And making an effort was the one and only way to actually get something out of it.

That was the crux. You. Only you could work on you. Nobody could force you, and if you weren't ready, then you weren't ready, and no amount of open-armed encouragement was going to change that.

Gary made an effort. He was on his way, trying to kick the coke and stay focused. His heart and mind were open to change. Cook made the occasional pull, but for the most part he was too busy making a play for the girls to really get down to his own business. Katie, more often than not, was texting her boyfriend that she was going to kick his ass when she got home. And Bobby? Well, Bobby was just not there at all. She didn't even try to disguise the lazy annoyance in her voice when she answered Carol's questions. She didn't seem in the least bothered by the fact that she'd taken other people's lives in her hands repeatedly while driving in the kind of condition that landed her upside down in ditches and trees. She only had a few days left to do at Mobius, and all she could talk about was how she was going to get drunk at the airport before she even got on the plane.

And that, in fact, is exactly what she did. The day she left, she had Diggs drive her to the airport in the morning a few extra hours before her flight was due to leave, so that she could spend that time in the bar. She sent Cook a message later that morning on his phone. There was no text attached. It was just a picture of a gargantuan Long Island iced tea.

So much for her process.

At noon, after process therapy, we ate our bagged lunches seated around the long table in the kitchen. Afterward, between one and two, we either met privately with our assigned therapist, or we met with Josie, who had her own paperwork to fill out for each of us, or, if it was Wednesday and we so desired, we could meet with the psychiatrist and get meds.

At two we had another group meditation session with Josie, Sam, or Carol, and sometimes all three, or we had rebirthing group, or we listened to a lecture on mindful living delivered by a Sri Lankan Buddhist monk who came in every other week to lend us his serenity. One day a week at this time we met with a nutritionist, who gave us information on caloric intake, body mass index, vitamin regimens, dietary supplements, carbs, fats, proteins, sweeteners, and so on.

This was all part of the mind, body, spirit aspect of the program, and whether, in the end, it changed your life or not (I found the monk pretty mindless rather than mindful, for example), I appreciated the effort that Dr. Franklin had made to offer us a variety of ways to approach our health. It was there for us to take advantage of or not, to incorporate or dismiss as we wished, and it wasn't usually very hard to skip out on these sessions if you really found them excruciating. You could, as I sometimes did, sneak into the meditation room, just off the main hall next to the art room, and ohm yourself into a state, or you could make yourself look busy over one of the self-help books on the shelves in the main seating area.

Three thirty usually rolled around pretty quickly, and then it was back into the van to the apartment where we usually had about an hour to ourselves before the evening activities. If it wasn't spa night, I often used this time for my workouts down at the apartment complex's minimalist gym, which was located next to the oval pool and Jacuzzi, where Cook and Bobby did their woozy cuddling.

If it was spa night, then I saved my workout for later and took a nap. The spa had a much larger, better-equipped gym than the apartment complex and a twenty-five-meter pool where I sometimes did laps. Petunia and I often spent most of our two hours at the spa working out, spotting each other in the weight room or riding the cardio machines.

After the evening's activity, we went back to the apartments, where I cooked myself dinner and ate it watching TV. I usually finished out the day in my room making notes about the day's events or combing the work of existential psychologists like Rollo May for juicy chewables to sleep on. I'd lie there drifting off, thinking hazily and more than a little self-satisfiedly of Kierkegaard's assertion that anxiety is our best teacher.

And then after a deep, restful sleep, I'd wake again to the sucking sound of the rubber seal breaking on the front door, and I'd wander sleepily out of my room to find Roger opening his yellow toolbox full of meds on the table in the kitchen.

As I said, it was predictable. It was simple. There was nothing to do but just be and breeze through the days unencumbered by responsibility yet untrapped by a locked ward. You had as much freedom as any program could grant you, and as much therapy and fresh air and entertainment as you were willing to grab.

On Saturdays and Sundays we slept in, and then they took us to the beach and to the movies, and we ate potluck lunches around the pool. If it rained we went to a museum, or we sat around in each other's apartments watching sportscasts and garbage TV.

People complained about the few small restrictions—that we had to go everywhere as a group, or we had to be driven around from place to place like bad-seed preschoolers. But after my experiences at St. Luke's and especially at Meriwether, I knew that these guys had no idea how good they had it. To me it was like a low-budget vacation or an ashram at the Motor Inn. It was all right. And given the alternatives, it was paradise.

I even got something out of it. Something real to take with me and use in times of distress. Call them tools, for lack of a better term. Or progress on the ongoing problem of me.

Best of all, I got a real therapist, someone who would be a person with me and challenge my views, nudge me off my brutal, grinding track and offer me a gentler alternative.

"Give yourself compassion," Carol said. "When you're feeling something intense, stop, observe the feeling, acknowledge your discomfort, and then give yourself compassion."

She saw me shaking my head.

"What? You don't like the word 'compassion'?"

"No. It's too delicate. It'll never work. My mean brain will just roll over that like a doll in the road."

"All right. Think of another word that you can relate to."

"I don't know."

I'd thought. The obvious, common words had come into my head. Kindness. Gentleness. Sympathy. But I had shaken them off with disgust. Then I'd thought, for some reason, of myself in the lobby at St. Luke's, terrified and crumpled, and I'd remembered that word. The word I had said as an exclamation, an invocation, a prayer. "Remember O most gracious Virgin Mary."

"Help," I'd said.

"Help," Carol had repeated. "Great. So," she had written it down on a sheet of paper for me, "stop. Observe yourself. Acknowledge your discomfort. Give yourself help."

"Right. Help," I'd repeated. "I can try that."

I had come back to the meanings of words. "Help." And now "try."

"Try that." "Just try."

I'd elongated the sound in my head. Trrrrryyyy. I had written it down in my notebook, and as I'd looked at it I'd seen that it was one of those words that looked off-kilter on the page the longer you stared at it. Three letters and the nonvowel vowel Y. It was like one of those words you see a lot in crossword puzzles because they fill in the three-letter gaps. Like emu or awl.

Try. It had a nice twist to it when I pronounced it again slowly to myself, like someone wringing out a rag between his fists. Tryyyyyyy. Squish. Dribble. Drip. Drip. Drip.

And then there was try, as in "Try the criminal." The trial. The judges in my head. They, too, had been in the lobby at St. Luke's. Pronouncing their sentence. Pointing their fingers. Relentless.

Ah. And there it was. Again. The pattern starting. This was how my brain went to the bad place. This was how I would end up in the tub. I would take a perfectly good sunny-day word like "try"—"Try it. You'll like it"—a word full of possibility and personal empowerment, and bring it around to Kafka in three minutes flat.

Thinking about it afterward, I could just hear what Carol would say, "Norah, listen to yourself."

Yes. Listen. Observe. See the downhill metal ball rolling, gathering speed until it is a bullet right in your path. Right in your brain. As fast as gravity. Then momentum. Then force.

Choose not to. I say this to myself a lot now after Carol. Choose not to go down that path. Take the dark thought pattern and bring it into the light. That was what perception therapy was all about.

The old thought is: Try.
The old perception is: I am on trial.
The old behavior is: Penalty.

The new thought is: Try
The new perception is: Try and try again.
The new behavior is: Go on.

When she got out of Mobius, Bobby only had about a week of freedom to enjoy before she had to do her time in jail. Since she and Cook were apparently an unofficial item by the time Bobby left, Cook had offered to let her stay at his beach house for that intervening week. He'd asked his sister to pick her up at the terminal.

Word was that Bobby had been so obliterated and belligerent by the time she landed, she'd nearly been arrested by the airport cops. She'd been outside on the curb ranting about lost baggage for about ten minutes when Cook's sister pulled up just in time to yank her into the car and drive off.

That was the last I heard of Bobby.

Now that she was gone, Cook had turned his attention back to Katie, who was basking in the prospect of another male to abuse. But Cook didn't mind. He didn't mind anything. He had a week to go and he'd be back on his sailboat making a trip to the Sargasso Sea, or some other place that seemed aimlessly appropriate. He was as supple and soft as the blond hairs that covered every visible inch of his body, like a golden down that signified his favored status with the gods. To look at him, you'd never know he'd been to prison. He looked like he'd been a lifeguard all his life, even *in* prison. He had a gift for finding the smooth passage, even through an ordeal. He had a talent for happiness, which might have been why he didn't really pay much attention in class. He knew how to turn negativity around. He was in the hammock already. What did he need with the Buddha.

I wondered if his equanimity was siphonable, like maybe his balls were full of quinine and that's why he wasn't susceptible to my disease, and if I could just tap some of that elixir, I'd be as sanguine and sun kissed as he was.

I wondered what his therapy sessions were like.

The thought is: Life is good.
The perception is: I'm made of nutmeg and cherries and malted milk.
The behavior is: Taste me.

Of course I knew this had to be an illusion. He wouldn't have been at Mobius if he'd had it all sorted out. Either that or he'd just gotten caught and been forced to do his time here like the others. He said he'd come of his own accord, but maybe that was crap.

Still he was there with the rest of us, and I was grateful for the enthusiasm he showed for the activities portions of the program. He was there in den chi bon, smiling and gesticulating inanely with Sam and Gary and me. He came to life in the art room after rebirthing when we drew our silly pictures, even though he couldn't draw any better than I could.

He took part enthusiastically when we made a Tibetan sand mandala one afternoon on the floor of the activities room. Earlier that week, Sam and Carol had asked each of us to draw a picture or symbol that we felt would be representative of our time at Mobius, something personally meaningful that would encapsulate what we had learned or remind us of the healing principles we should try to reconnect with in times of stress. They gave each of us a square of white cardboard, nine inches by nine inches, and asked us to fit our picture or symbol into that space. In order to make the mandala, we placed all of our small squares of cardboard side by side on a larger piece of cardboard on the floor and re-created the images on them, this time using colored sand, which we poured from the narrowed snouts of plastic bottles. As Sam and Carol instructed us, the sand mandala was a lesson in cooperation and impermanence, cooperation because it is a collective form of art, and impermanence because the sand is never fixed to the base. The wind can blow it away.

My symbol was a chair. It was my reminder to stay put, to stay with the feelings, not to run or try to escape through sex or drugs, to inhabit myself and my dreamy sea house for the first time.

Gary's symbol was an eye. A huge eye. He said it was for vision and seeing clearly. Other people made abstract symbols whose meanings I didn't investigate. Some had drawn mountain scenes with the sun rising above them or calming bucolic vistas as seen from a cottage window. That kind of thing.

It took us a few hours to finish tracing our own designs, and to fill in the open spaces at the center and edges of the large piece of cardboard underneath. It was like being in fourth-grade art class again, except without the mess. It was a relaxing way to spend an afternoon, and, more to the point, it was a way to calm the critical mind by occupying it in the relatively menial task of pouring sand.

Once engaged in this way, the mind stops watching the rest of you so closely, and your thoughts can amble unsupervised and unjudged. This will sound strange, and yet I'm sure it was the point: it was a bit like being high. That, for me, anyway, had always been the attraction of drugs, to stop the brutal round of hypercritical thinking, to escape the ravages of an unoccupied mind cannibalizing itself. Klonopin had done that. By chemically shutting out thought, it had stopped the whirling, overwhelming, expectant world and brought me to a tiny still point of focus right in front of me.

Working on the sand mandala had the same effect. The part of my brain that would normally have been obsessing about my failures and inadequacies, or the passage of unoccupied, unimproving time, or the pointlessness of going on, was busy thinking about how to trace the drawing with grains of sand.

Again, the material is meaningful. First, sand is not easy to manipulate precisely. It takes patience and concentration. What's more, it forces you, as I had learned by the end of my time at St. Luke's, to shrink your world, in this case from the overwhelming bucket or beachful to the single, manageable, even fascinating grain.

Sam and Carol were always trying to teach us, according to the Buddhist tradition, to be present, in the moment. This, they urged, was the way through our pain. But the novice rarely grasps this as anything but rhetoric. The conscious, micromanaging mind is just too omnipresent, too used to splashing around disruptively like a brat in a pool.

But making the mandala, which is an art practiced by Tibetan monks all over the world, showed me, not abstractly but concretely, what being present really meant. It put me there. Focus your mind on a task, the more menial and the smaller the component parts the better, and the shift is inevitable. As idiotic office managers are so fond of repeating, you will almost certainly find God in the details.

To preserve the tidiness of the activity room, instead of turning on a fan when we had finished the mandala and watching the beautifully patterned colored sand drift artificially along the baseboards, we poured it instead into several large pans that we planned to take to the beach the next day so we could toss it up and out over the water.

As it happened, the next day was my last full day at Mobius, so the sand-tossing ceremony made a fitting end to my stay. Instead of doing den chi bon in the exercise room as usual that morning, Sam and Carol took us to the site of an Indian mound in a nearby park. The mound overlooked the beach and was shaded by tall whispering palms. At the very top there was a flat clearing covered with loose soil. Sam set up his iPod speaker on a bench to the side of the clearing. He gave us each a receptacle—a bucket, a coffee can, what have you—and told us to walk down to the beach to gather sand.

When we came back, he told us to outline a large circle on the ground with a trail of sand. The circle had to be large enough for us all to stand along its circumference and still have plenty of arm and leg room to do den chi bon. Once we had finished outlining the circle, and had chosen our positions along it, Sam told us to make another trail of sand leading from each of our positions to the center of the circle, thereby forming spokes in a large wheel. Once we had done this, we took up our positions again along the circumference, and Sam took up his at the center.

Sam was wielding a long wooden staff that he had obviously fashioned for similar ceremonies. Gary had done this at least once with Sam. He claimed at one point to have had visions of spirits appearing on the mound in the form of wolves. Nobody else saw them, naturally, and nobody believed that they were there. But Carol had taken some photographs during the ceremony, and when she developed them, sure enough, you could see wolves in the circle. That was the story, anyway. I never saw the photos myself, and would have remained an unbeliever even if I had, but I did believe in the ceremony's power to unleash suppressed emotion, and that's all I was hoping for.

Being outdoors in that setting, standing atop a mound of crypted culture, made it easier somehow to let loose and connect with your own buried past. The open sky made you feel as though you could curse a blue streak without it bouncing back, and all that borrowed native juju seeping up through the soil was hard to beat when you were getting down and dirty with your inner child.

After we'd performed the usual den chi bon exercises, Sam took up his staff, aligning himself in turn with each spoke in the wheel, facing each of us one by one, and dancing up along the length of the spoke until he was close enough to kiss whoever was standing at the end of it. Then he invited each of us into the center of the circle for a little private mano a mano with him and the staff.

Actually, he didn't quite invite each of us. He didn't bother with Katie. When he made his way up her spoke, she looked at him like she'd beat the living shit out of him if he came any closer, so, no doubt knowing her history, he thought better of the gesture and backed off.

But the rest of us had a turn inside, an invitation to grab hold of the staff and try to wrestle it away from Sam while we put one lowered shoulder to his chest and leaned in hard against his resistance. Or as hard as any of us would. Almost everyone, even Petunia, whom I'd expected to mate more willingly with his demons, just moaned gamely and went through the motions, too embarrassed to really sumo in front of the group, or maybe just too emotionally impacted to purge the load.

By this point, I was a little more lubricated. I went at it with everything I had. When it was my turn, and Sam made his way to me, twirling and thrusting his staff, and grunting from the bottom of his throat, I said jokingly, "You're a brave man, Sam," and stepped into the circle.

Writhing against him, digging my toes into the dirt and pushing with all the strength in my legs, I barked, growled, and bellowed so hard and so loud that I scraped my throat raw. All the rage that I'd felt in Carol's office and during rebirthing came charging out. So much so, that I very nearly took a bite out of Sam's shoulder.

We went at it this way for at least five minutes, which feels like a hell of a long time when you're wrestling someone with superior spiritual skills. Sam encouraged me to drain myself, saying, "Come on. Let it out." And I did, until I couldn't make another sound or push against him any harder. And then, as the emotion slowed, so did we. Our grips on the staff loosened, and we swayed slowly to a stop, breathing heavily, leaning against each other gently, and then not at all, until we were standing again fully upright, our breath coming back, our hands only lightly on the staff. Sam led me back to my place in the circle, returned to his place at the center, put aside the staff, and tapered out the ceremony as usual, calling us in closer so that we could hold hands and close our eyes and breathe together as the music ended.

Then in silence, we took the sweepings from the sand mandala and walked to the water's edge. Each of us grasped a handful of the sand, ready to throw it out into the water, expressing our guiding thought for the day as we did so. Since it was my last day, mine was a guiding thought for the coming weeks and months, and maybe even years. In keeping with the symbolism of the chair that I had traced on the sand mandala, and the theme of inhabiting myself that I had been developing through-out my stay at Mobius, I came back in my mind to one of those four-letter words that I had written in caps in my notebook and underlined for emphasis: STAY.

Stay with it. Stay with the hard stuff. Stay with you. Accompany you. Help you. Rely on you. It was everything all in one. Occupying the empty center. Giving myself—could I say it now?—compassion. Assistance. Walking through the mask of rage, the false front, to the sanctuary behind it and living there.

"I choose to be here," I said, and threw my handful of colored sand into the water.

The morning I left, Diggs drove me to the airport. I said my farewells to Carol and Sam and Josie with long hearty hugs and just as hearty thanks. Carol gave me her number and told me to call if I wanted to set up phone therapy sessions in the future. Dr. Franklin shook my hand and told me to come back any time.

"We're always here for you," he said, and meant it in more than a commercial sense.

And I thanked him just as sincerely, thinking, in stark contrast to the way I felt when I left the other places I'd been, that I wouldn't be at all averse to coming back to Mobius for a tune-up if I needed one. They were good people doing good work, even if their clientele wasn't always as receptive as one would have hoped. Their success rate was probably still higher than at most other places. That is, if you measure success in more than neurotransmitters.

They were doing everything right as far as I could see: integrating mind, body and spirit; granting freedom, and yet providing sanctuary; using medication, but not overusing it; offering the healing routine of a structured day and intensive personal therapy, but not hemming you in with rote bureaucratic restraints and petty forms of control.

Most of all, they seemed to have fostered and implemented the belief that therapy and biochemistry are not either-or propositions, that the body and the mind are not separate. They did not inundate clients with pills, thinking that medicine was the only way to affect the brain. But rather they used meditation and talk and compassion to reach the brain through language and thought. They understood that words and ideas have physical life, that the things you say to someone in therapy and the things they say to you, or the things you think about in meditation, can and do have a physiological effect on the brain, an effect every bit as powerful as the endorphins and adrenaline you release in physical exercise or the serotonin and dopamine you manipulate when you take drugs.

When Carol told me that there was nothing wrong with me, those words entered my brain and brought about a chemical response that took the form of relief and tears. And who's to say that the emotion and the physiological response were separate things, one becoming the other, the relief, translating into tears. Who's to say that they weren't in fact the same thing. Simultaneous. Emotion as physical response, a physical response brought about by another human being's sympathetic thoughts spoken aloud. Brain chemistry affected, even improved, by good therapy.

This, I saw as the doorway to a new life: eventually free of, or at least less ruled by, drugs; a life where routine tasks, being present, and giving my full attention to detail could calm me; where talk, laughter, and compassion could counter both the habitual force of my negative experience and whatever might be chemically awry in my brain. Whether it was congenital or acquired, it didn't matter. I could fight it with new skills, new practices that treated me as a whole person, porous to the world but not submissive to it, alive and reactive to slings and arrows, sticks and stones, and even the cruel names that could actually hurt me, but never, never again just passively diagnosed in a waiting room or cowering paralyzed in the bathtub.

CONTINUUM

I began this project with the intention of exposing institutions. That was my prejudice. I had been to the bin my first time in genuine distress, had languished there, and had left with the intention of lobbying for change. I wanted to show, by doing, that locked psych wards are not conducive to recovery or good health. In fact, to my mind, quite the opposite was true. You could take a perfectly sane, well-adjusted person, lock him in the hospital for a few weeks, or even days, and his mental as well as his physical health would be virtually guaranteed to deteriorate.

Now, at the far end of a long haul, having spent my time at Meriwether and St. Luke's, and finally at Mobius, I still believe this to be true. Institutionalize someone and he will become institutionalized. Lock him in and down, and he will do the same. Institutions don't heal—they hold. At best, as I found at St. Luke's—which incidentally, I would not quite characterize as an institution, since it was not a hospital—mental wards neutralize the person and the world in such a way that some small comfort in terror may be found, if you are willing to find it.

But then, holding or neutralizing is all that most psychiatric facilities were ever really intended to do, and, having completed my journey through the system, I can see now that I was supremely naïve to believe otherwise. Not naïve about the system, but about people.

On one level, the system is the system, ruled largely by the laws of economics: competition, overhead, profit and loss, etc. Everyone knows that, whatever the treatment you are in for, private hospitals tend to be better than public ones, and specialty clinics or spalike facilities are better than private hospitals. Privatizing or specializing anything, from schools to public works, tends to improve facilities and quality of service across the board. This, too, is no secret, though it may be a matter of heated political debate.

But there is something else at work in the system, and this is the part I hadn't counted on. My first night in Meriwether, as I looked around me at the semisqualor and the degraded clientele of the public hospital, I wondered about cause. I wondered whether the system is the way it is because people are the way they are, or the other way around. Now I know that the answer is both. As I have just said, the system is the way it is mostly for economic reasons, and it brings down the people in its care. But the system is also the way it is because people—patients—are the way they are, often lazy, stubbornly self-indulgent, passive, and irresponsible, and they bring down the level of care accordingly.

The system does not aim to heal patients, partly out of cheapness and lack of effort, but also because the people who run these institutions have learned through experience that patients cannot be healed by institutions, or, for that matter, by any outside force. They know what I now know: nothing and no one can do for a person what he will not do for himself, even if he is crazy.

I was wrong initially to think that institutional staff and administrators do not understand the role of the will in healing. On the contrary, they understand it only too well. They know what it took my visit to Mobius to teach me, that no amount of money or luxury or therapy will do anyone any good if he is unwilling to participate in his own recovery. In that, Carol and the folks at Mobius were absolutely right. No one can heal you except you. But, and here is the heart of the matter, the vast majority of people don't want to participate in their own recovery. They are unwilling to try, even when they are given every advantage, every freedom, and an abundance of what was lacking in Meriwether, namely, compassion and the human touch.

The people I knew at Mobius had everything that the people at Meriwether didn't. And yet, with the exception of Gary, they refused to change. They went through the motions resentfully, and then got drunk or stoned again as soon as they had the chance, or went on in superficial, halfhearted sobriety, but without having changed underneath. And why? Because they hadn't come to Mobius of their own free will. They were there either because their families had sent them, or because they'd been arrested and were facing prison time. Rehab was part of their sentence. But you cannot sentence people to recovery. You cannot cajole them into it either. Charity, or therapy, or enlightened treatment, is wasted on people who don't want to or can't change.

That is not to say that Mobius could not do a world of good, and had done so (if the testimonial letters I'd seen posted in the kitchen were any indication) for a number of people over the years. But these were willing clients. Mobius could do nothing for you if you didn't participate, and neither could any other place, however swank or progressive.

In my experience, whether you were dealing with a psychotic, indigent, inner-city population, a depressed and addicted middle-class rural population, or a depressed and addicted upper-middle-class suburban population, the number of people in any group who were willing to take responsibility for their own lives and behavior is always small. So even, for example, if you had taken someone like Mr. Clean and transported him to a place like Mobius, he probably wouldn't have been any more likely than Katie or Bobby to get something out of it. Equally, you could have taken someone like Katie or Bobby and had them waste time and money at a place like Meriwether just as easily as they wasted it at Mobius.

And this, I think, must be where so much of the cynicism in the system comes from. Why waste therapy and resources on people who will actively resist, and so derive no benefit from them anyway? Why not just medicate the bejesus out of people, when medication is the one thing that requires no effort or willpower to have an effect? If people aren't going to heal, because they don't want to heal, then containment is the most any system can do for them and for us. And containment is necessary. Bobby and Katie couldn't be left to keep driving under the influence, and Mr. Clean and Mother T couldn't be left to wantonly disturb the peace.

Now how much willpower Mother T and Mr. Clean, as individuals, could have exerted over their conditions I have no way of knowing. I doubt the doctors could know that either, precisely because it was a matter of individuality. Psychosis, as a condition, isn't necessarily beyond self-help. The psychotics that I met at St. Luke's, people like Karen, had shown as much, as, arguably, had John Nash in his assertion that his own mental illness was in part the effect of a mind on strike. The will could play some role even in the schizophrenic mind, but how much, it seems, would depend on the person. Beyond that, clearly, medication could and did help tamp down the hallucinations and delusions of the psychotics I met, even if it did so largely by hobbling the brain.

But from what I saw in Meriwether, St. Luke's, and Mobius and what I experienced in my own struggles to cope with mental distress, a person's condition, whatever it was, whether depression, psychosis, or addiction, has less to do with his prospects for recovery than his personality, his willingness to change. The same was true of social class. Yes, it made a difference to be educated and supported by family and friends. Yes, it made a difference to have better food and exercise and therapy. But this alone was not enough.

Facilities matter. Everyone should have a clean bathroom and nutritious food and fresh air. Those are basic needs and rights. I still believe, as I did at the outset, that the system could do a lot better, and it could do so cheaply and easily with only minimal effort. Even if you don't expect patients to improve, and even if you loathe them on some level for their learned helplessness and indulgent immaturity, or even for simply being sick, you need not treat them with contempt. Kindness is not expensive, even if it is often trying. Therapy should be made available to people who want it, as should recreational activities and hugs and human contact.

But in the end, this is not the solution as I see it. The system, flawed as it is, is not solely, or perhaps even primarily, responsible for (or capable of bringing about) the health and well-being of the individual. The individual himself is. The luxuries or advantages that any psych facility might offer are what philosophers would call necessary but not sufficient conditions for mental health and recovery. With an individual's effort, they can make all the difference. Without it, they are virtually useless.

Now, I realize that all of this sounds terribly pessimistic. And it is, if you remain focused on the system. If, as I did at the outset, you think that the system is broken, and, more to the point, you think, as I also did at the outset, that throwing more and more money and human resources at the problem will bring about miraculous recoveries, you will be sorely disappointed. The patients themselves will thwart you. In this, Mobius was the ultimate case in point. Even if every Meriwether were made into a Mobius, a lot of people still wouldn't improve, except possibly through passive submission to the dictatorial effects of medication. Circumvent the will with a pill, as so many institutions and practitioners do, and that's the most you can hope for.

Sad. Very sad. But realistic.

If, however, you consider the flip side of this sad reality, the scenery looks a lot brighter. If you come to the conclusion, as I have, that you are at the helm of your mental and physical health, that you have more control than anyone over your own well-being, then the power to heal is put into your own hands. And what could be more optimistic and empowering than that? You do not depend on the institution, even if, when you are ready to work at it, you can be helped by places like Mobius or, indeed, harmed by places like Meriwether. The lesson is much the same in both places. Fend for yourself. For, as elaborate as the therapy at Mobius seemed, the message was simple. We are not helping you. We are teaching you that only you can help you. The message was similar at Meriwether, even though it came in the form mostly of neglect and hard knocks: Don't ask us to fix you, because we can't.

And so, in conclusion, I can offer only the same advice and the same report. Do it yourself.

This book turned inward more and more as it went along, for the most part, relinquishing even the vaguest objectivity. And it did so, not only because I was overwhelmed by the private emotional struggles that led me to pursue this project in the first place, but also because, philosophically, I began to feel that the point of interest, the point of healing, and the target of rebuke was less the institution, or the world as it is, than the individual. As it has done before, my immersive journey has brought me back to myself, and most of what I can say at this point is personal. I cannot tell you that Mobius healed me, because it didn't. I cannot tell you that I have healed myself, because I have not. I am not healed. But I am fighting. And I am fighting, not with the aid of better facilities, therapies, and therapists, but alone.

I have a motto for that fight: *Tertium non datur.* In Latin it means, "The third is not given." Or alternatively, "There is no third possibility." I first saw these words while at Mobius. Bobby had them embroidered on the back of her jacket. When we rode to and fro in the white van, I often sat behind her and read the phrase again and again. It became a mantra for me by the end of my stay.

One day I asked her what it meant, and she offered the literal translation. The third is not given. She said she had read it somewhere in an assigned text in school and had internalized its meaning as "Blaze your own path" or "Make your own way." In other words, don't do the expected thing, the prescribed thing. Do it yourself in whatever fashion suits you best.

It was a philosophy she lived by, though clearly, given where she'd put it, the phrase was not a reminder to self. Rather it was like some kind of bumper sticker, pasted there for the benefit of whichever bored fellow pilgrim happened to be stuck behind her in line, in class, in church, or, in this case, in a short bus full of life-skill spastics paying for the privilege of getting their shit together.

I looked up the phrase later and learned that it's a principle of logic called the law of the excluded middle. It means that something is either X or not X, or, as it is more commonly heard in general conversation, you can't be a little bit pregnant. You either are or you aren't. There is no middle ground.

The law of the excluded middle doesn't have anything to do with blazing your own path, at least not when it's used in its traditional sense. But for my purposes at Mobius, Bobby's interpretation was perfect.

The third is not given. There was all the rebel hope in the world in that phrase when you learned it from Bobby. It meant that the script was not yet written. It meant that there was a middle way between resignation and folly, between my nightmare au naturel and the tinker-bludgeon approach of modern alchemic psychiatry. It was a place in my mind where I could put all of my aspirations and keep them alive, stocking my vision of the future with the belief that I could exert some influence over it, and over my condition.

This is most of what I took away with me from Mobius, and from this project as a whole. The gist of it, anyway. Action. I am not bound by my diagnosis. I can help myself, and I will.

I, always the patient, am not condemned if only I can participate. If fortune is a wheel of fire, then I will not be bound upon it, but instead I will grasp it firmly with both hands and drive.

The metaphor holds in all respects. The fact that I am driving the car doesn't mean that the road will always be smooth or that I can control other drivers, the terrain, the weather, flats, malfunctions, darting animals, and other acts of God. But it gives me the vital sense of getting somewhere under my own power, of refusing to accept passively a wandering servitude to medical whim and the lonely defects of personality or birth.

But it is not a wholesale rejection of biology and its entailed determinism either. When it comes to medication, I am going to take what I can use, if it helps, but in the lowest possible doses, and I will do so knowing, through my own experience and investigation, about the pitfalls that the doctors should have told me about in the first place.

By this point I feel I have little choice, anyway. I don't know whether my brain chemistry has changed as a result of taking medication. I can't prove it, certainly. But I strongly suspect it. How could it not have, adapting itself to constant chemical alteration over the course of more than a decade? Is this permanent? I don't know that either, and neither do any of my doctors.

I know that when I go off medication I feel far worse than I ever felt before I took it, and I have never been able to stand the downside for more than a few months, so I don't know how long my brain might take to recalibrate, if it can.

But, be that as it may, I am still left with work to do. I am still left with the consideration of what my participation means, and what this so-called middle way really entails, aside from popping the evilly necessary, or occasionally desirable, pill now and again.

Primarily, it means effort. That's the simplest way to say it. Constant effort. We tend to think of happiness (and by happiness I also mean health or overall well-being) as a gift, and sometimes it is, a pure gratuity. But most of the time it comes about because you've done the work, prepared the ground to allow it in or tended it carefully once it has arrived. You have to practice happiness the way you practice the piano, commit to it the way you commit to going to the gym.

You don't do it most of the time because it feels good to do it. You do it because it feels good to have done it. Or, more precisely, you do it because repetition lays the groundwork. It is the prerequisite for feeling good. Happiness is not a reward. It's a consequence. You have to work at it every day.

Part of this, for me, means literally going to the gym. Being in good physical condition, getting my heart rate up for at least forty minutes, stretching, doing yoga and other strength exercises. This has a direct effect on my mood. When I'm terrified, when I'm really down and feeling like crap, I take myself to the gym. It's the first thing I do. I don't even think about it. I don't debate or consider whether I'm up for it. I do it. Automatically. And every time, even if the workout feels like hell while I'm doing it, I always feel better when I'm done. If I go in at an emotional 4, I come out at a 6 or 7. Sometimes just the act of having accomplished something that is hard, that takes willpower, makes me feel good about myself. It may be the only thing of substance that I accomplish in a day, but it's something and it clobbers the fear and the loathing and the futility.

If the question is, What's the point? The answer is, Just do it. Doing it is the point. Don't think. Do.

I have learned to apply that principle to almost every aspect of my life. So, for example, I don't work at my writing because I love it. I work at it because I know that work, focusing and exercising my brain in very much the same way as I exercise my body, brings about a certain fulfillment and contentment in me that is lacking when I go too long without intellectual stimulation. Giving my brain something to occupy it tends to keep it from obsessing so much about my failures, or about impending disasters. I believe this to be true of all of us. Our brains are hungry, in constant need of stimulation, and when we don't feed them enough, especially when we feed them the junk food of bad television and other mindless distractions, they turn on us and begin to cannibalize themselves for nourishment, much the way our bodies consume our own muscle and fat when we starve them.

My brain did this a lot while I was at St. Luke's. It spiraled in on itself and tangled me in knots because I succumbed to intellectual inertia. I didn't feed myself, and so I fed on myself. Once that had happened, it was doubly hard to pull myself out, and that is why so much of my effort in managing my depression is given over to maintenance, to keeping things going. In this, the emotional world mimics the physical one. It is far easier to keep going when you are already going than it is to start going when you have stopped or fallen into reverse.

I don't often feel like working or doing something that's good for my brain, but I try to push myself to do it nonetheless, because, as with physical exercise, I always feel better when I've done it.

Likewise, I often don't feel like socializing, and I often find myself on the verge of canceling engagements with friends. Sometimes I do cancel them. But almost invariably I regret it. I resent the effort it takes to maintain relationships or meet the tedious obligations that family and friendships can impose, and yet I know that isolation is very bad for me. I know that my happiness depends, in large part, on human contact and intimacy. And so, as with everything else, I do it and reap the reward, or I don't do it and suffer the consequences.

It's all of a piece. Together, the pieces bring about the whole, and the sense of wholeness that is essential to staving off depression. The pieces and the bringing about are mine. It is up to me to tend to my wholeness. I do it or I don't. That's it. Sometimes I do well and sometimes I do poorly, but the point is, I do. The success or the failure is my own.

As for last words on the subject, as for cure, that's a fantasy. You don't finish. You continue. And you don't do it—you are not forced to do it— because you are mentally ill. You do it because that's how living works. Maybe depressives like me have to work a little harder at happiness. Maybe psychotics like Karen have to work a lot harder. But everyone has to work at it. Everyone has to try, even people who have everything. Probably they most of all.

I'm not saying that eating right and exercising, nurturing your heart and challenging your brain, will save you. It won't. There is no saving, of course. You never "arrive." You move. You get on with it. That's the prescription.

In the end, and after a long, long trip, there's only one thing I can tell you about happiness, about well-being, as I understand it. You want to be happy? You want to be well? Then put your boots on.

ACKNOWLEDGMENTS

I would like to thank my agent, Eric Simonoff, for being, as usual, so much more than an agent; my editors, Molly Stern and Wendy Wolf, for their unflagging support, guidance and editorial acumen; Viking president, Clare Ferraro, who has been the kindest of fostering mothers; my publicists Jump Coleburn and Ann Day, who make it all turn out beautifully; and my friend and cohort Laura Tisdel, who also just happens to work at Viking. I owe my life, body, and soul to my beloved friend Claire Berlinski, who has done more for me over the years than anyone could or should ever have been expected to. I owe this and a whole hell of a lot more than I can ever repay to Lisa McNulty. In addition I would like to thank Bruce Nichols, Adam Bellow, and by no means last or remotely least, my family: Alex, Ted, Mom, Dad, and Kristen.